SUBMARINES

SUBMARINES

FROM EARLY SUBMERSIBLES TO NUCLEAR-POWERED SUBMARINES

DAVID ROSS

amber
BOOKS

This Amber edition published in 2024

First published as *The World's Greatest Submarines* in 2016

Copyright © 2016 Amber Books Ltd

Published by Amber Books Ltd
United House
North Road
London
N7 9DP
United Kingdom
www.amberbooks.co.uk
Facebook: amberbooks
YouTube: amberbooksltd
Instagram: amberbooksltd
X(Twitter): @amberbooks

ISBN: 978-1-83886-493-4

Project Editor: Michael Spilling
Picture Research: Terry Forshaw
Design: Andrew Easton

Printed in China

PICTURE CREDITS:
Alamy: 25 (Print Collector), 174 (EPA), 199 (EPA)
Art-Tech: 65, 72, 73, 81 top, 104, 118, 119, 122, 130, 131, 135, 138, 139, 158
BAE Systems: 202, 203
Cody Images: 6, 8, 17, 28, 29, 41, 44, 45, 48, 49, 52, 56, 57, 60, 64, 77, 81 bottom, 84, 85, 88, 89, 96,
    97, 105, 123 bottom, 126, 134, 142, 143, 150, 171, 175, 182, 183, 186, 190, 191, 218, 219
Dreamstime: 162 (Per Bjorkdahl)
Getty Images: 92 (De Agostini)
Kockums: 163
Library of Congress: 10, 37
Netherlands Ministry of Defence: 166, 167
U.S. Department of Defense: 7, 114, 127, 146, 147, 151, 154, 155 bottom, 159, 178, 179, 187
U.S. Navy: 12, 13, 20, 21, 36, 68, 69, 100, 101, 108, 109, 113 both, 194, 195

All artworks Art-Tech except for the following:
Amber Books: 177, 180/181, 184/185, 208/209,
Amber Books/Tony Gibbons: 14/15, 16, 18/19, 62/63, 78/79, 132/133
Amber Books/Patrick Mulrey: 22/23, 38/39, 86/87, 156/157, 188/189, 192/193, 196/197, 204/205,
    212/213, 216/217
BAE Systems: 200/201
John Batchelor: 176/177

Note on distances and weight
Nautical miles (nm): 1nm is equivalent to 1.85km or 1.15 miles. A knot is the measurement
of speed at sea: the number of nm travelled by a ship in one hour.
Gross Register Tons (GRT): a measurement of a ship by its internal volume. One GRT equals
2.83m^3 (100 cubic feet). It is not a measure of weight or displacement.

Contents

Introduction

Submarines, which some navies once considered too unlike proper warships to merit names of their own (Germany still sticks with numbers), have become the principal strategic weapons' platforms in world armaments.

In preserving a global or regional balance of power, their ability to deliver a 'second strike' in the event of their nation being attacked is indisputable. Their size, technical complexity and powers of endurance and of destruction are awesome, as is the cost of developing, building and maintaining them.

In 1623 the Dutchman Cornelius Drebbel was recorded as having built a submersible craft in London, which was rowed under the River Thames for some distance by 12 oarsmen. The French inventor Denis Papin used an air pump of his own design to control the buoyancy of a submersible vessel in 1696 – things were getting more scientific. Some 80 years later, during the American War of Independence, the American David Bushnell constructed the *Turtle* and inaugurated the era of submarine warfare. But it was with the American Civil War (1860–65) that

development really began. In the American Civil War the prospects for submarine tactics were promising enough for individual groups or companies, especially on the Confederate side, to engage in building submersibles to be used as privateers.

The self-propelled torpedo, introduced by the English inventor Robert Whitehead in 1866, opened up new opportunities for submarine warfare, and in the 1870s serious work began on powered submarines. As so often with pioneer projects, early efforts were frustratingly unsuccessful, but dogged belief in the future potential kept the work going. In 1887 the U.S. Navy offered $2 million towards construction of the best submarine design, then transferred the prize to surface ships. A turning point came in 1890 when the submarine *Gymnote*, designed by the Frenchman Gustave Zédé, passed unseen beneath a battleship to break through a blockade. Surface-fixated officers began to revise their views, and anti-submarine protection became a hot issue.

Crewmen on the walking deck of Simon Lake's submarine *Protector*, built in 1902.

USS *Connecticut* (SSN22), second of the Seawolf class, commissioned on 11 December 1998, under way in the Pacific Ocean. *Connecticut*'s motto is 'Arsenal of the Nation'.

Achievement of the large internal combustion engine, powered initially by gasoline, then kerosene and finally diesel, for surface running, backed up by battery-powered electric motors for subsurface travel, made the sea-going submarine a viable proposition in the 1900s. At this stage it was still a surface vessel that could dive for brief periods, rather than an undersea craft that could also travel on the surface. Its strategic value became fully apparent in the course of World War I. With the land war deadlocked on the Western Front, the British Navy was enforcing a tight blockade of German ports. The German naval command responded with a policy of 'unrestricted submarine warfare', at first partial, then total, on ships approaching the British Isles. The effect of this in 1917 was enormous – over 3,210,000 tonnes of shipping were sunk in February–June of that year, and in Britain both food and vital war supplies were reaching danger level, until the belated introduction of convoys and improved counter-measures in the detection and destruction of submarines began to reduce the toll.

In the ensuing decades, which encompassed World War II and numerous more localized outbreaks of warfare, the role of the submarine did not essentially change, although much ingenuity was lavished on peripheral concepts like submarine aircraft carriers. The snorkel, a Dutch invention adopted by Germany, making it possible to run diesel engines and recharge batteries without surfacing, was a key development in 1943. Two further developments – the introduction of the jet-propelled missile and the construction of a compact nuclear reactor – transformed the role of the submarine in the course of the 1950s. The nuclear-powered submarine could remain submerged, its position unknown, as long as its crew's food supply lasted, could travel any distance without having to refuel, and could carry the increasingly large guided missiles of the Cold War era.

In its various forms it still fulfils that role and looks likely to do so far into the 21st century. In recent years, though, it has become clear that both development and construction of submarines has slowed down. In part this is due to economic considerations, but the ever-increasing technical complexity of an up-to-date submarine is also responsible. The efforts to make a submarine virtually undetectable underwater have resulted in equipment of great refinement, sensitivity and expense.

The construction and maintenance of nuclear submarines requires a stronger and larger technical-industrial base than most nations can provide, and recently there has been a renewed interest in non-nuclear submarines, encouraged by important developments in air-independent engine design, long-term underwater staying power, reduced detectability and greater manoeuvrability.

Submersibles and Submarines

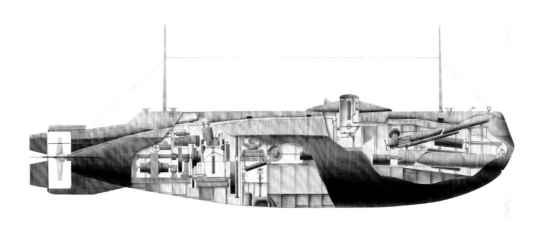

A drawn timeline of submarine design would show a very long flat line stretching from dim antiquity to around 1600, rising slightly from then to 1860, with a marked step up in the 1860s and another in the 1880s–1890s. By 1910 the modern submarine with diesel and electric power was present and although much enlarged and fitted with a wide range of new equipment over the next 50 years, it remained recognizably the same type of vessel. The 1920s and 1930s saw a range of experiments with specialized craft, but the prime line of evolution was towards the long-range attack boat. The diesel-electric submarines of 1943 onwards, although equipped with sonar, radar and fire-control systems, and armed with far more effective torpedoes and deck guns, would still have been understandable to the submariners of 1910.

Opposite: A German U-boat crew enjoy a meal on deck in the open air during the early years of World War II.
On operational patrol, crews would spend many weeks within the cramped confines of their submarine.

🇺🇸 **The Turtle** (1775)

The world's first submarine craft specifically designed and built for military action was deployed off New York Harbour during the American War of Independence on 6 September 1776. Its mission was to sink a British man-of-war with a displacement a thousand times greater than its own.

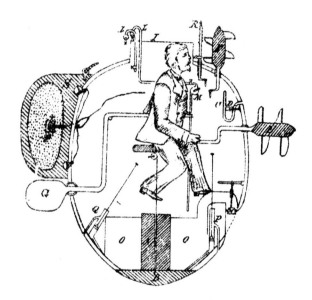

The *Turtle* was the brainchild of David Bushnell (1740–1824), who was determined to create the most effective submersible vessel yet built. The son of a Connecticut farmer, he became a mature student at Yale where his interest in scientific matters, including explosives, was well known. Work at a Saybrook shipyard to pay for his college course perhaps sparked his interest in submersibles. The concept of a submarine was unfamiliar, and one contemporary reference refers to the craft as a 'water machine'. Benjamin Franklin was informed of the project to construct the *Turtle* and he

Sectional and plan drawings of *Turtle*, made in the 19th century, based on contemporary descriptions.

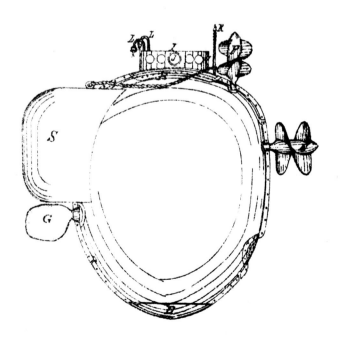

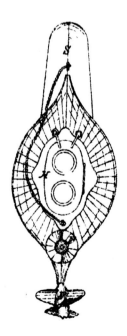

A remarkable range of controls and devices was incorporated within the *Turtle's* tight framework. The operator could barely turn around.

Air tubes
The air tubes are among *Turtle* firsts; also the use of water as dischargeable ballast (at the base of the craft); and the use of 'glow in the dark' needles on barometer and compass dials.

Bomb and detonator
Note the release cord. Two clockmakers worked with Bushnell on the firing mechanism, modifying a clockwork-timing device to trigger a flintlock mechanism whose sparks would ignite the priming powder in the pan, which in turn would set off the gunpowder. The operator would set this device when releasing the mine from the submarine, allowing himself enough time to get well away.

Propeller
Turtle's propeller was not of the screw type as shown, but a bladed paddle type, hence the reference to 'oars' in descriptions from the period.

One-man operation
The multiplicity of levers and handles shows the problem of one-man operation: to maintain depth and trim while also working the awl would have been extremely difficult.

Ballast
Ballast pumps and outlets.

Keel
The lead keel could be detached for emergency surfacing.

took a close interest, gave advice and may have seen a demonstration.

Remarkable craft

A detailed description of this remarkable craft survives in letters from Dr Benjamin Gale from November 1775 to February 1776. He noted that: "The Body, when standing upright in the position in which it is navigated, has the nearest resemblance to the two upper shells of a Tortoise joined together." The operator entered through a brass-domed lid, secured by screws and with eight glasses for all-round viewing. Two brass tubes were fitted to admit fresh air when required and a ventilator at the side released 'air rendered unfit for respiration' (believed at the time to be heavier than fresh air). Equipment included a barometer, for depth measurement, and a compass. "In the barometer and on the needles of the compass is fixed fox-fire, i.e. wood that gives light in the dark" – this was from a suggestion of Franklin's, as a candle would have been quite impracticable. Ballast was nine cwt (502kg) of lead "part of which is so fixed as he can let run down to the Bottom, and serves as an anchor". A sounding lead was fixed at the bow. A foot-operated valve admitted water to a ballast tank from which it could be pumped out again: "To bring the machine into a perfect equilibrium with the water, he can admit so much water as is necessary, and has a forcing pump by which he can free the machine at pleasure, and can rise above water, and again immerge, as occasion requires."

An opened-out full-scale replica of the *Turtle*, at the Submarine Force Museum, Groton, Connecticut. The propeller has a more authentic form.

Specification

Dimensions:	Length: 2.29m (7ft 6in); Beam: 0.9m (35in); Height: 1.83m (6ft)
Displacement:	Surfaced – 0.55 tonne (0.54 ton); Submerged – 1 tonne (0.98 ton)
Propulsion:	Two-blade foot-worked paddle-propeller
Speed:	Walking pace
Range:	c. 1km (0.62 mile)
Armament:	68kg (150lb) gunpowder keg with clockwork fuse
Complement:	1

Bushnell had carried out tests to establish that gunpowder would explode under water, and had also perfected a clockwork mechanism that made his mine an effective time bomb. This must have been set in motion before the mission set off, as the mine was mounted externally: "Three magazines are prepared; the first, the explosion takes place in twelve – the second in eight – the third in six hours, after being fixed to the ship. He proposes to fix these three before the first explosion takes place. He has made such a trial of the effects of the explosion of gunpowder under water ... as has exceeded his most sanguine expectations, and is now convinced his magazines will contain three times so much powder as is necessary to destroy the largest ship in the navy."

With Sergeant Ezra Lee as a volunteer in the operator's seat, *Turtle* was towed out in the dark by rowing boats to a position close to the blockading squadron and then submerged to approach the British flagship HMS *Eagle,* a 64-gun, third-rate ship of the line. All the systems worked as planned, except that the drill failed to penetrate the timber of the ship's hull. *Eagle* was not copper-sheathed, but the drill may have met an iron rudder-support or simply have been inadequate for its purpose.

Lee had to retreat without completing his mission. His craft was spotted and pursued, but by his own account he detached the mine, which exploded, and he and *Turtle* made it safely to shore. At least one further attempt on a British vessel also failed to attach the mine. *Turtle*'s subsequent fate is not entirely clear. A vessel carrying it was sunk by the British, but Bushnell may have salvaged his craft. If he did so, it was not used again.

Operation of the *Turtle* placed a heavy demand on its pilot, who had to work all of its equipment, keep a lookout, make tactical decisions and use his arms and legs in strenuous activity. George Washington, while commending the exercise as "an effort of genius", realized that it expected too much from a single operator. Yet although it came very close to success, Bushnell did not attempt to build another submarine and instead transferred his attention to floating mines.

A replica of the *Turtle* was built in 1976, and in 2003 another fully working replica was constructed using materials of 1775, and this successfully travelled under the surface. One of the reasons for this was to counter scepticism from British sources that the celebrated attack of 1776 had ever been made, as the records of the British blockading fleet have no reference to it.

Hand-operated

The hand-worked propeller could be reversed for backwards travel and a second set of blades on a vertical shaft enabled the pilot to trim the vessel. There was also a hand-worked rudder. The mine was carried externally, and described as "... so contrived, that when he comes under the side of the Ship, he rubs down the side until he comes to the keel, and a hook so fix'd as that when it touches the keel it raises a spring which frees the magazine from the machine and fastens it to the side of the Ship; at the same time, it draws a pin, which sets the watchwork agoing which, at a given time, springs the lock and the explosion ensues."

The stabilising effect of the weighted keel was vital. If the vessel had 'turned turtle' the result would have been fatal for the pilot.

CSS Hunley (1863)

The intensity of the struggle in the US Civil War forced submarine builders to work fast and take risks. The Confederate submarine *Hunley* underwent three sinkings, drowning its eponymous designer, before it became the first submarine to sink a surface craft.

Although trained as a lawyer, Horace Lawson Hunley (1823–63) had already built two submarines before designing and building this one, at first unnamed but sometimes referred to as 'Fish Boat'. He was thus familiar with the problems of submarine operation and had even considered powered propulsion before reverting to manual cranking in the interest of simplicity and practicality. Based on plans by Hunley, James R. McClintock and Baxter Watson, the vessel was

constructed in 1863 in Mobile, Alabama, for the Confederate Army. Also involved was E.C. Singer, who had patented an underwater contact mine.

Riveted iron plates

The boat's hull shape, with a vertical stem and stern, anticipated later submarine designs. When the *Hunley* was raised in 2000, it was found to be constructed of iron plates

Armament
Torpedo spar, with spike and release cord.

Though on a smaller scale, *Hunley's* elongated hull form anticipated that of later submarines more closely than most of the early designs.

riveted to a purpose-built frame tapered fore and aft to provide 'streamlining' to help it move easily and unobtrusively under the surface. The final configuration was about 10m (32ft) long, 1.2m (4ft) wide and 1.5m (5ft) deep.

A tiller worked the rudder. Ballast consisted of iron bars bolted to the bottom of the hull and tanks at either end, which could be opened manually to allow the boat to submerge. Hand-operated pumps were used to discharge water to allow it to surface. To move the craft to Charleston, it was cut in half, loaded on railcars and covered up for the journey from New Orleans. With the boat's arrival in Charleston on the morning of 12 August 1863, a suitable mooring from which to strike out at the enemy fleet was sought, and preparations and training continued for attack on the Union ships. Horace Hunley filed a requisition for nine grey-jacketed uniforms, three to be trimmed with gold braid, to be worn by the crew during their nocturnal patrols, noting that the men were "on special secret service and that it is necessary that they be clothed in the Confederate Army uniform."

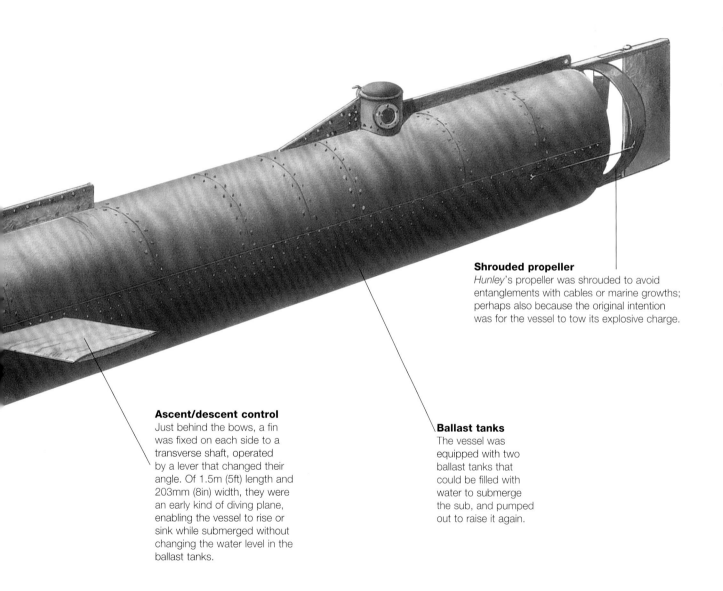

Shrouded propeller
Hunley's propeller was shrouded to avoid entanglements with cables or marine growths; perhaps also because the original intention was for the vessel to tow its explosive charge.

Ascent/descent control
Just behind the bows, a fin was fixed on each side to a transverse shaft, operated by a lever that changed their angle. Of 1.5m (5ft) length and 203mm (8in) width, they were an early kind of diving plane, enabling the vessel to rise or sink while submerged without changing the water level in the ballast tanks.

Ballast tanks
The vessel was equipped with two ballast tanks that could be filled with water to submerge the sub, and pumped out to raise it again.

CSS Hunley

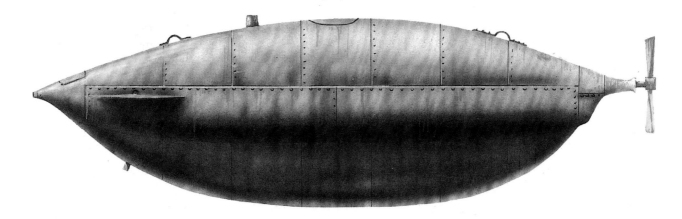

The Confederate military took over the submarine from its private builders and owners shortly after its arrival, turning it over to the Army. In fact during its entire career, *Hunley* was under the control of the Confederate Army, although Horace Hunley and his partners remained involved in its further testing and operation. Its early excursions were disastrous.

On 29 August 1863, the crew of 'Fish Boat' were preparing to make a test dive when Lieutenant Payne accidentally stepped on the lever controlling the diving planes while the boat was running on the surface (another account suggests it was swamped by the wake of a tender craft). This caused it to dive with hatches still open. Payne and two others escaped, but the other five crewmen drowned. The submarine was salvaged and training exercises resumed. On 15 October 1863,

Contemporary with *Hunley* is the preserved 'Bayou St John submarine' at Louisiana State Museum. *Hunley's* predecessor, *Pioneer*, was of very similar appearance.

it failed to resurface after a mock attack, drowning Hunley and seven other crewmen. It appeared to have dived too sharply and the bow had become embedded in the seabed mud. The Confederate forces once more salvaged the submarine and returned it to service.

After the second disaster, General Beauregard, commander of Charleston's defences, placed restrictions on the vessel, requiring it to operate only as a surface ship. He wrote: "After this tragedy I refused to permit the boat to be used again; but Lieutenant Dixon, a brave and determined man, having returned to Charleston, applied to me for authority to use it against the Federal steam sloop-of-war *Housatonic*, a powerful new vessel, carrying eleven guns of the largest calibre, which lay at the time in the north channel opposite Beach Inlet, materially obstructing the passage of our blockade-runners in and out."

Attack on *Housatonic*

The final attack was made on the steam-powered blockade ship *Housatonic* of 1260 tonnes (1240 tons) on 17 February 1864. Now named in commemoration of Horace Hunley (although sometimes referred to as the CSS *Hunley*, it was never officially commissioned as such) the boat was submerged, but near enough the surface to create a disturbance that was spotted by a lookout, but taken to be a plank or a porpoise. Too late this mistake was rectified, the anchor chain was slipped

Specification

Dimensions:	Length: 12m (40ft); Beam: 1m (3ft 4in); Draught: 1.2m (3ft 11in)
Displacement:	Surfaced – 6.8 tonnes (6.7 tons)
Propulsion:	Hand-crank shaft, single screw
Speed:	Surfaced – 4 knots (7.4km/h; 4.6mph); Submerged – approx. 2 knots (3.7km/h; 2.3 mph)
Range:	c. 4.8km (3 miles)
Armament:	One spar torpedo containing 41kg (90lb) of gunpowder
Complement:	8

Artist's impression of the attack, with *Hunley* still very close to *Housatonic* when the mine explodes.

Refined construction

Later observers would admire the quality of the engineering. Rivets were sanded almost flush with the submarine's exterior to reduce friction, which was important both to avoid detection and to ease its movement. With Union ships blockading Charleston Harbor, the boat was planned as a stealth weapon that would approach a target ship undetected and attack it with a Singer-type spar torpedo attached to a 6m (20ft) pole protruding from its bow. The torpedo was placed by ramming the victim, penetrating the hull then backing off, using a long cord to trigger the explosive.

and the 'porpoise' came under musket fire, which had no effect. The torpedo was rammed against the ship, detached and fired. Traces of copper wire found with *Hunley*'s hull suggest that detonation may have been electrical rather than mechanical. The effect was immediate: in five minutes after the explosion, *Housatonic* was sinking in flames. But although *Hunley* was reported to have sent a light signal confirming success, that was its last action – it sank close to its victim, drowning all the crew.

First located in 1970, its position confirmed in 1995, *Hunley* was raised in 2000 and is currently under conservation at the Warren Lasch Conservation Center in the former Navy Yard at Charleston. Approximately 10 tonnes of encrusted sediment have been removed and on-going analysis of the hull and its contents are expected to shed further light on the vessel's design and its method of attack.

USS Intelligent Whale (1863)

The only surviving US Civil War submersible built in the North, *Intelligent Whale* was intended as a business speculation, but was also an innovative craft using the most advanced technology of its time.

Intelligent Whale was the result of a speculative exercise in 1862 by a group of entrepreneurs who hoped to operate privateer vessels as was being done by the Confederate forces. Its designer was the inventor Scovel S. Merriam and construction began in secret, probably at Springfield, Massachusetts, in late 1863. Mild steel, cast and wrought iron from the West Point Foundry, New York, were used, with the hull formed of 46 plates 13mm (0.5in) thick. President Lincoln's refusal to use privateers doomed their American Submarine Company, but construction continued

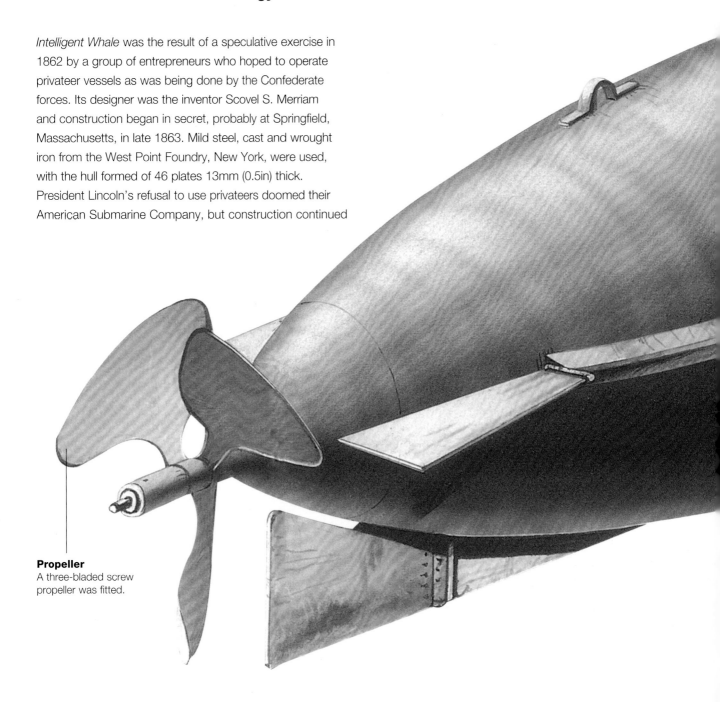

Propeller
A three-bladed screw propeller was fitted.

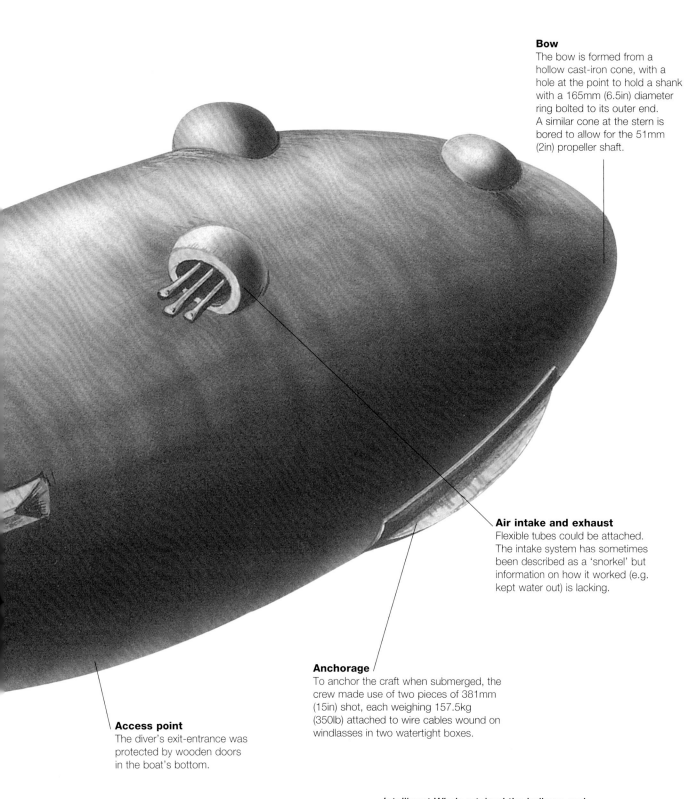

Bow
The bow is formed from a hollow cast-iron cone, with a hole at the point to hold a shank with a 165mm (6.5in) diameter ring bolted to its outer end. A similar cone at the stern is bored to allow for the 51mm (2in) propeller shaft.

Air intake and exhaust
Flexible tubes could be attached. The intake system has sometimes been described as a 'snorkel' but information on how it worked (e.g. kept water out) is lacking.

Anchorage
To anchor the craft when submerged, the crew made use of two pieces of 381mm (15in) shot, each weighing 157.5kg (350lb) attached to wire cables wound on windlasses in two watertight boxes.

Access point
The diver's exit-entrance was protected by wooden doors in the boat's bottom.

Intelligent Whale retained the bulbous and whale-like hull form typical of most early submarine designs.

in the hope of interesting the U.S. Navy in the craft (in February 1864 the *Hunley*'s sinking of *Housatonic* caused a sensation). But later in 1864 the Navy rejected it. An overrun on construction costs of some $45,000 caused a series of disagreements and lawsuits between owners and builders.

Under new owners, led by the lawyer and arms dealer Oliver S. Halsted, work continued on the vessel during

A photograph taken at the Brooklyn Navy Yard in the 1930s. The towing or mooring ring can be seen, as can the craft's relatively flat bottom.

1865 and 1866. In April 1866 it underwent a successful trial, anchored at a depth of 4.8m (16ft). General Thomas W. Sweeney exited the vessel in a diving suit, attached a 'torpedo' to a scow anchored nearby and returned to the submarine. The weapon was detonated using a lanyard and a friction primer, and sank the scow. Despite this, the Navy took no interest. For another four years intermittent work was done on the hull, stored on land at the New Jersey works of Hewes & Phillips, while simultaneous disputes went on about the ownership.

A further official inspection was made in October 1869, resulting in a favourable report, and a contract for purchase was drawn up, subject to successful trial at Brooklyn Navy Yard by 1 January 1870. This contract referred to the craft for the first time as *Intelligent Whale*. The price was to be $50,000, with a down payment of $12,500. A trial did not in fact take place until 20 September 1872 and was not a success, with leaks occurring as soon as it began to dive.

Specification

Dimensions:	Length: 8.92m (29ft); Beam: 2.21m (7ft 3in); Draught: 1.2m (3ft 11in)
Displacement:	Surfaced – 46.7 tonnes (46 tons); Submerged – not known
Propulsion:	Single screw, geared hand-crank
Speed:	c. 4 knots (7.4km/h; 4.6mph)
Range:	17nm (31km/19 miles)
Armament:	Mine – 11.2kg (25lb) of gunpowder
Complement:	6

The inspection committee concluded that: "As a practical instrument of warfare it is utterly useless." No further money was paid over but *Intelligent Whale* remained at the Brooklyn Navy Yard.

'Intelligent Elephant'

A description dating from September 1872 notes that the vessel was known at the Navy Yard as the 'Intelligent Elephant': "… built of iron, with air and watertight compartments for its regulation and control. At the bottom of the boat, amidships, is a flat gate, the upper parts and the end being round and tapering. The water being kept from entering the vessel while it is open by compressed air. Out of this gate someone is expected to pass and place a torpedo under a vessel, an electric wire being attached and connected with a battery in the boat and thus fired. It is estimated that the air compartments will contain enough compressed air enough to last 10 hours in use under the water. The water compartments are filled for sinking the boat by opening a valve, and can be ejected by pumps or forced out by compressed air being let in, there being a connection between both compartments. The boat will hold 13 persons and has been tried in the Passaic River with that number on board. Six men are sufficient for working it, its motive power being produced by part of them through the agency of a crank."

The observer noted that when under water the boat had no ventilation other than from the compressed air holders, and that foul air could be exhausted by the use of thumb valves. Ballast tanks were fitted at the bow and stern, and four large air pumps were mounted. Around 1874 a flexible pipe linked the hull to a floating air intake "the size and shape of a wild duck", a design presumably intended as camouflage. Also among its equipment were a compass, depth gauge and air pressure gauge. Two ball anchors were mounted to stabilize the vessel underwater while the minelayer went about his task. A low conning tower, with four viewing ports, protruded at the top and from here the pilot could operate the rudder controls and the two diving planes. Eight further ports were fixed in the hull, two on each side being made to project, enabling an observer to see forwards and aft.

Operator error or design flaws?

John P. Holland, leading submarine designer of the next generation, believed that *Intelligent Whale*'s operating problems stemmed from incompetent handling rather than technical faults. Although the vessel's design did not lead to further development, close examination of the hull has yielded much information about the construction methods and operating systems of an 1860s' submersible. An internal framework of seven circular frames and nine horizontal stringers supports the 467 hull plates in a symmetrical pattern. The plates themselves are fixed to the frame by over 3000 rivets. The conning tower is formed of a single metal casting, inserted into the hull from above.

The hull, moved to Washington Navy Yard in 1965, is currently on display in the New Jersey Militia Museum.

Gustave Zédé (1893)

The French were the most innovative submarine designers of the later 19th century, with the marine engineer Gustave Zédé (1825–91) a leading figure. His electrically-propelled *Gymnote* was the French Navy's first submarine in 1888. It made over 2000 dives.

Zédé played a large part in the design of *Gymnote*, a small steel-hulled vessel of 18m (59ft) length, powered by a 55hp (41kW) electric motor and capable of 6 knots (11km/h; 7mph). It was very much a test-craft, and carried no armament. In 1898 it was reconstructed with a raised conning tower and was used in tests and training along with *Gustave Zédé* until 1907.

In many ways the design looks forward to that of submarines of the later 20th century, notably in the propeller-rudders configuration, though, of course, without the technical sophistication of the later boats.

Power supply
The submarine had electric drive only, taking its power from batteries.

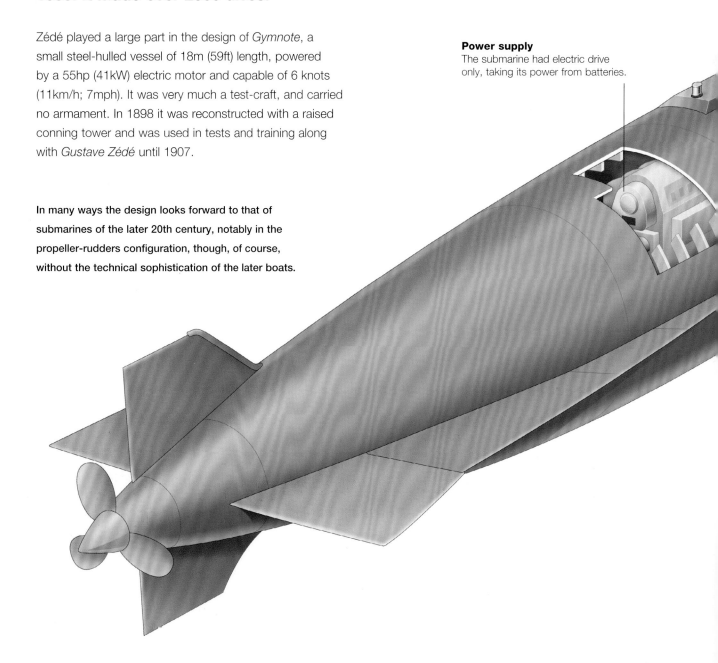

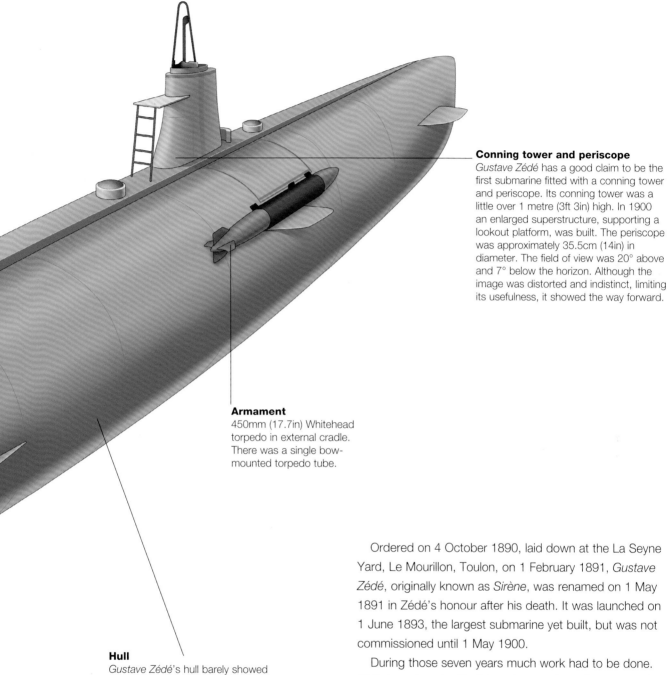

Conning tower and periscope
Gustave Zédé has a good claim to be the first submarine fitted with a conning tower and periscope. Its conning tower was a little over 1 metre (3ft 3in) high. In 1900 an enlarged superstructure, supporting a lookout platform, was built. The periscope was approximately 35.5cm (14in) in diameter. The field of view was 20° above and 7° below the horizon. Although the image was distorted and indistinct, limiting its usefulness, it showed the way forward.

Armament
450mm (17.7in) Whitehead torpedo in external cradle. There was a single bow-mounted torpedo tube.

Hull
Gustave Zédé's hull barely showed above the water when surfaced, with only the walk-platform visible. For 10 years after launching, it was the largest submarine in the world. To contemporaries, it was 'a giant'.

Ordered on 4 October 1890, laid down at the La Seyne Yard, Le Mourillon, Toulon, on 1 February 1891, *Gustave Zédé*, originally known as *Sirène*, was renamed on 1 May 1891 in Zédé's honour after his death. It was launched on 1 June 1893, the largest submarine yet built, but was not commissioned until 1 May 1900.

During those seven years much work had to be done. At first equipped with diving planes only at the stern and intended to submerge at an angle of 50°, its performance was erratic, and while undergoing tests with a committee of experts on board the first dive was a failure. At first the boat would not submerge, then it hit bottom at an angle of 30° in 18.3m (60ft) of water. Effective dive depth was 15m (50ft). However, determined to maintain their technical lead, the French Admiralty allowed the engineers to persist in their efforts to put things right. Three additional hydroplanes

Gustave Zédé

were added on each side to prevent it from pitching down, and it went on to make over 2000 dives.

The single hull was made of bronze roma-metal, non-magnetic and also considered more corrosion-proof and less brittle than steel. Cylindrical in general shape, the *Zédé* differed from most submersibles of the time by

Gustave Zédé **skims the surface of the water, sometime after reconstruction in the late 1890s.**

having differently-shaped fore- and after-parts. The basic framework was made from 76 round ribs connected by longitudinal braces. Instead of one ballast tank in the centre, the *Zédé* had two. Water was expelled from the tanks by compressed air obtained through the action of two Thirion pumps, each worked by an electric motor. The pumps also supplied the air necessary for breathing and for the discharge of the torpedoes. Diving and steering were managed on the same principle as that employed by Gustave Zédé in *Gymnote*, the rudders being in a similar position just forward of the propeller.

The boat was electrically driven with power supplied by a bank of batteries. Two 360hp (268kW) Sautter-Harlé DC electric motors operating at 250rpm were coupled to the single propeller drive shaft. Together the motors weighed 27.4 tonnes (27 tons). The original Laurant-Celvieva battery configuration was of 720 cells weighing 132 tonnes (130 tons) and capable of delivering 1800A at 300V. When the charging current was turned on the battery exploded, causing serious damage to the stern structure and starting a violent fire. After nearly two years, with a new battery layout consisting of 360 cells, the *Gustave Zédé* was able to go on its first trials; but

Specification

Dimensions:	Length: 48.5m (159ft); Beam: 3.2m (10ft 6in); Draught: 3.2m (10ft 6in)
Displacement:	surfaced – 264 tonnes (260 tons); submerged – 274 tonnes (270 tons)
Propulsion:	Two Sautter-Harlé 360hp (268kW) electric motors, battery powered; single screw
Speed:	Surfaced – 12 knots (22km/h; 14mph); Submerged – 6.5 knots (12km/h; 7mph)
Range:	Surfaced – 220nm (407km; 253 miles) at 5.5 knots (10km/h; 6 mph); Submerged – 105nm (194km; 121 miles) at 4.5 knots (8km/h; 5mph)
Armament:	One 450mm (17.7in) torpedo tube, 4 Whitehead torpedoes
Complement:	19

the designed speed of 15 knots (28km/h; 17mph) was reduced to only 8 knots (15km/h; 9mph), although this was later improved to 12 knots (22km/h; 14mph). The boat had no alternative power source on board that could be used to recharge the batteries, unlike other contemporary designs such as the *Holland VI,* which had a petrol engine as well as batteries.

A serious hazard for the crew was the battery's liability to discharge poisonous acid vapour, but it was learned how to bring this problem under control. In December 1898 *Gustave Zédé* made the 65.6km (41 mile) journey between Toulon and Marseille unaided, showing the capacity of its electric-only motors, to join in Mediterranean Fleet exercises, and made two successful mock attacks on the battleship *Magenta*. In April 1901 it made a demonstration dive at Toulon with French President Loubet on board.

Combat trials

On the evening of 2 July 1901 the submarine left Marseille without the lookouts stationed on the quay being able to notice its departure. A naval tug towed it to a position off Ajaccio harbour in Corsica, where it submerged in the early morning of the 3rd, entering the harbour undetected. A battleship squadron was just weighing anchor to leave on practice manoeuvres, and *Gustave Zédé* fired an unarmed torpedo at the *Charles Martel*, flagship of the Second Division, striking the hull. An observer wrote: "The presence of the submarine was not suspected until a curious shock was sustained and a white furrow was perceived on the surface of the sea. Then, two hundred yards away, a black cylinder, which was the optic tube of the submarine, was noticed. This sudden and unforeseen attack, which had been so skilfully conducted by Lieutenant Jobard, aroused general enthusiasm … There is no doubt that she successfully torpedoed the *Charles Martel*." The admiral in command, although warned in advance that the submarine would be joining the exercises, refused to take it seriously and disallowed the claim. But the event soon became widely known, and confirmed the role of the submarine as an integral element in a modern fleet.

Favourable press coverage

A British newspaper report on 21 February 1899 noted that *Gustave Zédé* made a speed of 6 knots (11km/h; 7mph) between Toulon and Marseille, even though there was quite a heavy sea and "everything was shut down on board, so that the crew were for seven hours under the same conditions as if the boat had been entirely submerged … She could not be sighted from a battleship at a greater distance than 2000 yards, and then while covering the intervening distance she would only appear intermittently for a few seconds at a time, so that the enemy could not watch her course or aim at her." It also noted that "experiments are being made with a periscope on the principle of the photographic camera, by which a telescopic tube raised above the water would afford a view of anything going on around it."

The submarine's arrival in Marseille (1898) drew a large crowd.

Argonaut (1897)

Simon Lake's wheeled submarine can fairly be called the precursor of all seabed-travelling vehicles, especially those engaged in non-military activities. It brought him riches and fame. But it has many other claims as a pioneering undersea craft.

Lake was born in Pleasantville, New Jersey, in 1866 and entered his father's foundry and machine shop in 1883, later becoming a partner in the business. Being interested in submersibles, in 1894 he tested his ideas with *Argonaut*

Junior, a small triangular vessel of pitch pine, 4.3m (14ft) long. When submerged to a shallow seafloor, a diver's door could be opened and he could retrieve articles or exit and re-enter the craft through a pressurized compartment. It ran

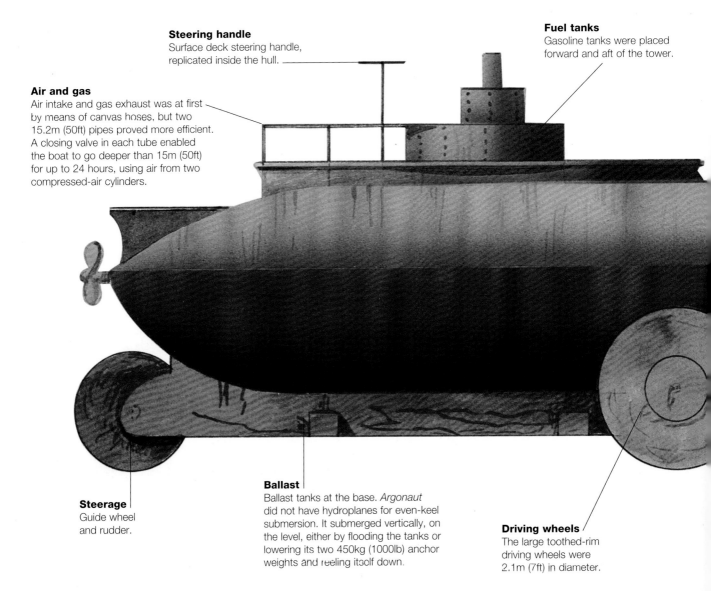

Steering handle
Surface deck steering handle, replicated inside the hull.

Fuel tanks
Gasoline tanks were placed forward and aft of the tower.

Air and gas
Air intake and gas exhaust was at first by means of canvas hoses, but two 15.2m (50ft) pipes proved more efficient. A closing valve in each tube enabled the boat to go deeper than 15m (50ft) for up to 24 hours, using air from two compressed-air cylinders.

Steerage
Guide wheel and rudder.

Ballast
Ballast tanks at the base. *Argonaut* did not have hydroplanes for even-keel submersion. It submerged vertically, on the level, either by flooding the tanks or lowering its two 450kg (1000lb) anchor weights and reeling itself down.

Driving wheels
The large toothed-rim driving wheels were 2.1m (7ft) in diameter.

on three wheels, the rear pair being turned by means of a hand crank.

Argonaut, built in 1897 in Baltimore at the Columbian Iron Works & Dry Dock Co., was a much more substantial vessel, incorporating most of the distinctive features of Lake's 1893 design, including a diver's air-lock, but with powered wheels for bottom crawling. The boat was driven by a 30hp (22kW) gasoline engine, even while submerged, when it used a hose supported by a surface float to supply combustion air. Although this device limited the depth to which *Argonaut* could operate under power, a supply of compressed air permitted even deeper excursions and bottoming for as long as 24 hours. Primarily intended for exploration and salvage, *Argonaut* travelled on the surface to pre-identified sites, where it would descend vertically, either by ballasting down or using haul-down anchors installed in the keel. Then it would trundle along the bottom on its powered wheels, towing the surface float.

An enthusiastic report in the *San Francisco Call* on 29 December 1897 noted that: "Submarine navigation seems to be an accomplished fact. In the presence of a thousand persons the *Argonaut*, built by Simon Lake of Baltimore, was recently submerged in twenty feet of water and remained at the bottom of the Patapsco River for four hours. The craft behaved admirably, fulfilling all the requirements claimed by the Inventor. As the vessel lay at anchor she looked very much like a miniature monitor. Her decks were covered with water, only the hollow masts towering above, supplying air to those inside. After an exhibition of her going powers above water the little craft took up a position a short distance from shore, and in two minutes after coming to a standstill went to the bottom in twenty feet of water and cruised around at the will of those inside. The party, which accompanied the inventor, say they experienced no unpleasant sensation. The only time at which the motion of the vessel was felt was when rolling along on a hard bottom. Then there was a slight vibration. The test was a severe one, as much of the bottom was muddy."

"Nevertheless the boat plowed through without any trouble. When at a full stop a diver entered an air-tight compartment and made his way out of the vessel. Those within were able to watch him as he moved about at the

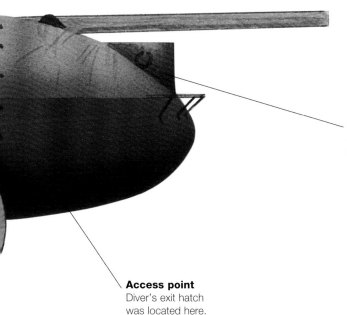

Lookout point
Forward lookout point. A light was mounted below.

Access point
Diver's exit hatch was located here.

Argonaut was a well thought-out and thoroughly practical undersea vessel, though its wooden wheels and frame could only be used on a fairly level and firm sea-floor not encumbered by rocks and gullies.

Argonaut

Argonaut on its coastal voyage of 1898, possibly approaching New York Harbour. Simon Lake is the man on the right.

Specification

Dimensions:	Length: 11m (36ft); Beam: 2.7m (9ft); Draught: 3m (10ft)
Displacement:	Surfaced – 59.9 tonnes (59 tons); Submerged – not known
Propulsion:	One White & Middleton gasoline engine, 30hp (22kW); single screw
Speed:	Surfaced – approx. 4 knots (7km/h; 4.5mph); submerged – 2 knots (3.7km/h; 2.3mph)
Range:	300nm (555km; 345 miles)
Armament:	None
Complement:	5

bottom of the river. A dinner was served under water, and the guests experienced no difficulty while eating."

"Three systems can be used for submerged travelling. With the masts, which are hollow, permitting air to come in on one side and go out the other, the vessel can work forty feet under water. In deeper water a hose is used, which answers the purpose of supplying air to the gasoline engine, and also supplies the crew. In water 100 feet deep the storage battery is depended upon for power and light and the compressed air reservoir for the air supply."

"When the hollow masts are submerged and water pours in, an automatic valve stops the flow. The diver obtains his supply of air from a tube running around the top of the vessel, which contains compressed air. He experienced no trouble either in going out or returning."

As the report noted, Lake found tube-masts more satisfactory as air intakes than the canvas hoses. After a series of local displays, Lake began using the boat to salvage sunken cargoes in Chesapeake Bay. Then in 1898 he took the boat into the open ocean, first for a limited excursion off Cape Henry, Virginia, and then for a longer cruise in which he sailed from Norfolk to Sandy Hook, New Jersey – the first successful open-sea voyage in a submarine. It was a slow two-month journey. At Hampton Roads, where mines protected the naval base (the Spanish–American War had just ended), *Argonaut* could have cut their moorings. It easily by-passed them, and laid its own demonstration cable across the Patuxent River, but when Lake offered the services of an *Argonaut* type to the Navy, it did not want to know. The boat travelled largely on the surface but submerged regularly to investigate promising wrecks or to scoop up edible shellfish. When a serious squall blew up, Lake avoided it by going under. At the journey's end he got a message of congratulation from Jules Verne, author of *Twenty Thousand Leagues Under the Sea*, who had been a source of youthful inspiration.

The year after the long coastal voyage, Lake had his vessel cut in half at the J.N. Robbins Dry Dock Co. in Brooklyn, given a new mid-section 6.1m (20ft) long, and a new schooner-like free-flooding superstructure above the pressure hull for better surface performance and to give it accommodation that would allow for a range of 3450nm (6389km; 3970 miles), and space for eight men. A new engine of doubled power was

fitted, along with a small 4hp (3kW) auxiliary. The modified craft was named *New Argonaut*, or *Argonaut II*, and based at Bridgeport, Connecticut, where Lake established the new headquarters of the Lake Submarine Company, essentially a marine salvage operation.

After staging several well-publicized sea-bottom excursions for local civic dignitaries (in 1898 he let a telephone line down to *Argonaut* and became the first person ever to a make telephone call from under water), he got down to recovering sunken cargoes in earnest. Over the next several years, he retrieved the contents of over 30 lost vessels in Long Island Sound, using patented improvements to *Argonaut II* and a new 'submarine wrecking car' that could be used to bring salvageable commodities, such as coal, to the surface for resale at a handsome profit.

The ultimate fate of *Argonaut II* does not seem to be recorded, but at the end of its working life it was presumably scrapped. Lake himself had moved on to other ventures. The success of his salvage boats did not result in orders for more, and perhaps reluctantly he looked to the better prospects offered by the military submarine (see *Protector*), turning the Lake Submarine Co. into the Lake Torpedo Boat Co.

Argonaut Junior

Lake's first design for a submersible was made in 1893 and never built (*see photograph, right*). It already reflected his interest in developing submarines primarily for commercial purposes, and particularly for marine salvage. It was intended to submerge on an even keel using a combination of judicious ballasting and horizontal control planes, and to operate largely on the sea bottom using a set of powered wheels for propulsion. The prime mover was to have been a compound steam engine, whose boiler would be shut down for submergence, after which compressed air would substitute for steam to turn both the propeller and the wheels.

USS Holland (1897)

Named for its Irish–American designer John P. Holland, this was the first submarine to be commissioned into the United States Navy. Among many other novel features, it was the first submarine to incorporate separate power sources for running on the surface and when submerged.

J.P. Holland established his reputation as a submarine designer with *Fenian Ram* (1875), a vessel built for US-based Fenian Irish independence fighters. On 3 March 1893 the US Congress approved the construction of a naval submarine. Holland's Torpedo Boat Company won the resulting design competition and gained a $150,000 contract to build the steam-powered USS *Plunger* on 3 March 1895. Hampered by interference from the naval authorities and with no confidence in steam propulsion for submarines, Holland effectively stopped

Below: USS *Holland* was the first submarine to be formally commissioned into any navy apart from that of France, which was first with *Gymnote* in 1888.

Propeller

One of J.P. Holland's fixed ideas was the propeller of the submarine should be placed beyond the steering gear. It was only with difficulty, after early testing of the *Holland*, that he was persuaded to have the large three-bladed screw moved inboard of the rudder.

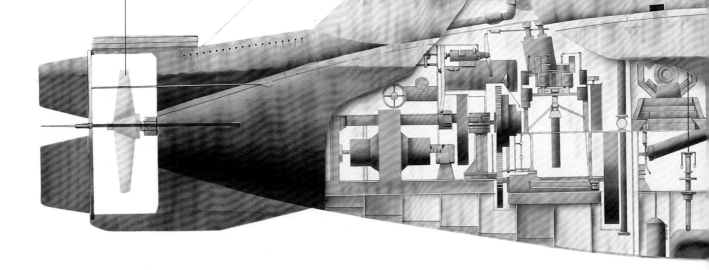

The fifth Holland submarine for Britain's Royal Navy, commissioned in 1902 and designated *Holland 5*. A periscope and torpedo tube were incorporated.

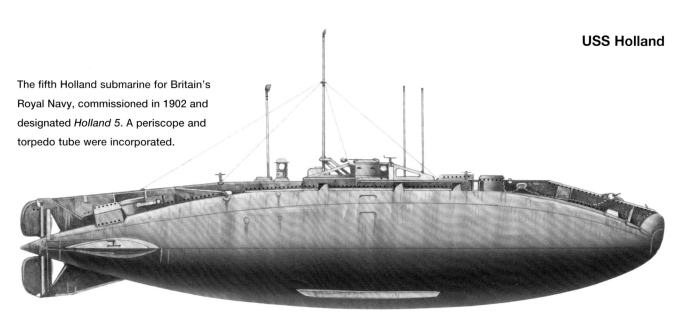

'Aerial torpedo'
The Zalinski cannon or 'dynamite gun' fired a level shot just above the surface. It was known as the 'aerial torpedo'. On 27 March 1898 in Staten Island Sound, the *Holland* tested its forward gun for the Navy. The gun was aimed at Tottenville on Staten Island and was charged with only 270kg (600lb) of compressed air instead of the 450kg (1000lb) Holland had wanted. When fired, the 1m-long (3ft 3in), 22.5kg (50lb) wooden dummy-projectile ran forward just under 300m (980ft).

Clinometer
Among the numerous aids pioneered on the *Holland* was the clinometer, devised by Frank T. Cable, which enabled the vessel's pilot to check the submarine's angle from the horizontal.

Power supply
As in subsequent submarines, the batteries in *Holland* were placed centrally close to the keel, their weight helping to maintain the boat's trim.

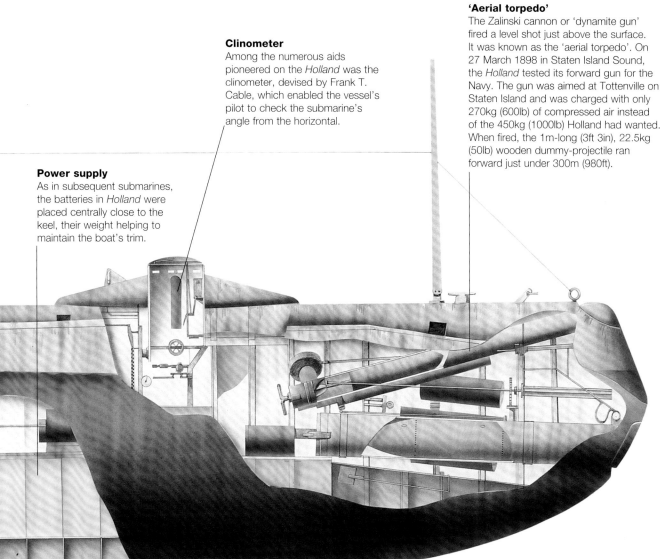

The first Holland design for Britain's Royal Navy, and the Royal Navy's first submarine, on trials in 1900. It is preserved at the Royal Navy Submarine Museum, Gosport, Hampshire.

Specification

Dimensions:	Length: 16.4m (53ft 10in); Beam: 2.6m (8ft 6in); Draught: 2.6m (8ft 6in)
Displacement:	Surfaced – 65 tonnes (64 tons); Submerged – 75 tonnes (74 tons)
Propulsion:	Otto engine developing 45hp (34kW) with one E.D. electric motor developing 75hp (56kW); single screw
Speed:	Surfaced – 8 knots (14.8km/h; 9mph); Submerged – 5 knots (9.2km/h; 5.7mph)
Range:	1150nm (2129km; 1323 miles)
Armament:	One 457mm (18in) bow torpedo tube, two torpedoes; two Zalinski pneumatic cannon (one later removed)
Complement:	6

work on *Plunger* to build a boat (his sixth) to his own exclusive design using a combination of electric and gasoline motors.

On 17 May 1897 this new boat was launched from Lewis Nixon's Crescent Yard at Elizabeth, New Jersey, its tapering cylindrical hull formed of iron plates round a series of steel frames set about 33cm (13in) apart. A flat superstructure provided a deck, with a tower of minimal height at around 46cm (18in), and 61cm (24in) in diameter forming both the entrance hatch and control position. A single three-bladed propeller was fitted, forward of the rudder and the two 'horizontal rudders' or diving planes. Internally it contained a 75hp (56kW) electric motor from the Electro-Dynamic Company of Philadelphia and a 66-cell Exide battery, as well as the 50hp (37.25kW) four-stroke Otto gasoline engine. There were six main compressed air tanks, with 0.9m³ (30 cubic feet) of air at 140kg/cm² (2000psi) and two smaller tanks at 3.5kg/cm² (50psi) and 0.7kg/cm² (10psi) respectively.

The flotation tanks had been rethought: in earlier submarines they lacked subdivision, simply made large enough to hold the required maximum of water, and

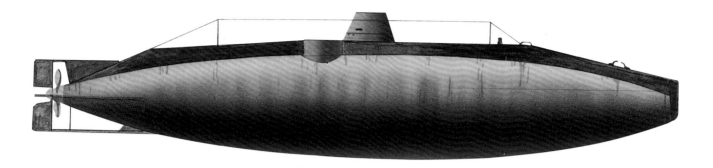

consequently were rarely totally filled, allowing the water to flow freely from one end of the tank to the other as the boat's angle changed, making it very difficult to keep a proper trim. In Holland's new boat the main storage tanks were of such a capacity that when entirely filled the boat would be brought to the awash condition only, and final adjusting of the buoyancy was made using a small tank with only a small free-water surface if not entirely filled, leaving the main ballast tanks either empty or full. The craft was capable of diving to 23m (75ft) and had a range of 40 nautical miles (74km; 46 miles) at a surface speed of 3 knots (5.5km/h; 3.4mph). After initial trials on 17 March 1898, streamlined wooden fairings were added fore and aft of the conning tower to help the water flow around it.

The vessel was designed for attack, with a single reloadable 457mm (18in) torpedo tube and two Zalinski

Night attack

Holland was used for training purposes at the Annapolis Naval College, although its career was relatively brief due to its lack of internal space, the difficulties of operating it and the availability of newer boats. Its most glorious moment was in the course of night exercises in Narragansett Bay on 25 September 1901. Holland slipped unseen past the scout ships of the 'enemy' fleet and made a run at the battleship Kearsarge with its torpedo tube open. At 100 yards (91m; 300ft) its commander, Lieutenant Caldwell, flashed a light and shouted, "Hello Kearsarge, you are blown to atoms. This is the submarine boat the Holland!"

HMS *Holland I* (1900) in profile. It was built in England to plans supplied by the Electric Boat Co.

210mm (8.2in) pneumatic cannon mounted fore and aft, not as deck guns, but within the hull structure (the aft one was removed in 1900). Various mishaps and consequent supplementary works ensued after the launch, and Holland's team also had to learn how to handle the boat, although it was evident that its potential was greater than that of any predecessor. In March 1898 the vessel made its first successful underwater runs in open water, which required considerable adjustments of the dry ballast in order to submerge in waters of greater salinity. There was no periscope, and position of the boat and of any target had to checked by the art of 'porpoising' – bringing the craft just above the surface for a few seconds before diving again.

US Navy's first sub

Holland's Irish–American political contacts proved helpful, despite rather tricky relations with the US Navy Board, whose *Plunger* project had been left high and dry. Inspections and tests carried out by the Navy confirmed that the 'Holland VI' answered its requirements and it was duly purchased for $150,000 on 11 April 1900, becoming the Navy's first submarine. On 12 October that year it was commissioned as USS *Holland*. Orders followed for a further six, all built at the Crescent Yard, and Holland's company, renamed the Electric Boat Company on 7 February 1899, was established as the country's premier builder of naval submarines. Decommissioned in July 1905, *Holland* was stricken from the Navy list on 21 November 1910. The hull finally went for scrapping in 1932.

Protector (1902)

In the 1900s, the Imperial Russian Navy sought to short-circuit its desire to create a submarine arm by buying in American technology. At the same time, Simon Lake was trying, unsuccessfully, to break the Electric Boat Company's monopoly of the US Navy market.

The Electric Boat Company had a rival in the Lake Torpedo Boat Company of Bridgeport, Connecticut, established in 1900 by Simon Lake, engineer, inventor and entrepreneur, and designer of the successful salvage submarine *Argonaut* (1897). Lake was the first marine engineer to develop 'controlled submergence' through air/water ballast tanks that allowed the vessel to submerge on a level plane, known as 'even-keel operation'. Lake had been demonstrating the advantages of his even-keel technology for a number of years, but by 1900 the Holland Company, now the Electric Boat Company, had well-established political connections, and Lake felt compelled to explore the possibility of foreign buyers for his submarines. Thus it happened that the even-keel

The US Navy could have had two rival submarine designs to compare, and combine their merits, but commercial and political pressure prevented this from happening

Exhaust vent
An exhaust funnel for the gasoline engines was mounted. Later Lake submarines would have a protective fairing built around the funnel to ease water-flow past it.

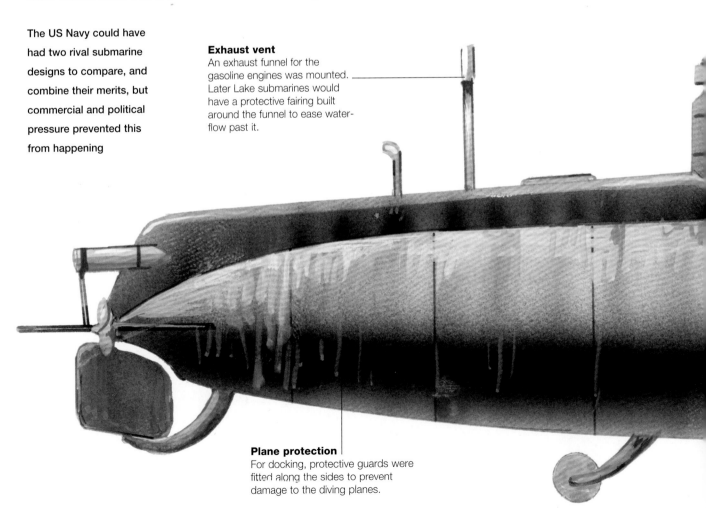

Plane protection
For docking, protective guards were fitted along the sides to prevent damage to the diving planes.

design was adopted by European navies before the U.S. Navy finally accepted it.

Lake's first military vessel, named *Protector*, was built as a speculation in the hope of gaining sales to the US Navy. Launched at Bridgeport on 1 November 1902, it was a steel-hulled boat, more powerful than the post-Holland A-class. *Protector*'s hull was almost shiplike, rather than cigar-shaped, although with a flat keel. It was also the first submarine with diving planes fitted amidships, just forward of the conning tower. Its four diving planes enabled it to submerge on a level keel, unlike the Holland boat that dived by the bow, and an automatic dry ballast release was fitted. A conning tower about 2m (6ft 6in) high was mounted centrally, big enough to hold a steersman and the operator of a novel piece of equipment, an 'omniscope', an

early kind of periscope. There was also a small dome-like sighting-hood.

Tanks in the tower held 6300 litres (1400 gallons) of gasoline fuel. It could surface by discharging water ballast using either compressed air, power or hand pumps, and the drop keel could also be released in case of emergency. Like Holland, Lake had adopted dual power, with internal combustion engines for running on the surface and charging storage batteries, and electric motors for underwater movement.

Accordingly, for operation on two shafts, *Protector* mounted two gasoline engines of 250hp (186kW) each and two 100hp (74.5kW) electric motors. It contained a lock-out dive chamber allowing submerged exit for the purpose of cutting cables or setting mines, and wheels for

Conning tower
One photograph of *Protector* shows the top of the tower railed and with a steersman's wheel at its forward end.

Access points
Access hatches were provided forward and aft of the conning tower. The airlock and diving compartments are located just behind the bows.

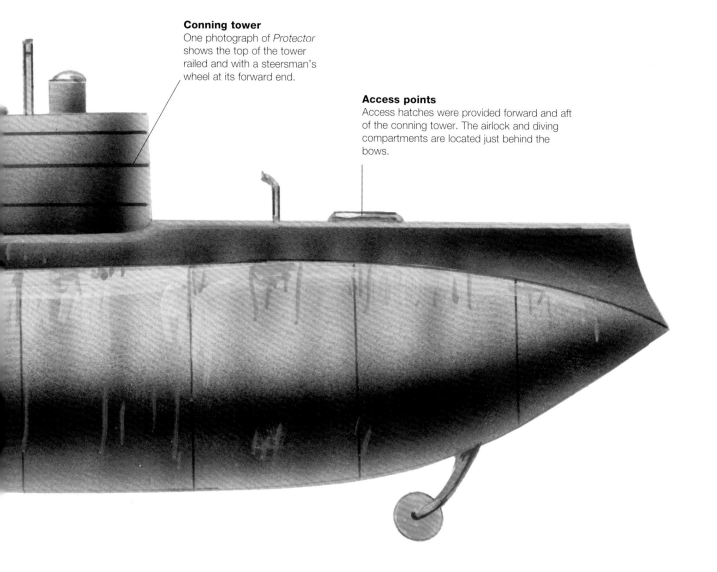

Protector

seabed crawling, although these were kept retracted into the hull.

The craft could make 11 knots (20.3km/h; 12.6mph) on the surface and 7 knots (12.9km/h; 8mph) submerged, with reported underwater endurance equivalent to a radius of 80km (50 miles), and was capable of diving to 46m (150ft) and of remaining submerged for 60 hours. During tests in Narragansett Bay, off the coast of Rhode Island, *Protector* travelled under ice 20cm (8in) thick, and broke through

Cutaway view of *Protector*, showing the omniscope in use. It was the first submarine to have a proper 'conning tower'.

it without ill effects. Internally *Protector* was much more comfortable than other submarines of the era. A small pantry separated the engine compartment and the 'saloon', which was entered through swing doors and had four upholstered bench seats where crewmembers could lie down.

Complex design

Lake's design was certainly superior to the Holland type in numerous specifications, but was possibly too complex for the liking of the U.S. Navy. Multiple features offered more possibility of things going wrong. Also, Lake, an ardent inventor, reputedly kept on making alterations so that the Navy was never wholly sure what it was being invited to buy. Attempts to set up a direct comparative trial with a Holland boat never came to fruition. The U.S. Army desired to purchase *Protector* and five others, but Electric Boat's political clout in Congress stymied this. Although a senior naval officer announced, "I am ready to admit that the 'Protector' outclasses anything which the government has", Electric Boat applied what Lake called "doubtful and reprehensible" efforts, with every kind of political influence, legal pressure, and personal contacts to hold on to its monopoly position. US government orders were not forthcoming and Lake looked abroad for business.

Specification

Dimensions:	Length: 19.8m (65ft); Beam: 3.35m (11ft); Draught: 3.35m (11ft)
Displacement:	Surfaced – 117 tonnes (115 tons); Submerged – 173 tonnes (170 tons)
Propulsion:	Two 250hp (186kW) gasoline engines; twin 110hp (82kW) electric motors; two screws
Speed:	Surfaced – 11 knots (20.3km/h; 12.6mph); Submerged – 7 knots (12.9km/h; 8mph)
Range:	1000nm (1852km; 1150 miles)
Armament:	Three 381mm (15in) torpedo tubes; one quick-fire cannon
Complement:	6

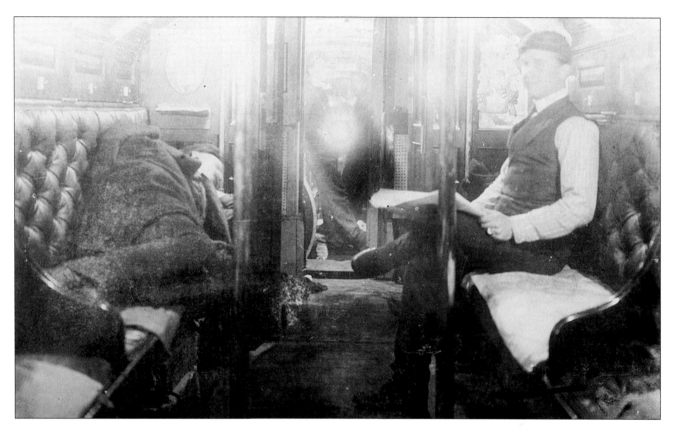

The saloon, looking past the pantry to the motor room. With no armament, more crew space was available.

Japan and Russia had already shown interest in US submarine prototypes, and Lake made an incognito visit to Russia in the winter of 1903–04. The Russian government had been attracted by the idea of large cargo-carrying submarines that could travel beneath ice and so give their ice-bound ports all-year commerce, but the war with Japan in 1904 focused all attention on military submarines. Courted by both warring sides – it was wrongly reported in June 1904 that the boat was bought by Japan – Lake chose the Russians, who bought *Protector* for $250,000. Shipped with its battery removed to Kronstadt (described as a coal shipment to evade regulations to do with the

USA's neutrality stance), *Protector* was commissioned into the Imperial Navy as *Oster* ('Sturgeon'), and transported in sections across Siberia by rail to Vladivostok on the Pacific coast. Its performance was highly satisfactory and Lake eventually secured a $4,000,000 contract for submarines. The Lake company sought further foreign contracts and Lake worked with the Austrian, German and British governments. But no more were built for Russia. All the *Oster*-class boats were decommissioned in 1913.

Russian sub division

The Russians also bought Electric Boat's 'Holland VII', named *Fulton*, for comparison purposes, and after tests in which French and German vessels also took part, decided that *Protector* was by a long way the best of the competition. Five similar boats, built to Lake's order at the Newport News Shipbuilding & Dry Dock Co., were shipped to Russia for reassembly. By the time they arrived in late 1905 the Japanese had won the naval war with Russia, but Russia now had the nucleus of a submarine division. One of the Protector class, *Kefal* ('Mullet'), was the first submarine to operate under thick ice cover, in December 1908, off Vladivostok.

🇬🇧 **B-Class** (1904)

By 1901 the British Admiralty had dropped its complacent attitude to submarines and began to take them seriously, both as a threat and as a potential new weapon. The B-class marked a real step forward.

The British Royal Navy was slow to take an interest in submarines, which some senior officers considered as unsporting, even piratical. Britain had no equivalent of J.P. Holland or the French submarine designers, and the fast surface torpedo boat was regarded as a more important development. Admiral Fisher, the reformist head of the

Royal Navy, was an advocate of submarines, although at first only for coastal patrol and defence. A contract was made in 1901 with the Electric Boat Company for the construction of five. This was the A-class, a small *Holland*-type vessel. It was followed in 1904 by the 11-strong B-class. All were built by Vickers at Barrow-in-Furness.

The B-class submarine was intended for coastal defence, with gasoline and electric battery propulsion. Maximum endurance at sea was three days in fine weather.

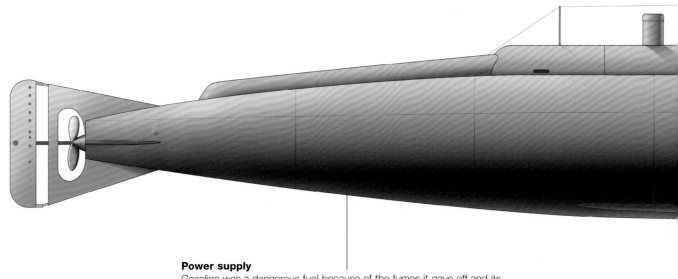

Power supply
Gasoline was a dangerous fuel because of the fumes it gave off and its high flammability. From around 1904 the French Navy was experimenting with diesel engines, but the Royal Navy did not use diesel until the advent of its D-class submarines, after the Electric Boat contract ended in 1910.

Displacing almost twice as much water as the A-class, the B-class was still of very limited capacity. The hull was single, with no internal bulkheads, and was pressurized for a maximum depth of 30m (100ft) although operating depth was 15m (50ft). Crew accommodation was minimal even for British submarines of the time. The horizontal 16-cylinder gasoline engine, built by Vickers, was a development of the Wolseley engine used in the A-class. The electric motor, operating on 100v DC, was also used as a starter motor for the gasoline engine and drove the same shaft. The original batteries allowed for four hours of submerged travel, although in World War I underwater patrols of up to 16 hours were achieved by B-class boats.

Two torpedo tubes were fitted, angled slightly downwards on the supposition that the missiles would be fired as the boat was surfacing. Diving speed was not yet recognized as a vital aspect: the B-class took three minutes to switch power and submerge, which was considered adequate at the time.

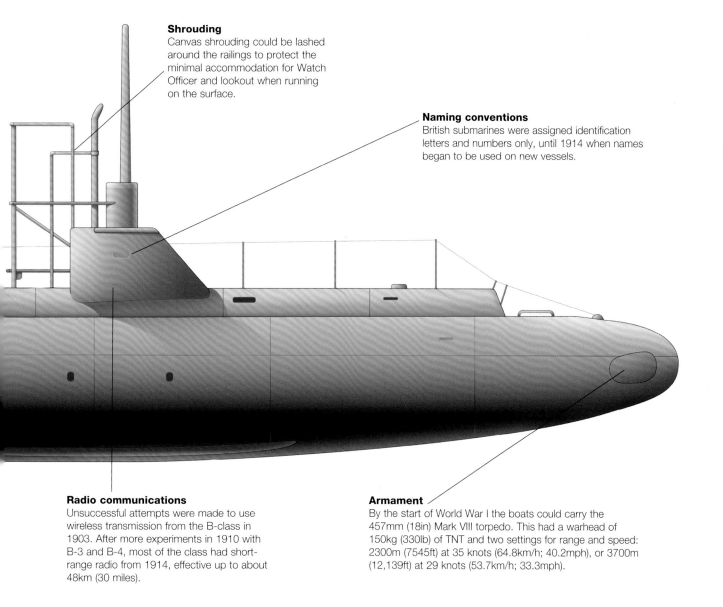

Shrouding
Canvas shrouding could be lashed around the railings to protect the minimal accommodation for Watch Officer and lookout when running on the surface.

Naming conventions
British submarines were assigned identification letters and numbers only, until 1914 when names began to be used on new vessels.

Radio communications
Unsuccessful attempts were made to use wireless transmission from the B-class in 1903. After more experiments in 1910 with B-3 and B-4, most of the class had short-range radio from 1914, effective up to about 48km (30 miles).

Armament
By the start of World War I the boats could carry the 457mm (18in) Mark VIII torpedo. This had a warhead of 150kg (330lb) of TNT and two settings for range and speed: 2300m (7545ft) at 35 knots (64.8km/h; 40.2mph), or 3700m (12,139ft) at 29 knots (53.7km/h; 33.3mph).

Specification

Dimensions:	Length: 41m (135ft); Beam: 4m (13ft 5in); Draught: 3.15m (10ft 4in)
Displacement:	Surfaced – 292 tonnes (287 tons); Submerged – 321 tonnes (316 tons)
Propulsion:	16-cylinder gasoline engine, 600hp (450kW) and electric motor, 180hp (130kW); single screw
Speed:	Surfaced – 12 knots (22.2km/h; 13.8 mph); Submerged – 6.5 knots (12km/h; 7.4 mph)
Range:	1110nm (2055km; 1277 miles) at 12 knots (22.2km/h; 13.8 mph), surfaced
Armament:	Two 457mm (18in) torpedo tubes, two reload torpedoes
Complement:	15

HMS *B-6* off Portsmouth Harbour. A compass binnacle is mounted on the quarter deck aft of the tower.

The limited endurance of the B-class and its ability to fire only four torpedoes led to its termination, and construction ceased in 1906 with the introduction of the slightly larger C-class. It was deemed inadequate as an attack boat and suited only to a defensive role. Some 10 years later its war service showed that despite its shortcomings the craft had been underestimated. Originally intended for coastal patrols in the North Sea and English Channel, six of the class were towed to Mediterranean bases, Gibraltar and Malta, in 1912. In that year *B-2* was rammed and sunk by the liner *Amerika* off Dover on 4 October 1912, with the loss of 14 lives.

On the outbreak of war in 1914, the class was already virtually obsolete, but saw considerable active service in

British waters, the Mediterranean and the Adriatic (with Venice as a base following Italy's entrance into the war in 1915). On 13 December 1914, *B-11* with Lt Norman Holbrook in command entered the Dardanelles Straits. Mines had been laid in the straits from just below Kepez Point to above Çannakale, but it was believed that submarines could pass through the minefields if they were fitted with gear for pushing aside the mooring ropes that anchored the mines to the seabed. *B-11* was hastily fitted with the necessary guards and wires.

Another of the problems *B-11* encountered in the Dardanelles was the presence of salt and freshwater layers at different depths, which upset the boat's trim and required frequent alteration of the balance between water and air in the ballast tanks to keep the submarine submerged and level.

Every two hours Holbrook brought *B-11* to periscope depth to fix his position. As they made their way in an atmosphere laden with oil and petrol fumes, the crew breakfasted – the men on tea, ham, bread, butter and jam, while their captain consumed half a lobster given to

him by a French submarine officer. With a single torpedo they sank the Turkish ironclad *Messudieh* off Chanak, and made a successful retreat, spending eight hours under water, and gaining the submarine service's first Victoria Cross for its commander.

Combat success

In the ill-fated Dardanelles campaign, the exploits of the submarines were among the few successful aspects. The B-class, by 1915 provided with a Maxim gun for surface defence, had several encounters with Austrian seaplanes in the course of 81 Adriatic patrols, and *B-11* captured a seaplane's crew on 17 January 1916. *B-10* was the first submarine to be sunk by air attack, during a bombing raid on Venice on 9 August 1916. Although refloated, it was further damaged by a fire and scrapped.

Five of the class were converted to surface patrol boats at Malta in 1917, renumbered *S-6, S-7, S-8, S-9* and *S-11*. The others were used only as training boats in the latter part of the war. Only *B-3* remained in commission until the end of the war.

Diving/surfacing control refinement

An important addition to the design, no doubt owing something to Simon Lake's advice, was the provision of a second pair of hydroplanes fitted just forward of the tower at first, then close to the bows, which enabled far easier diving, surfacing and depth-keeping. With no bulkhead to close off the engine room, and no ventilation for the crew space, protection from engine exhaust fumes became a vital consideration. A cage of mice was carried as a crude monitor of carbon monoxide levels: mice died more quickly than men. Battery gas also remained a hazard.

Right: In HMS *B-5*, the observation platform was extended aft on some members of the class, supported on metal struts, hidden here by canvas shrouding.

▬ U-9 (1910)

Although already an obsolescent design, *U-9* caused a sensation in the early weeks of World War I by sinking three British cruisers in the North Sea in the course of a single hour.

Laid down at the Kaiserliche Werft, Danzig (Gdansk), in 1908, *U-9* was the first of four built to a design that was already out-dated by its launch on 22 February 1910. This applied particularly to its kerosene-powered engines. Although less flammable than gasoline, kerosene burned with a lot of smoke and, as with the gasoline engine, a dismountable exhaust pipe was required to lift this away from the boat. The engines could not be reversed and battery power was needed to go backwards.

German submarine design at first followed French models, but by 1908 the U-boats were already showing distinctive features.

Submarines were not built around the needs of their crews: the men had to adapt to a situation close to intolerable. One of *U-9*'s officers gave an account of the living conditions:

"The storage battery cells, which were located under the living spaces and filled with acid and distilled water, generated gas [hydrogen gas] on charge and discharge: this was drawn off through the ventilation system. Ventilation failure risked explosion, a catastrophe that

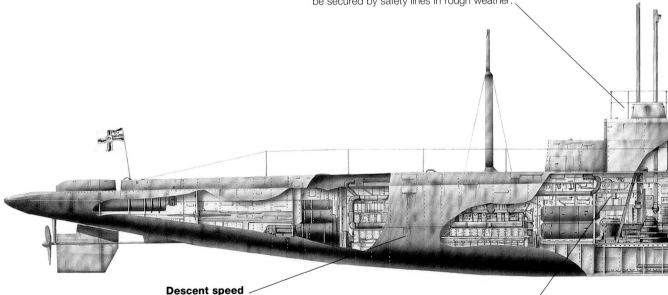

Battle bridge
The top of the conning tower was the 'battle bridge', occupied by a watch crew of officer, petty officer and seaman lookout. They had to be secured by safety lines in rough weather.

Descent speed
These early double-hulled U-boats had a very slow dive-time: *U-9* required seven minutes. This was not seen as a problem until wartime conditions prevailed, especially when facing the disguised merchantmen known as Q-ships, and later air attacks.

Air intake/release
The diving station consisted of 24 levers on each side of the submarine, allowing air to be released from or forced into the ballast tanks.

occurred in several German boats. If seawater got into the battery cells, poisonous chlorine gas was generated …
The central station was abaft the crew space, closed off by a bulkhead both forward and aft. Here was the gyro compass and also the depth rudder hand-operating gear with which the boat was kept at the required level, similar to a Zeppelin. The bilge pumps, the blowers for clearing and filling the diving tanks – both electrically driven – the air compressors were also here. In one small corner of this space stood a toilet screened by a curtain and, after seeing this arrangement, I understood why the officer I had relieved recommended the use of opium before all cruises which were to last over twelve hours…"

"The Watch Officer's bunk was too small to permit him to lie on his back. He was forced to lie on one side and then, being wedged between the bulkhead to the right and the clothes-press on the left, to hold fast against the movements of the boat in a seaway. The occupant of the berth could not sleep with his feet aft as there was an electric fuse-box in the way. At times the cover of this box sprang open and it was all too easy to cause a short circuit

Armament
From 1915 *U-9* would be fitted with a 37mm (1.46in) SK L/40 deck gun.

Power supply
Batteries were placed below the living space and were constantly monitored for release of poisonous hydrogen. Ventilation tubing ran along both sides of the boat.

Crew members stand at the salute as *U-9* returns to its base, somewhere off the Baltic coast.

by touching this with the feet ... Since the temperature inside the boat was considerably greater than the sea outside, moisture in the air condensed on the steel hull-plates and the condensation had a very disconcerting way of dropping on a sleeping face, with every movement of the vessel. Efforts were made to prevent this by covering the

Specification

Dimensions:	Length: 57.3m (188ft); Beam: 6m (19ft 7in); Draught: 3.5m (11ft 6in)
Displacement:	Surfaced – 431.8 tonnes (425 tons); Submerged – 610 tonnes (601 tons)
Propulsion:	Four Körting kerosene engines; electric motors, single screw
Speed:	Surfaced – 14.2 knots (26.2km/h; 16.3mph); submerged – 8 knots (14.8km/h; 9.2mph)
Range:	3356nm (6215km; 3862 miles) at 8.6 knots (15.9km/h; 9.8mph)
Armament:	Four 450mm (17.7in) torpedo tubes, two reloads; one 37mm (1.5in) deck gun
Complement:	29

face with rain clothes or rubber sheets. It was in reality like a damp cellar."

Submariners were paid at a higher rate than the crews of surface ships, but in terms of discomfort and danger, they certainly earned it. In its own way, the sharing of hardships and hazards generated a strong team spirit in most crews.

Attack sub

In August 1914 *U-9* was commanded by an exceptionally able officer, Kapitänleutnant Otto Weddigen, who was the first submarine commander to reload his torpedo tubes while submerged. Early on 22 September 1914 *U-9* sighted the British cruisers *Cressy*, *Aboukir* and *Hogue* steaming NNE at 10 knots (18.5km/h; 11.5 mph) without zigzagging. Patrols were supposed to maintain 12–13 knots (22.2–24km/h; 13.8–14.9 mph) and zigzag, but the old cruisers were unable to maintain that speed and the zigzagging order was widely ignored. *U-9* manoeuvred to attack and at about 6.25 am fired a single torpedo at *Aboukir*, striking it on the port side. *Aboukir* rapidly suffered heavy flooding, developed a 20° list and lost engine power.

At first *Aboukir*'s captain thought that he had been mined and signalled the other cruisers to close and assist but he soon realized that it was a torpedo attack and ordered them away, but too late. It was soon clear that she was a lost cause and the order was given to abandon ship. As *Aboukir* rolled over and sank, half an hour after being attacked, *U-9* fired two torpedoes at HMS *Hogue*, hitting

Crew standing on deck, *U-9* sets off on a patrol. The location may be the Kiel Canal.

it amidships and rapidly flooding the engine room. *Hogue* had stopped to lower boats to rescue the crew of *Aboukir*, its captain thinking that as he was the other side of *Aboukir*

Double-hull construction

Drawing on French practice, Imperial Germany's U-boats (*U-1* was launched on 4 August 1906) were double-hulled. This was considered to have several advantages: the external hull could be made to any shape and similar to that of a surface ship and so give better surface speed than the single circular hull form. A greater reserve of buoyancy and better seaworthiness resulted. The spaces between the two hulls could be used for water ballast. Since the external shape was that of a surface vessel, surface stability was greater than in single-hulled boats. Strength of the pressure hull could be increased by web frames fitted between the hulls. Placing the frames outside the pressure hull allowed for greater space inside. The outer hull could provide a decked top that made it easier for the crew to moor the boat and to get some exercise; and eventually provided room for a gun emplacement.

from *U-9* he would be safe. But *U-9* had gone right round *Aboukir* and launched two torpedoes at *Hogue* from a range of only 270m (900ft). The firing of the torpedoes affected the submarine's trim and as it briefly broke surface it was fired on by *Hogue* without effect.

Hogue sank within 10 minutes as *U-9* headed for HMS *Cressy*, which had also stopped to lower boats but got under way again on sighting a periscope, firing at the submarine also without effect. At about 7.20 a.m. the *U-9* fired two torpedoes, one of which hit *Cressy* on the starboard side and the other missed. The damage was not enough to sink the ship, but *U-9* made a turn and fired its last torpedo that also struck home, and the cruiser sank within a quarter of an hour. Weddigen's ability to run rings round the cruisers is an indication of how little trouble the British took with anti-submarine drills in 1914. The elderly cruisers were slow and unwieldy: their inability to run fast in zigzag formation left them as virtually sitting targets. Survivors were picked up by several nearby merchant ships including the Dutch *Flora* and *Titan* and two British trawlers, before the Harwich force of light cruisers and destroyers arrived. In all 837 men were rescued, but 1459 died.

U-9 was the only U-boat to be awarded an Iron Cross by the Kaiser. It was withdrawn from active duty in April 1916 and used for training purposes. With the rest of the German fleet it was surrendered in November 1918 and broken up at Morecambe, England, in 1919.

HMS E-11 (1914)

The E-class submarines were the main element in the Royal Navy's attack submarine force during World War I, operating in the North and Baltic Seas, the Mediterranean and the Dardanelles. In some respects inferior to U-boats, they still gave distinguished service.

An improved version of the previous D-class submarine, with higher freeboard and increased reserve buoyancy, the first of the class, *E-1*, was launched in November 1912. Its appearance was typical of British design at the time, with bulbous sides, a flat-surfaced 'walking deck' and a low, squat tower giving minimal protection against waves and wind when running on the surface. Diving planes were fitted at the bow and stern. It was the first British submarine class to be provided with transverse bulkheads, dividing the boat into three compartments and increasing its survivability. Diving depth, originally estimated to be 30m (100ft) proved in action to extend to over 60m (200ft). In the Dardanelles *E-12* reached almost 75m (245ft). Ultimately 58 were built, in three groups. *E-1* to *E-8* had a single bow torpedo tube, another at the stern, and two tubes mounted on the beam (beam tubes were not used in subsequent RN classes). From *E-9*, two bow tubes were fitted, along with a 12-pounder deck gun. *E-9* to *E-20* formed a second group and *E-21* onwards formed the

third and largest group, although the differences between it and Group 2 were slight, apart from six boats that were fitted out as minelayers.

By 1914 the British Admiralty was well aware of the strategic possibilities of the ocean-going submarine – and of Britain's lack of such vessels. *E-9* to *E-24* were built with funds originally earmarked for a battleship, HMS *Resistance*, that was never laid down. *E-11* was the third vessel in the second group. Built by Vickers at Barrow-in-Furness, it was launched on 23 April 1914 and completed

Exhaust vent
Diesel engine exhaust, alongside walk-deck.

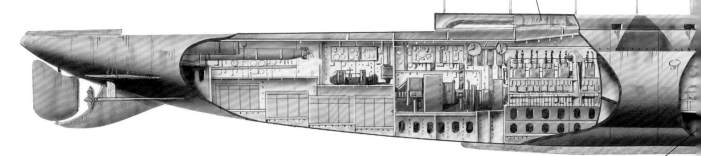

Beam tubes
The beam tubes fired to port (forward tube) and starboard (after tube) respectively. They were opened laterally to load the torpedoes. Impracticable in action, they were hard to aim and required the boat to come to a stop for firing.

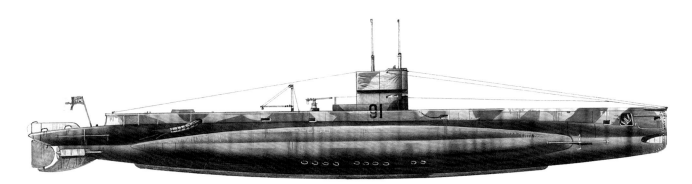

on 19 September that year. Conditions on board the E-class submarines were basic and extremely cramped. There was just one bunk that the three officers shared, while the ratings slung hammocks where they could. The heads (toilets) were more often than not a bucket. But this was typical of submarines at the time.

E-11, commanded by Lieutenant-Commander Martin Nasmith, was first deployed in the North Sea, and prevented by German craft from entering the Kattegat to join other British submarines in the Baltic. In December

Above: Twelve-pounder QF guns were installed on the walking deck, either immediately aft of the tower or on the extreme end of the deck.

Below: Various alterations were made to the towers and periscope fittings of this hard-worked class in the course of 1914–1918 war service, as a result of damage or service requirements.

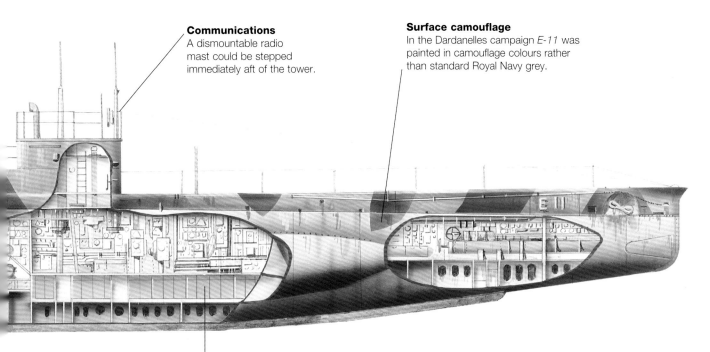

Communications
A dismountable radio mast could be stepped immediately aft of the tower.

Surface camouflage
In the Dardanelles campaign *E-11* was painted in camouflage colours rather than standard Royal Navy grey.

Power supply
E11 was fitted with two battery-sets for the electric motors, each consisting of 112 cells, with a combined weight of around 230 tonnes (226 tons).

1914 it supported the British raid on the Cuxhaven Zeppelin base. In May 1915 it joined in operations at the Dardanelles and in the Sea of Marmara. Entering the Dardanelles Straits on 19 May in the hope of encountering the German battleships *Goeben* and *Breslau*, the boat had to dive below 30m (98ft) to pass below three minefields. On

Submarine symmetry: the inner ends of an E-class's forward torpedo tubes (two were fitted from *E-9* onwards).

Specification

Dimensions:	Length: 55.17m (181ft); Beam: 6.91m (22ft 8in); Draught: 3.81m (12ft 6in)
Displacement:	Surfaced – 677 tonnes (667 tons); Submerged – 820 tonnes (807 tons)
Propulsion:	Two Vickers diesel engines developing 1600hp (1192kW), two 420hp (313kW) electric motors, two screws
Speed:	Surfaced – 14 knots (25.9km/h; 16.1mph); Submerged – 9 knots (16.6km/h; 10.3mph)
Range:	3579nm (6628km; 4118 miles) at 10 knots (18.5km/h; 11.5 mph)
Armament:	Five 457mm (18in) torpedo tubes; one 6pdr QF deck gun
Complement:	30

surfacing, the battleships were not to be seen. Evading two destroyers that attempted to ram his boat, Nasmith went on to capture a dhow, lashing it to the top of his conning tower in order to disguise his progress. The submarine was already painted in camouflage colours.

Dardanelles success

On 20 May Nasmith managed to put a boarding party aboard a sailing ship and torpedoed a Turkish gunboat at the expense of nothing more than a bullet hole in the *E-11*'s periscope. The Turkish ammunition ship *Nagara* was *E-11*'s next victim, on the 24th, blown up by a demolition charge after the crew had been ordered to abandon it. Another Turkish coal-carrier was pursued into the nearby port of Rodosto and torpedoed. Later that day he retrieved the prize crew from the sailing ship, which had run aground and was being fired on by Turkish cavalry.

On 25 May *E-11* lay off Istanbul, ready to attack the supply ships in the Bosporus – the first hostile craft to enter the Golden Horn in 500 years – and sank the Turkish transport *Stamboul*. On 28 May it sank a large transport using demolition charges again. On the return passage *E 11* passed again under the three minefields, snagging a

E-11 and its crew, probably at Mudros port, Lemnos, Greece, in 1915. Nasmith is the officer in the middle. Wartime fittings include the wave-deflector and the extended upper platform on the tower.

Diesel power

Vickers had originally obtained a licence to build MAN diesel engines in 1904, although they were not installed in British boats until the D-class of 1907–10. Diesel engines did not require an electric ignition system, caused less in the way of toxic gases and with a flash-point above 300°F the fuel was far less liable to explosion. The Vickers diesels were described as highly practical: if one cylinder failed, it could be disconnected from the crankshaft and the boat could proceed on reduced power. Two E-types were supplied to the Royal Australian Navy as AE1 and AE2. They travelled to Australia under their own power: a tribute to the efficiency of their diesel engines.

moored mine and towing it into open water before surfacing to disentangle the cable.

During a 20-day patrol Nasmith had sunk one gunboat, two ammunition ships, two transports and two further supply ships. Nasmith became the third submarine commander to be awarded a VC in the Dardanelles campaign. On 8 August 1915 E-11 sank the Turkish pre-dreadnought Barbaros Hayreddin with torpedoes.

By the war's end, all boats of E-class and later were given 1kW or 3kW Poulsen wireless sets, affording ranges of 320km (200 miles) submarine-to-submarine, and 480–640km (300–400 miles) between shore stations and submarines. High-power shore stations could be received over 800–960km (500–600 miles). One transverse torpedo tube was taken out to make room for the radio gear. Some of the class were also fitted with the Fessenden Morse code underwater signalling system. E-11 survived the war, although 19 of the class were lost. It was sold for scrapping in 1921. Its damaged search periscope is displayed at the Royal Navy Submarine Museum, Gosport.

▬ **UC-25** (1916)

The Imperial German Navy's Type UC-II consisted of 64 small but powerfully-armed submarines, which turned out to be perhaps the most versatile and effective U-boats of World War I.

Drawn up by the Development Section of the U-boat Inspectorate as Project 41, the class was a developed version of UC-I, the first operational minelaying submarines (Russia's *Krab*, although an earlier design, was later in service). The UC-1s were single-hulled vessels designed for coastal operations, with limited sea-keeping abilities. UC-II, designated Project 41, were larger, double-hulled and, although still considered 'coastal', had improved range and seakeeping. UC-II boats were capable of crash-diving in 40 seconds, with a test depth of 50m (164ft). The pressure hull was formed of steel plates 11mm (0.4in) thick.

Bigger than its UC-I predecessor, the UC-II class was still a compact vessel with scant space for its 26-man complement.

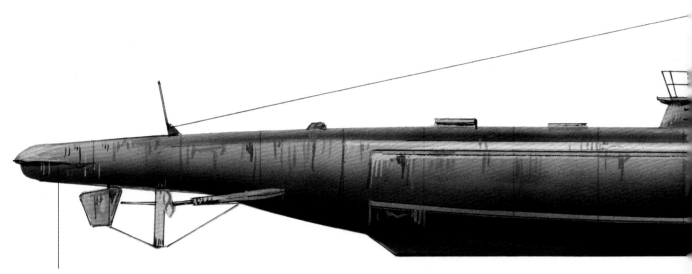

Rear torpedo
A single stern torpedo tube was fitted.

The least satisfactory aspect of the design was that the conning tower was not armoured and there was no means of sealing it off from the control room below. In the forward section 18 mines were held in six vertical chutes.

Mass-produced type

UC-II could be considered the first mass-produced submarine type, with five yards involved in construction. *UC-25* was first of a batch of nine built at the Vulcan Works in Hamburg. Launched on 10 June 1916, it was commissioned only 18 days later, entering service as part of the 5th (later *Kurland*) U-boat flotilla in the Baltic Sea. Under the command of Kapitänleutnant Johannes Feldkirchner it laid mines in the Gulf of Finland

against Russian shipping. In March 1917, still under Feldkirchner, it was one of two UC-II boats deployed to the Mediterranean, travelling under its own power to join the *Mittelmeer II* flotilla at Pola, on the Austrian Adriatic coast. On the way it sank three small enemy craft.

A U-boat base had been set up at the Austrian naval base of Pola since 1 April 1915, as *U-boot Sonderkommando Pola*. Two small UC-I submarines had been transported there in sections by rail, assembled and launched. Later that year the base was upgraded to *Deutsche U-boot Halbflotille Pola*, with a further operational base far to the south at Cattaro (Kotor). At that time, although Austria–Hungary and Italy were at war, Germany and Italy were not. Until Italy formally declared war, German submarines operated

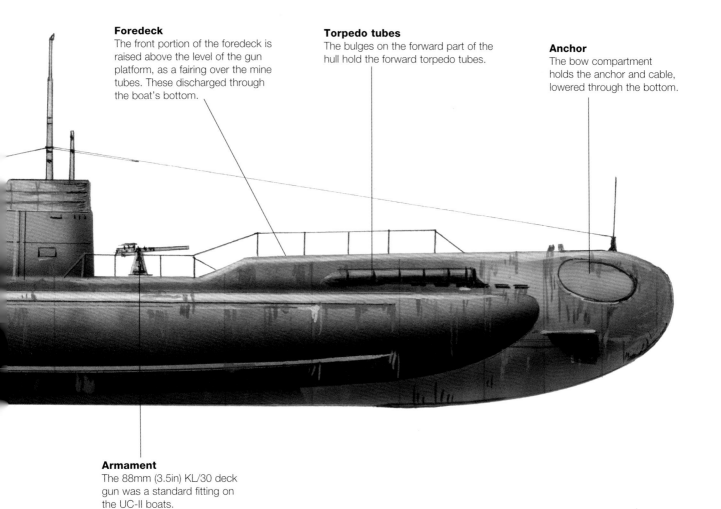

Foredeck
The front portion of the foredeck is raised above the level of the gun platform, as a fairing over the mine tubes. These discharged through the boat's bottom.

Torpedo tubes
The bulges on the forward part of the hull hold the forward torpedo tubes.

Anchor
The bow compartment holds the anchor and cable, lowered through the bottom.

Armament
The 88mm (3.5in) KL/30 deck gun was a standard fitting on the UC-II boats.

Specification

Dimensions:	Length: 49.45m (162ft 3in); Beam: 5.28m (17ft 4in); Draught: 4m (13ft 1in)
Displacement:	Surfaced – 400 tonnes (390 tons); Submerged – 480 tonnes (470 tons)
Propulsion:	Two 6-cylinder diesel engines, 500hp (370kW); two Siemens-Schukert electric motors, 460hp (340kW); twin screws
Speed:	Surfaced – 11.5 knots (21.2km/h; 13.2 mph); submerged – 7.2 knots (13.3km/h; 8.2mph)
Range:	9260nm (17,149km; 10,656 miles) at 7 knots (12.9km/h; 8mph)
Armament:	Three 500mm (20in) torpedo tubes, 7 torpedoes, 18 UC200 mines; one 88mm (3.5in) deck gun
Complement:	26

A Type UC-II boat at an unidentified base, probably Pola as the submarine is rigged for breaching defence netting.

against Italian targets under the Austro–Hungarian flag and with Austrian identification numbers. Such 'false flag' incidents were among the causes of Italy's declaration of war on Germany in May 1916. Even in 1917 *UC-25* was allotted the Austrian number *U-89*. In 1917 Germany proclaimed a policy of unrestricted warfare in the Mediterranean, including U-boat attacks without warning.

Submarine barrier

The main Allied defence against the Adriatic-based U-boats was an anti-submarine barrier formed of trawlers and anti-submarine nets laid across the Straits of Otranto. This was only partially effective. The Straits were too wide at 71km (44 miles), and too deep for such a barrage to be successful, and to

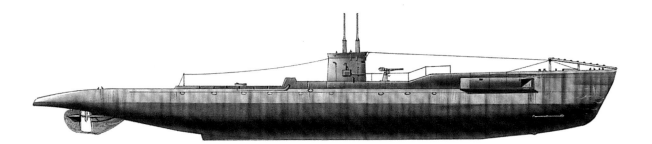

UC-II class *UC-74*, commissioned on 26 November 1916 and based at Pola from 7 March 1917, was at sea when Germany surrendered. It made for Kiel, but ran out of fuel and was interned at Barcelona on 21 November 1918. Later handed over to France, it was broken up in 1921.

patrol it consumed a huge effort and tied up many of the Allied ships. Only two U-boats were caught in the barrage in all the time it was in operation. Meanwhile, the merchant ships continued to suffer huge losses. In 1916, the Allies lost 415 ships in the Mediterranean, a total of 1,061,828 tonnes (1,045,058 tons), half the tonnage of all Allied ships sunk anywhere.

Italian raid

On 15 May 1917 Feldkirchner took UC-25 in support of Austrian surface ships making a raid to break the Otranto barrage. The British cruiser HMS *Dartmouth* was torpedoed and disabled by UC-25, which earlier that day had laid mines off Brindisi, one of which sank the French destroyer *Boutefeu*. On 4 July the British sloop HMS *Aster* was sunk by another of *UC-25*'s mines.

In March–August 1918 Karl Dönitz, future supreme commander of the U-boat fleet, became captain of *UC-25*, his first command. On a mission between 17 July and 7 August 1917 it slipped through the Otranto Barrage, narrowly avoiding air attacks with depth charges south of Corfu. Entering the Sicilian harbour of Augusta it sank a ship that Dönitz possibly believed to be the British depot ship HMS *Cyclops*, but which was later identified as an Italian cargo vessel (*Cyclops* spent the war at Scapa Flow). *UC-25* sank four enemy ships and damaged another.

Between 19 October 1916 and 5 August 1918 *UC-25* was responsible for the sinking of 21 ships

totalling 19,637 tonnes (19,328 tons) and heavy damage to a further seven of 35,336 tonnes (34,870 tons). The *Kriegstagebuch* or war-log of *UC-25*, listing observations, encounters and hits, survives in the German state archives.

In late October 1918, with negotiations going on for an armistice between Austria and the Allies (signed on 3 November) and an Allied–German armistice also imminent, German U-boats based at Austrian ports were ordered to make their way back to Kiel, if possible; otherwise to a Spanish port. Those that could not be readied for a long voyage were to be destroyed. *UC-25* was one such, and was scuttled at Pola on 28 October.

In all, 33 of the UC-II boats were lost during the war and a further three sank while in transit from Germany to Britain in 1919.

On-board conditions

On cruises and patrols, *UC-25* travelled on the surface whenever possible, and could be steered from the bridge, but it was not designed for a long sea voyage and the crew found minimal comfort on board. A shower might be possible on deck using seawater. With a choppy sea running, breaking water in the conning tower felt like wet cement thrown into one's face. Inside was the continuous throbbing of the engines, diesel fumes and the all-pervasive dampness. Lighting was poor. Cooking a meal was almost impossible, except in calm weather when it could be prepared on deck. Hygiene was virtually impossible to maintain. Many men suffered from bronchitis and ear and lung diseases.

Deutschland (1916)

First as a cargo-carrier that made two voyages across the Atlantic, then as armed submarine cruiser *U-155*, *Deutschland* demonstrated the rapid development of German U-boat design and technology during World War I.

The success of the U-boats in the Atlantic encouraged the German Navy to plan and build large, long-range submarines armed with powerful guns as well as torpedoes (more ships were sunk by gunfire than by torpedoes). On the surface, however, the British held command of the seas, enforcing a shipping blockade on German ports. To evade the blockade, the *Deutschland* class of merchant U-boats was also introduced. Ostensibly belonging to a commercial venture, the *Deutsche Ozean-Reederei* company, the submarines were in fact manned by

experienced U-boat crewmen and reserve officers provided with civilian documents.

Design and construction were supervised by Oberingenieur Rudolf Erbach. *Deutschland* was laid down in the Flensburger Schiffsbau Yard in Flensburg on 27 October 1915, launched on 28 March 1916, completed at Krupp's Germaniawerft in Kiel and commissioned on 19 February 1917. Its cost was around 4 million Reichsmarks. The craft was double-hulled with a broad deck above the outer hull. Two folding radio masts were fitted. Diving time

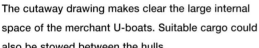

The cutaway drawing makes clear the large internal space of the merchant U-boats. Suitable cargo could also be stowed between the hulls.

Exhaust vent
Diesel engine exhaust pipe.

Propellers
New larger propellers were fitted as part of the U-boat conversion in the hope of improving speed. The diesel and electric motors could drive the shaft simultaneously, although only for limited periods, to obtain maximum speed.

was from 50 to 80 seconds, with an operating depth of 50m (164ft).

On 23 June 1916 *Deutschland* left Wilhelmshaven carrying around 700 tonnes (690 tons) of high value cargo – gemstones, concentrated dyestuffs, chemicals and pharmaceuticals, all of which had an eager market in the still-neutral USA. Its arrival at Baltimore on 9 July caused an international dispute. The British and French demanded it should be impounded as a warship or potential support vessel for warships, while the Germans insisted it was a cargo vessel. In a propaganda coup for Germany, the American government concurred with the Germans and *Deutschland* was allowed to discharge and load cargo. It left on 2 August, with vital items for the war economy: 346 tonnes (341 tons) of nickel, 94.5 tonnes (93 tons) of tin and 353.5 tonnes (348 tons) of crude rubber, most of the rubber being stored outside the pressure hull. Of the 8450 nautical miles (15,649km; 9724 miles) of its double journey, 190 (352km; 219 miles) were made submerged.

Its sister-boat *Bremen* set off from Kiel for the United States on 21 August, but never arrived: its fate remains a mystery. *Deutschland* made a second visit, to New London, Connecticut, between 1 and 17 November 1916, accidentally ramming and sinking a tug as it left US waters. By December 1916 relations between Germany and the USA had worsened, and *Deutschland* was dry-docked for conversion to a military vessel, armed with six external torpedo tubes mounted in two tiers inside the outer casing, and angled out at 15°, and two 150mm (5.8in) deck guns. A tween-deck was fitted in the cargo space to provide accommodation for a war crew above a torpedo storage area. Its roomy interior enabled it to carry 30 torpedoes, although with its external tubes *Deutschland* could reload only on the surface. The torpedo tubes of the other converted merchant submarines were fitted inside the pressure hull.

In the course of 1917 the *U-Kreuzer Flotille* (*U-151* to *U-157*) was formed, comprising the three ex-merchant

Attack periscope
As *U-155* an attack periscope tube was set in the deck forward of the tower.

Derricks
The derricks over the cargo hatches were dismountable.

Mercantile form
The profile shows the boat in its original unarmed mercantile form. Three were built like this and four were converted to combat boats while under construction. Addition of two 150mm (5.9in) deck guns radically changed the appearance.

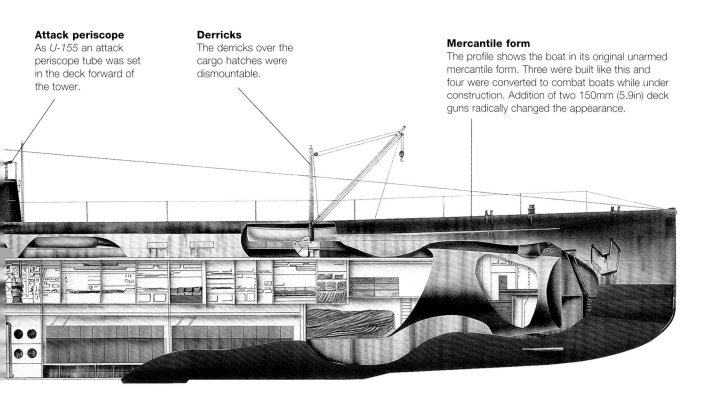

Engine-room passageway in *U-155*. Note the massive spanners stowed at the side.

Specification

Dimensions:	Length: 65m (213ft 3in); Beam 8.8m (28ft 10in); Draught 5.3m (17ft 5in)
Displacement:	Surfaced – 1536 tonnes (1512 tons); Submerged – 1905 tonnes (1875 tons)
Propulsion:	Two six-cylinder Viertakt diesel engines 800hp (588kW), electric motors; twin screws
Speed:	Surfaced – 12.4 knots (22.9km/h; 14.2mph); submerged – 5.2 knots (9.6km/h; 5.9mph)
Range:	13,130nm (24,316km; 15,109 miles) at 9 knots (16.6km/h; 10.3mph)
Armament:	Six 500mm (20in) torpedo tubes, 18 torpedoes; two 150mm (5.9in) deck guns
Complement:	29 (merchant); 56 (military)

boats and four that had been converted to U-boats while still under construction. Its purpose was to attack shipping in the western Atlantic and lay mines (they could each carry 14) off the American coast. On 10 February 1917 *Deutschland* was deleted from the merchant register and on the 19th became *U-155*, attached to the cruiser flotilla. By then it had been refitted at Wilhelmshaven with torpedo tubes and deck guns. Its size also enabled it to carry 20 men as prize crews for captured ships.

Azores patrol

Some of the class made long voyages south to the Azores and the African coast, where they operated generally unmolested against shipping operating in the area, although *U-154* was torpedoed by the British submarine *E-35* off the coast of Portugal in May 1918. From 24 May 1917, under the command of Kapitänleutnant Karl Meusel, *U-155* made its first patrol, off the Azores, remaining at sea for 105 days and sinking 19 ships, only one by torpedo. After this patrol, two internal bow torpedo tubes were fitted. In the course of three patrols it sank 43 ships with a total of 122,361 tonnes (120,434 tons), and damaged three ships with a total of 9225 tonnes (9080 tons).

Deutschland enters the port of Baltimore, July 1916. The US flag is at the foremast, the Imperial German flag at the aftermast, with the German Merchant Navy ensign at the stern.

U-155 armament

Six torpedo tubes were fitted beneath the deck and outside the pressure hull. Although two internal bow tubes were later installed, little use was made of them. *U-155*'s guns were large enough to tackle an armed merchant vessel or an anti-submarine Q-ship, although their recoil put heavy stress on the mountings made in a deck not intended for such a purpose. Despite its slow speed, the exploits of *U-155* were sufficient to promote the idea of the U-boat cruiser. One of its commanders, Korvettenkapitän Ackermann, noted that "even such clumsy and slow vessels as the former merchant submarines, when handled correctly, are equal to their tasks both surfaced and submerged, all of which justifies the construction of even larger U-cruisers than are now in construction" – although these were, of course, intended to be both faster and more manoeuvrable than the Deutschland class.

In August 1918, the former *Deutschland* sailed again, under the command of Korvettenkapitän Ferdinand Studt, with orders to cruise off the eastern Canadian coast, laying mines and cutting telegraph lines. *U-155* was the last U-boat to go hunting in North American waters, but this cruise was much less successful than the 1917 mission. The lack of any 'choke point' where merchant shipping was forced to congregate made its task difficult, and its presence failed to impede the flow of transatlantic shipping. It sank three merchantmen, but was itself damaged on 13 September rendering it temporarily unable to dive. It returned to Germany on 12 November 1918, the day after the Armistice.

Ceded to Britain, *U-155* was towed up the Thames on 2 December 1918, and after a collision with a passing steamship, during which both vessels received minor damage, it was moored in St Katherine's Dock next to Tower Bridge. Admission to view it cost one shilling. *U-155* was sold by the Admiralty in March 1919 and was later passed on to a company that towed it around Britain for exhibitions at seaside resorts. These were a financial failure, and in September 1921 the vessel was finally taken to be broken up at Birkenhead. Even then it still was responsible for deaths. During its breaking-up an explosion killed five young fitter's apprentices. Many souvenir artefacts were made from the scrap metal.

▬ U-139 (1917)

The first of a class of three long-range attack submarines, this was the last German submarine to sink an enemy ship before the war ended in 1918. Its design influenced the post-war submarine designs of other navies.

Even before the entry of the United States into World War I, the German naval command was interested in long-range submarines as an element in the total U-boat force. A new design was introduced, under the name of Project 46, even bigger than the *Deutschland* type, but this time with a wholly military purpose. Three boats were ordered

in August 1916 from Germaniawerft, Kiel. *U-139* was the first, launched on 3 December 1917, and commissioned on 18 May 1918. It was double-hulled with the pressure hull 25mm (1in) thicker than usual, in order to permit diving to greater depths. Four bow and two stern torpedo tubes were fitted, but the main armament was the two

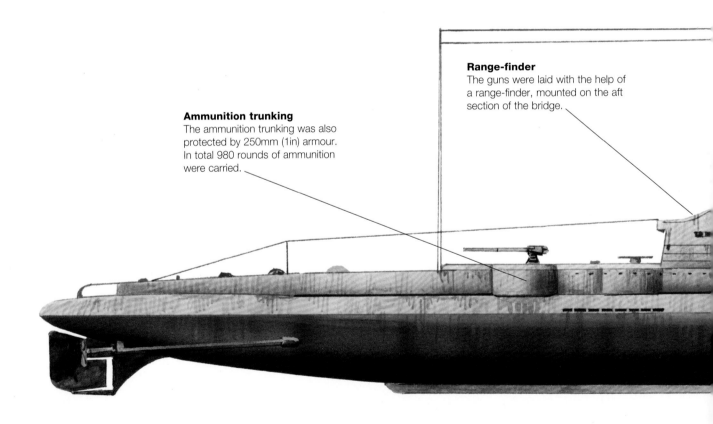

Range-finder
The guns were laid with the help of a range-finder, mounted on the aft section of the bridge.

Ammunition trunking
The ammunition trunking was also protected by 250mm (1in) armour. In total 980 rounds of ammunition were carried.

150mm (5.9in) deck guns, set on barbette-type mountings extending from a central fairing. The guns could be laid by a range-finder on the aft section of the bridge. The conning tower's command centre was protected by 90mm (3.5in) armour against the guns typically carried by armed merchant ships. The superstructure was also raised by 2m (6ft) so that a shell hitting it would not penetrate the pressure hull. Power was provided by two Germania diesels, one MAN-Brown Boveri diesel and two AEG electric motors.

With the USA a belligerent from April 1917, the *Kaiserliche Marine*'s interest in long-range submarines that could bring the war right to American waters was greatly stimulated. The exploits of the converted Deutschland-type *U-151* during April 1917, sinking ships and cutting telegraph cables off the north-eastern USA, suggested that a U-boat bonanza was to be had there, but the number of U-boats with sufficient range was small, and the Americans swiftly adopted defensive measures.

The two completed Type 139 submarines, *U-139* and *U-140*, were dispatched on long-range cruises, south across the Equator, and to the west across the Atlantic, operating independently. *U-139*'s first and only cruise

The profile shows *U-139* with its radio masts raised and aerial wires in position. Radio communication was a major help in long-distance operations.

Target optics
The attack periscope used a system known as UZO (*U-Boot Ziel Optik*, 'U-boat target optics') incorporating a Stadimeter split-prism range-finder that gave a double image of the target and a range calculation up to 6000m (19,685ft). With the help of a target bearing ring around the periscope tube, giving the compass bearing in degrees in relation to the U-boat's bow, the depth, speed and bearing of a torpedo had to be rapidly worked out on a slide-rule before firing.

Armament
As the French *Halbronn*, *U-139* kept its deck guns, but the fairing round the conning tower was removed, leaving the armoured 90mm (3.5in) tower form.

Specification

Dimensions:	Length: 94.8m (311ft); Beam 9m (29ft 9in); Draught: 5.2m (17ft)
Displacement:	Surfaced – 1961 tonnes (1930 tons); Submerged – 2523 tonnes (2483 tons)
Propulsion:	Two diesel engines delivering 3300hp (2458kW); electric motors, 1780hp (1326kW); twin screws
Speed:	Surfaced – 15.8 knots (29.2km/h; 18.1mph); submerged – 7.6 knots (14km/h; 8.7mph)
Range:	12,630nm (23,390km; 14,534 miles) at 8 knots (14.8km/h; 9.2mph)
Armament:	Six 508mm (20in) torpedo tubes; two 150mm (5.9in) guns
Complement:	62

U-139's sister ship *U-140* alongside an American warship. It was transferred to the USA in 1919 and sunk as a target in 1920.

took it southwards into the Atlantic. Encountering an Allied convoy on 1–2 October 1918, it sank three small merchant ships and damaged the armed escort *Perth*. From this engagement comes an unsubstantiated story that one ship came down on top of the submarine, forcing it towards the seabed. All tanks were blown empty by compressed air in the effort to wrest *U-139* free, and it disengaged and shot to the surface. Damaged, its periscopes bent, it managed to make its escape.

Early in the morning of 14 October, *U-139* spotted the Portuguese steamer *São Miguel*, en route from Madeira and escorted by the naval trawler *Augusto de Castilho* of 495 tonnes (487 tons), armed with two Hotchkiss cannon of and 47mm (1.8in). The U-boat surfaced and opened fire, but was hotly engaged by the trawler in a two-hour battle, while the passenger ship was able to

Prominent on this profile of U-139 are its two 150mm (5.9in) deck guns.

Lothar von Arnauld de la Perière

U-139's commander was a remarkable submariner, Korvettenkapitän Lothar von Arnauld de la Perière, who as captain of *U-35* had achieved a unique record of ships and tonnage sunk. With a total of 452,120 tonnes (445,000 tons) of enemy shipping sunk, he remains the most successful wartime commander ever. Entrusting *U-139* to this most distinguished officer showed that great things were expected from the boat. He gave it a name, *Kapitänleutnant Schwieger*, in memory of the U-boat commander who had sunk the *Lusitania* and later died in action. Performance of his new command was not entirely to his satisfaction. Arnauld de la Perière considered *U-139* to be clumsy underwater, unable to be swung round quickly into firing position "as is necessary for a craft that aims its shot by aiming itself."

make its escape. Eventually, the badly damaged trawler surrendered, but *U-139* continued firing and the crew abandoned ship. *Augusto de Castilho* was then boarded and sunk by explosive charges, becoming the war's last U-boat victim.

Revolution and peace

U-139 remained in action until the general recall of U-boats on 20 October, and returned to find Kiel in the midst of a naval mutiny. For a time it was taken over by a sailors' soviet (revolutionary council). All told, it had sunk four ships with a total tonnage of 6897 tonnes (6788 tons) and severely damaged another of 2542 tonnes (2502 tons). In post-war reparations it was handed over to France, and served until 1935 in the *Marine Nationale* as *Halbronn*, its design influencing the French interest in large submarine cruisers.

Design drawings from Project 46 found their way to Japan, and had considerable influence on the design of the *Kaidai* long-range fleet submarines. Drawings were also supplied to Russia in 1926, but the Soviet Navy was not interested in submarines of this type at that time. One relic of *U-139* survives: its bronze ship's bell, in private ownership.

Surcouf (1929)

Intended as an oceanic commerce raider and built to beat international restrictions, this huge submarine carried a floatplane and was the largest in the world from 1929 until 1943. The cause of its loss, with no signal or message, remains unclear.

The final design for *Surcouf*, intended to be the leader of a new class, was drawn up by the *Service Technique des Constructions et Armes Navales*. Chief designer was Jean-Jacques Roquebert, who played a leading part in the formation of France's post-war submarine fleet. Laid down at Cherbourg naval dockyard on 3 October 1927, *Surcouf* was launched in secret on 18 October

1929. As usual with French submarines, it had a double hull. The superstructure had a massive appearance, with the conning tower located behind a double gun turret and forward of the aircraft hangar. On the surface it was powered by two Sulzer diesel engines of 3800hp (2831kW). The electric motors, delivering 3400hp (2533kW), were supplied by the Compagnie Générale

Armament
The 203mm (8in) guns and gun-laying equipment were not new, as many guns in good condition were available from decommissioned surface ships. The twin turret weighed 185 tonnes (182 tons) and could be ready to fire within three minutes of surfacing, sending a 120kg (264lb) shell a distance of 27,500m (90,223ft).

Holding cell
Although the design provided for a 5m (16ft) motorboat, it was unusable and *Surcouf* never carried one on active service. The submarine was also said to have prison space for 40 men, but this was also usable as a cargo space.

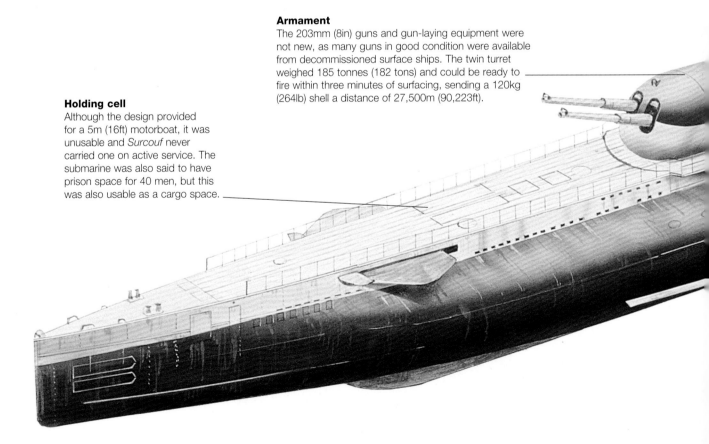

Electrique of Nancy. Large fuel capacity gave it a range of 10,000 nautical miles (18,520km; 11,507 miles) and it was equipped to stay at sea for up to 90 days. Six forward torpedo tubes were installed, four of 550mm (21.4in), two of 400mm (15.6in), and two externally-mounted triple sets, formed of one 550mm tube and two of 400mm. It carried 22 torpedoes and 640 shells for the 203mm (8in) guns. Its maximum operating depth was 80m (262ft), but diving time, in excess of two minutes, made it vulnerable to air attack.

Fitting out and testing took much longer than anticipated, revealing many problems of design and operation. These included breakage of the rudder and damage to the steering gear, a tendency to roll heavily (up to 25°), leaks from the tanks outside the pressure hull, breakage of the diesel engine mountings, and stifling heat in warm climates due to inadequate ventilation. *Surcouf* was eventually ready to undergo test dives in the course of 1931, and from 31 December 1932 was attached to the 1st Submarine Flotilla at Cherbourg. It was formally

Floatplane
A Besson MB-41-0 floatplane with a 400km (248 mile) range was originally carried in a hangar behind the tower. After a crash-landing in July 1933 it was replaced by an MB-41-1 model. Both were wood-framed. In 1938 a Breguet gyroplane was tested as a possible replacement.

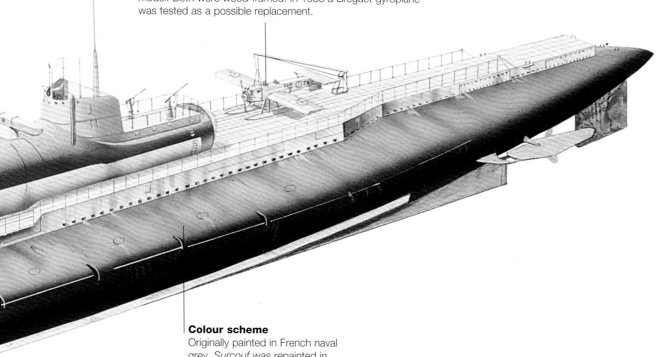

Colour scheme
Originally painted in French naval grey, *Surcouf* was repainted in 'dark Prussian blue' from 1934 until 1940. From then it was painted in two-tone grey.

Surcouf was more than an expensive prestige symbol. From the beginning, the French Navy had led the way in the development of submarines and this was intended as the leader of a class that combined surface and sub-surface capacities for attack.

Specification

Dimensions:	Length: 110m (360ft 10in); Beam: 9.1m (29ft 9in); Draught: 9.07m (29ft 8in)
Displacement:	Surfaced – 3302 tonnes (3250 tons); Submerged – 4373 tonnes (4304 tons)
Propulsion:	Two diesel motors 7600hp (5700kW), two electric motors 3400hp (2500kW); twin screws
Speed:	Surfaced – 18.5 knots (34.2km/h; 21.2mph); submerged – 8.5 knots (15.7km/h; 9.7mph)
Range:	10,000nm (18,520km; 11,507 miles) at 10 knots (18.5km/h; 11.5mph)
Armament:	Eight 551mm (21.7in) and four 400mm (15.75in) torpedo tubes; two 203mm (8in) guns; two 37mm (1.5in) guns, four 8mm (0.3in) Hotchkiss machine guns
Complement:	118

This photo, possibly on the occasion of *Surcouf's* commissioning, shows the gun turret without the streamlined casing that was fitted for seagoing service.

commissioned in 16 April 1934, although many of the defects noted above had not been fully addressed. It transferred to the 4th Submarine Squadron at Brest from 1 June that year. In 1935, now attached to the 2nd Submarine Flotilla, it made a transatlantic voyage to the Antilles.

Refit

A major refit was carried out at Brest in 1936–37, when its radio masts were removed. Until 1939 its use was largely for 'showing the flag' purposes at colonial ports and even so was hampered by frequent mechanical and operational problems. It was difficult to keep the vessel trimmed while submerged and it rolled violently in a surface swell. In September 1939 it crossed the Atlantic again to Fort de France, Martinique, and acted as escort to a convoy of British and French ships on the return journey. From

October 1939 it was refitting at Brest and in June 1940 was hastily brought to seagoing condition as the Germans advanced across France. Quitting Brest just before the port fell to the Germans, *Surcouf* made for Plymouth. Still in need of refitting and arming, made difficult by its unique design and the lack of suitable parts in Britain, the submarine was in no state to go anywhere.

Free French service

But with other French naval vessels, on the night of 3 July 1940 it was forcibly taken over by the British Navy in 'Operation Catapult'. The crew resisted and there were two British and one French fatality. Refitting then went ahead, and on 27 July the submarine was formally transferred to the Free French Naval Forces (FNFL), and after a training stint in the Firth of Clyde operated primarily on convoy work in the Atlantic. On 24 December 1941 it was part of the French squadron that wrested control

of the St Pierre and Miquelon Islands, off Newfoundland, from the Vichy French, causing a serious diplomatic row with the still-neutral USA. On 2 February 1942 it was redirected to the Pacific and left Halifax, Nova Scotia, for Tahiti. It made a call at Bermuda, but on 18 February *Surcouf* disappeared with all hands in deep water in the Caribbean Sea. The cause of the disaster remains disputed. An American freighter, *Thompson Lykes*, reported colliding with a submarine in the same area on that night, and this remains the official American account. It has also been suggested that *Surcouf* was sunk by 'friendly fire' from Panama-based US fighter-bombers, two Northrop A-17s and a Douglas B-18, which reported attacking a large submarine – presumed to be German or Japanese – on the morning of the 19th.

Under the flag of Free France, *Surcouf* made 15 raids, 15 patrols, five convoy escorts and travelled 56,327km (35,000 miles).

Design limitations

From around 1920, French naval designers and strategists had been considering the construction of a large, well-armed, floatplane-carrying class of submarine. Unlike surface ships, there was no international accord on the size of submarines until the London Naval Treaty of January 1930, which fixed limits: each signatory country (France included) was allowed to possess no more than three large submarines, each not exceeding 2800 tonnes (2755 tons) standard displacement and with guns not exceeding 155mm (6.1in) in calibre. *Surcouf*, already launched although not fitted out, was specially exempted from the rules, but the proposed six others of the class could not be built. *Surcouf* remained a one-off.

Surcouf, carrying the designation number 17P, close to the Royal Navy's submarine base at Faslane, on the Firth of Clyde, in 1940.

USS Nautilus (V-6) (1930)

The US Navy, like the British and French, felt the lure of the big cruising submarine. The ability of the U-151 and U-139 types to strike at the American coast had made a deep impression. Drawing on the U-boat designs, nine submarines, known as the V-boats, were built between 1919 and 1934.

In fact the nine formed five separate types. Originally designated only by the letter 'V' and a number, they received names from 1931. The basic aim was to find an acceptable 'fleet boat' design, on the lines of the German cruisers. The first designs, V-1 to V-3, later named Barracuda, Bass and Bonita, was not considered a success, partly because of unreliable and underpowered motors, and they failed to make the required surface and submerged speeds of 21 knots (38km/h; 21.4mph) and 9 knots (16.6km/h; 10.3mph). USS V-4, later named Argonaut, was the United States' only submarine minelayer.

USS V-6 was launched at Mare Island, California, on 15 March 1930 and commissioned on 1 July that year,

Armament
The deck guns were designed for the secondary battery of Lexington-class battle cruisers and South Dakota-class battleships, but were only installed in Omaha-class cruisers. They fired a 47kg (105lb) shell to a range of 21,310m (69,914ft) at their maximum elevation of 25°.

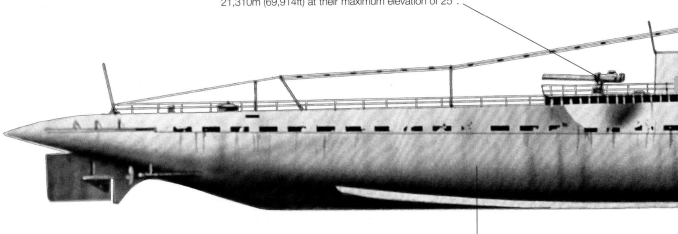

Fuel reserves
With extra fuel in some ballast tanks, Nautilus had an extended operating range of 25,000nm (46,300km; 28,769 miles) at 5.7 knots (10.5km/h; 6.5mph).

While there was certainly a spirit of experiment and inquiry behind the various V-boat designs, internal naval politics were also a factor. But the US Navy learned some useful lessons.

one of very few large American submarines of the period. The name *Nautilus* was given in February 1931. *Nautilus* carried the heaviest artillery of any US submarine. Two 152mm (6in) deck guns were carried, forward and aft of the tower, requiring built-out Mark 17 wet mountings, and capable of firing a 47kg (105lb) shell to a maximum range of 21,310m (69,914ft), at the maximum elevation of 25°. To its original six 533mm (21in) torpedo tubes, four externally mounted tubes were added in a 1941–42 refit. It could carry up to 38 torpedoes, with 12 mounted externally.

While the large V-boats incurred criticism for poor handling qualities, their besetting problem was the inadequate performance of the engines. Like other V-boats, *Nautilus* had a powerplant of original German MAN design, but built by the Navy's BuEng (Bureau of Steam Engineering): two direct drive 10-cylinder 4-cycle main engines of 2350hp (1750kW) main engines, two

6-cylinder 4-cycle auxiliary engines of 450hp (340kW) each and two Westinghouse 800hp (600kW) electric motors. As with *Bass*, the diesel and electric drives could be run together for short periods. These engines were replaced in 1941–42 by a full diesel-electric system (see Specification). The original two 120-cell Exide ULS37 battery sets were replaced by two 120-cell Exide UHS39B batteries.

Pacific service

Long-range scouting missions had been envisaged for *Nautilus*, with the boat's reconnaissance abilities enhanced by carrying a seaplane. Plans for the seaplane were dropped and it never undertook the scouting missions, but it and V-5 *Narwhal* gave useful service. *Nautilus* as SS-168 was deployed to Pearl Harbor, where it was flagship of Submarine Division 12, then relocated to San Diego as flagship of SubDiv 13 from 1935 to 1938 before returning

Freeboard
Nautilus had a high freeboard, with the gun deck raised above the outer hull, giving the guns a wider bearing and greater range.

Longboats
A 1931 cutaway diagram of *Nautilus* shows two longboats carried just beneath the gun deck, forward of the bow gun. These were not retained.

Embrasures
Modification of *Nautilus* was complete by 31 March 1942. It included addition of four external torpedo tubes two facing aft, two forward. Embrasures were made in the upper side of the outer hull, just in front of the forward gun, for the new forward tubes.

USS Nautilus (V-6)

Specification

Dimensions:	Length: 113m (370ft 9in); Beam: 10m (32ft 10in); Draught: 4.8m (15ft 9in)
Displacement:	Surfaced – 2773 tonnes (2730 tons); Submerged – 3962 tonnes (3900 tons)
Propulsion:	From 1942 – four GM 16-278A two-cycle diesels each of 1600hp (1200kW), two GM 8-2168A diesel generators of 400hp (300kW) each; two Westinghouse 1270hp (950kW) electric motors; twin screws
Speed:	Surfaced – 18 knots (33.3km/h; 20.7mph); Submerged – 11 knots (20.3km/h; 12.6mph)
Range:	9380nm (17,371km; 10,794 miles) at 11 knots (20.3km/h; 12.6mph)
Armament:	Six 533mm (21in) torpedo tubes; two 152mm (6in) guns
Complement:	88

The relative size of *V-6* is clear as it rests alongside an S-class boat in a fitting-out basin, probably Mare Island.

to Pearl Harbor. Shortly before World War II, *Nautilus* was modified to carry 90,000 litres (20,000 gallons) of aviation gasoline to refuel seaplanes at sea, but it never performed this service.

In the war it had an eventful career, making a total of 14 patrols across a wide extent of the Pacific. Its most dangerous moments came on 4–5 June 1942 as the Battle of Midway was about to begin, when it was spotted by a Japanese formation of four warships. Two torpedoes were fired at the battleship *Kirishima*, but one missed and the other misfired, and the submarine was harried by depth charges from destroyer escorts. *Nautilus* went on to attack the damaged aircraft carrier *Kaga*, striking it with a torpedo that failed to explode. On 25 June it sank the Japanese destroyer *Yamakaze,* and the auxiliary minesweeper *Musashi Maru* two days later. With the converted V-type minelayor *Argonaut* it supported the unsuccessful Makin

68

Raid on 16–18 August 1942. There were further secret missions connected with invasions and personnel retrieval, on one of which *Nautilus* was hit by 'friendly fire' from the destroyer USS *Ringgold* on 26 November 1943, sustaining damage to the conning tower but still managing to proceed with its mission. With the end of the Pacific War in sight, *Nautilus* was decommissioned at Philadelphia on 30 June 1945 and scrapped in 1946.

One of the V-boats' achievements was to make air-conditioning a standard feature of American submarines, starting with USS *Cuttlefish*. AC was fitted to *Nautilus* in its 1942 refit. Damp and humidity had always been features of submarine life, but a drier atmosphere was needed as more sophisticated electrical equipment came into use. Crew comfort, although better on American submarines than others, was as ever a secondary consideration.

Ten-year experiment

The value of the V-boats in the story of American submarine development has been much argued over, with some suggestions that the 10-year experiment merely showed the US Navy what it didn't need. As often, political considerations played a part – all save one of the nine were built at the US Navy's own yards. The US Navy was not the only navy to invest in large, expensive submarines that formed classes of only one or two boats. Only Nautilus and its sister Narwhal proved to have a useful wartime role because of their size and consequent ability to carry up to 100 troops for shore landings and their guns' ability to provide supporting fire. But they were surpassed in all respects except sheer size (until the next Nautilus in 1954) by the series of submarine classes that followed, when the demands of impending and then actual war concentrated the minds of designers on providing the US Navy with large numbers of effective and reliable combat submarines.

Early stage of *V-6*'s construction at Mare Island, California, in 1929.

☒ U-32 (Type VIIA) (1937)

Type VII in its various configurations was the most successful submarine class of World War II and formed the backbone of the U-boat force. Like many other military designs, the original Type VII was quickly modified to provide longer range, better performance and revised armament.

Type VII inaugurated a new generation of German attack submarines. Only 10 were built before an improved design was completed, and they became designated as Type VIIA. It was an effective design from the start, able to dive in less than 30 seconds and operate at a depth of 100m (330ft), with capacity to go as deep as 220m (720ft) in an emergency. Built to withstand water pressure up to a crush depth of 250m (820ft), the single-

hull design was reinforced with 82 steel ribs. Ballast tanks were situated internally and externally, with the main tank just below the control room inside the hull. External tanks were fitted at the bow and stern, and additional saddle tanks were later fitted to the sides of the hull. Diesel fuel tanks were situated inside the pressure hull to avoid leakages from depth charge attacks. The earliest variants were also fitted with serrated net cutters on the bow, a

Designed in 1933–34, launched in 1936–37, the ten Type VIIA boats formed the small nucleus of what would become the world's largest submarine fleet.

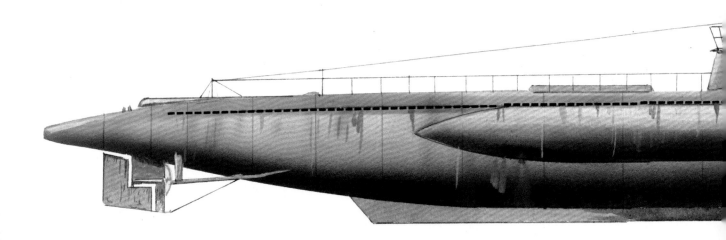

specification carried over from World War I boats, but these were discontinued.

With five torpedo tubes and 11 torpedoes, or 22 TMA mines (33 of the smaller TMB type), they had considerable striking power. On the Type VIIA, the stern torpedo tube was situated externally, and could be reloaded only in port. For surface fighting it had an 88mm (3.4in) fast-firing gun with around 160 rounds of ammunition. On battery power its two Brown Boveri GG UB 720/8 double-acting electric motors could propel it submerged for two hours at 7.7 knots (14.2km/h; 8.8mph) or 130 hours at 2 knots (3.7km/h; 2.3mph),

and on the surface its two supercharged MAN 6-cylinder 4-stroke diesels gave it 17.7 knots (32.7km/h; 20.3mph). Manoeuvrable, responsive and seaworthy, it was probably the best submarine of its day.

Like other U-boats and surface ships it was fitted with the *Gruppenhorchgerät* (GHG) passive sonar hydrophone array, 24 mounted on each side, making it possible to identify a vessel's engine type, propeller speed and course. It could pick up the noise of a single vessel at 20km (12 miles) or a convoy 100km (62 miles) away. The VIIA's main shortcoming, corrected in later versions with increased bunkerage capacity, was a relatively restricted

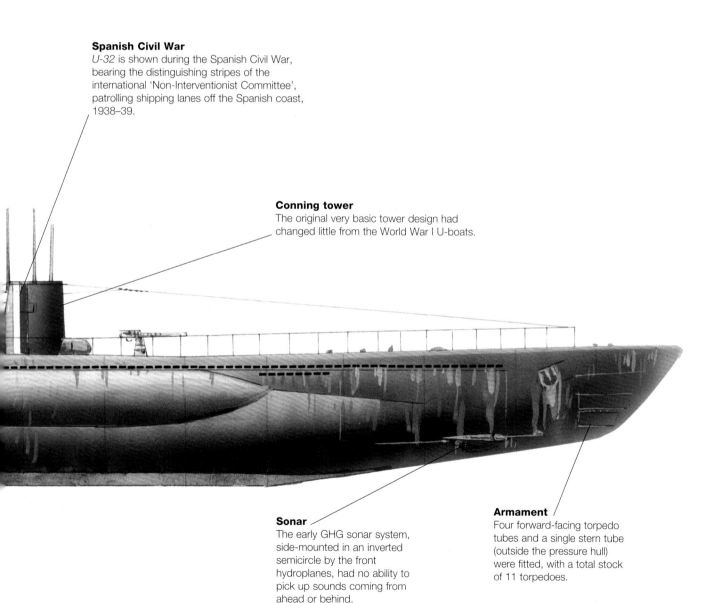

Spanish Civil War
U-32 is shown during the Spanish Civil War, bearing the distinguishing stripes of the international 'Non-Interventionist Committee', patrolling shipping lanes off the Spanish coast, 1938–39.

Conning tower
The original very basic tower design had changed little from the World War I U-boats.

Sonar
The early GHG sonar system, side-mounted in an inverted semicircle by the front hydroplanes, had no ability to pick up sounds coming from ahead or behind.

Armament
Four forward-facing torpedo tubes and a single stern tube (outside the pressure hull) were fitted, with a total stock of 11 torpedoes.

Kiel harbour on the eve of war, 1939. *U-27*, *U-33* (alongside tender) and *U-34* can be seen. Two Type IIA submarines are in the background.

Specification

Dimensions:	Length: 64m (209ft 11in); Beam: 5.8m (19ft); Draught: 4.4m (14ft 5in)
Displacement:	Surfaced – 636 tonnes (625 tons); Submerged – 757 tonnes (745 tons)
Propulsion:	Two MAN M 6 V 40/46 four-stroke, six-cylinder diesel engines, 2310hp (1700kW); two BBC GG UB 720/8 double-acting electric motors, 740hp (550kW)
Speed:	Surfaced – 16 knots (29.6km/h; 18.4mph); Submerged – 8 knots (14.8km/h; 9.2mph)
Range:	4300nm (7963km; 4948 miles)
Armament:	Four bow, one stern 533mm (21in) torpedo tube, 11 torpedoes; one 88mm (3.5in), one 20mm (0.8in) gun
Complement:	42

operating range of 6200 nautical miles (11,482km; 7134 miles). As with preceding types, internal accommodation was extremely cramped, and comfort and amenities for the crew were virtually non-existent.

Atlantic raider

U-32, last of the 10 Type VIIA boats, was laid down at the Deschimag (AG Weser) Yard in Bremen, launched on 25 February 1937 and commissioned on 5 April that year. It was attached to the 2nd 'Salzwedel' U-boat Flotilla on 15 April and remained with that group throughout its career. When war was declared in September 1939, it was one of the few German submarines ready for combat on the high seas. The flotilla was based at Wilhelmshaven and merged from 1 January 1940 with the 6th 'Hundius' flotilla. In June 1940 it transferred to Lorient, France. *U-32* undertook nine war patrols, in the course of which it sank around 20 ships. Its first mission was minelaying in waters off the British Isles, and en route it sank its first victim, a British cargo ship, by gunfire on 18 September 1939. But its commander, Kapitänleutant Paul Büchel, was deterred by the sight of British patrols and failed to lay its mines in the specified area. On returning he was relieved of command.

Under Oberleutnant Hans Jenisch, *U-32* had a more distinguished record. In total it sank 20 ships, with a gross registered tonnage of 116,836, and damaged a further five. On 1 September 1940, it attacked a convoy about 40 nautical miles (74km; 46 miles) north north-east of Rockall in the Atlantic, striking the new light cruiser HMS *Fiji* with a torpedo. It claimed the largest vessel to be sunk by a U-boat, the liner *Empress of Britain* (42,348 gross registered tons), en route from Cape Town to Liverpool. On 26 October 1940 the liner had been spotted off north-west Ireland by German planes, whose bombs started a fire. Although this was put out, the ship was abandoned except for a skeleton crew and was under tow by two tugs with an escort of two destroyers. Four Type VIIA boats, including *U-32*, returning to Germany for training duties, were in the area

and ordered to find and sink the *Empress*. Excellent radio communications between the Atlantic U-boats and Admiral Dönitz's operational headquarters made it possible for such opportunistic diversions to be made (the Allies had not yet broken the German naval codes).

U-32 traced the liner using passive sonar and followed it for 24 hours before closing to fire three torpedoes from a distance of 600m (1968ft). One detonated prematurely, but two struck, causing a massive explosion. The tow lines were slipped and *Empress of Britain* sank.

On 30 October *U-32* attacked the British freighter *Balzac*, which put out an alarm call that brought the destroyers *Harvester* and *Highlander* to the scene. The U-boat was forced to the surface by 20 depth charges and it came under searchlight-directed fire from the warships' 120mm (4.7in) guns. Unable to dive, it was scuttled at the commander's orders. Nine crewmen died, and 33 survivors, including Jenisch, were picked up.

Secret research and development

The design of the World War II U-boats before the war was carried out in clandestine fashion in the 1920s, then somewhat more openly from the early 1930s under a cover project named *Entwicklungsaufgaben auf dem Gebiete des Motoren-Versuchsboot-Wesens* ('Development exercises with engine-trial vessels'). During this period the Types IA, II A–D, VII and IX were built. The construction methods employed in building the new U-boats were very much as in 1914–1918, with the hull completed first and then everything for the interior, including the engines, inserted in parts through the narrow hatches and assembled inside. It took about 10 months to build a Type VII U-boat.

U-30, *U-31* and *U-32* moored at Kiel. The activity on deck suggests they are about to set off on a training exercise.

⚅ U-47 (Type VIIB) (1938)

U-47 made world headlines and won glory in Germany by a daring entry into the Scapa Flow naval anchorage in the Orkney Islands on 14 October 1939, when it sank the battleship HMS Royal Oak before making a successful getaway.

An improved version of the Type VIIA, the 24 Type VIIBs had a slightly lengthened hull and larger saddle tanks. This enabled a greater fuel capacity, which increased the range from 4300nm (7963km; 4948 miles) to 6000nm (11,112km; 6904 miles). It was divided into three compartments by two pressure-proof bulkheads and subdivided into six rooms by

Twin rudders
Type VIIB had twin rudders rather than the single rudder of the VIIA boats, and its stern tube was brought inside the pressure hull.

Armament
The early VIIBs had their 20mm flak gun mounted on the aft deck. This was not ideal as the tower created a dead firing zone, and it took time to get the gun into action and for the crew to return inside the U-boat in an emergency. For these reasons, it was decided to move the gun to the aft end of the conning tower. Re-siting took place over the winter of 1939–40. To accommodate the gun, the rear of the platforms had to be completely rebuilt.

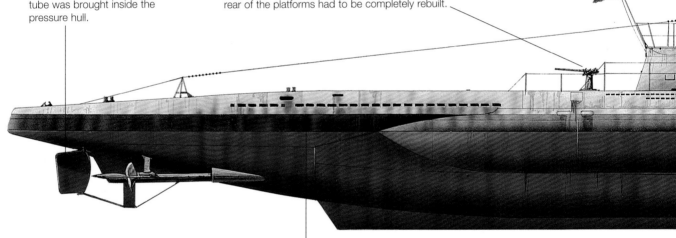

Power supply
Diesel engines in Type VIIB submarines were normally either MAN Type M6 V40/46 with forced induction by Buchi supercharger, developing 1400hp (1043kW) and weighing 39.1 tonnes (38.5 tons) or the slightly heavier Germania Werft GW Model e.v. 40/46 also with forced induction, the same power rating and weighing 44 tonnes (43.4 tons).

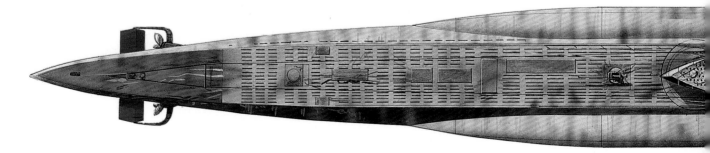

watertight bulkheads. Ballast was provided by three main tanks situated internally and externally of the pressure hull. Two of these could be used as reserve fuel tanks. The main tank was just below the control room, inside the pressure hull. Superchargers were fitted to the diesel engines, increasing surface speed by about 1 knot (1.8km/h; 1.1mph). Torpedo capacity was also increased from 11 to 14 – two were stored externally in pressure-tight containers underneath the upper deck. To improve on manoeuvrability and the turning radius, twin rudders were fitted directly behind the propellers. This new arrangement allowed the single stern torpedo tube to be brought inside the pressure hull, making internal reloads at sea possible.

U-47 was laid down at Krupps Germaniawerft, Kiel, on 27 February 1937, launched on 29 October 1938 and commissioned on 17 December 1938. It was assigned to the 7th 'Wegener' flotilla at Kiel. In September 1940 the flotilla was transferred to St Nazaire, France. From the first, its commander was Oberleutnant (later Korvettenkapitän) Günther Prien. When war broke out in September 1939 *U-47* was already on patrol and sank three ships on 5, 6 and 7 September. In its second patrol, a highly secret and carefully prepared project, it penetrated the naval anchorage of Scapa Flow in the Orkney Islands on 14 October. U-boat chief Karl Dönitz was the mastermind, using intelligence provided both by aerial photographs

With the same armament as the VIIA, but carrying three additional torpedoes, the VIIB design drew on experience to provide a more effective attack submarine.

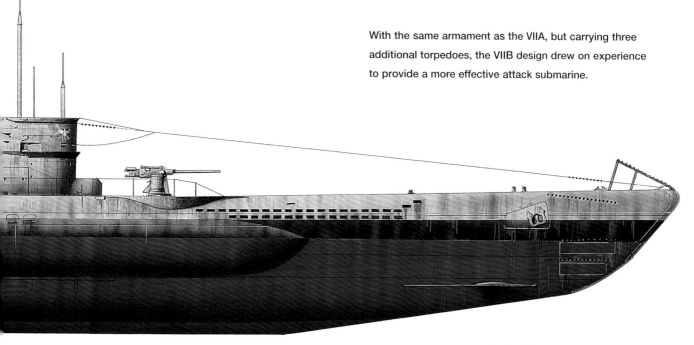

Surface camouflage
Colours of wartime U-boats varied at different times, but were almost always in shades of grey, usually in two tones. *Dunkelgrau* 51 ('dark grey', although actually more like medium grey) above the surfaced waterline, and *Schiffsbodenfarbe III Grau* ('hull colour grey') below.

Protection
Protectors were fitted to forward and aft diving planes.

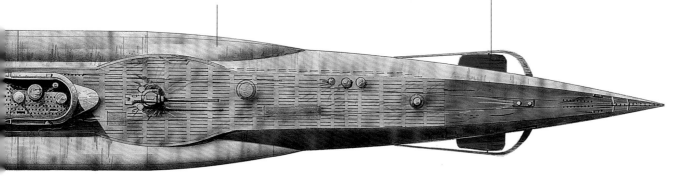

U-47 (Type VIIB)

supplied by the Luftwaffe and reports submitted from *U-14*, under Kapitänleutnant Wellner, who had been patrolling the area between 13 and 29 September as part of an ongoing reconnaissance operation. Preen was invited to carry out the action in *U-47* and accepted with enthusiasm.

Royal Oak sunk

The submarine was carefully prepared. All excess items, even food, were unloaded, and new G7e electric wakeless torpedoes were deployed. The battleship *Royal Oak* was hit by four torpedoes and sank with the loss of over 800 crew. Although by chance most of the British fleet had left Scapa Flow two days previously, and *Royal Oak* was an elderly battleship, the venture was one of the most daring, skilful and hazardous ever carried out by a submarine and made a tremendous propaganda victory for the Nazi regime.

U-47 made a further seven patrols, all under Prien's command, in the North Atlantic. On 12–17 June 1940 it led a 'wolfpack' massed attack operation of seven U-boats, codenamed 'Prien' against Convoy HX-47. Five ships were sunk. This was the first such attack of the

The frontal view shows the bulges of the Type VIIB's increased fuel capacity.

war, other than the 'Hartmann' attack of October 1939, and was made possible by the collapse of France, giving Germany bases on the French west coast and the use of powerful land-based transmitters, capable of sending messages from *Befehlshaber der Unterseeboote* (BdU, 'U-boat Command') to U-boats far out in the Atlantic.

Also by this time, Dönitz had a nucleus of effective U-boats and was able to initiate his thought-out wolfpack

Specification

Dimensions:	Length: 66.5m (218ft); Beam: 6.2m (20ft 3in); Draught: 4.7m (15ft 6in)
Displacement:	Surfaced – 765 tonnes (753 tons); Submerged – 871 tonnes (857 tons)
Propulsion:	Two GW diesel engines, 2800hp (2100kW), two AEG GU 460/8-276 double-acting electric motors, 740hp (550kW); twin screws
Speed:	Surfaced – 17.2 knots (31.8km/h; 19.7mph); Submerged – 8 knots (14.8km/h; 9mph)
Range:	surfaced – 8700nm (16,112km; 10,011 miles) at 10 knots (18.5km/h; 11.5mph)
Armament:	Five 533mm (21in) torpedo tubes, 14 torpedoes; one 88mm (3.5in) gun, one 20mm (0.8in) flak gun
Complement:	44

This AA gun configuration was tested on U-84, with a separate platform for a second 20mm (0.8in) gun aft of the tower. It was not adopted, but improved defence against aircraft was a constant concern.

Celebration, complete with band, on board *U-47* after the Scapa Flow exploit in October 1939.

Wolfpack tactics

The first wolfpack boat to find a convoy was designated as the 'shadower' – its job was to maintain contact and to report the convoy's position back to U-boat Command (BdU), then remain out of visible range, often submerging by day and travelling on the surface by night. When enough boats had gathered, BdU would give the signal to attack, normally at dusk when the U-boats' low silhouettes made detection difficult. With the signal given, individual commanders were free to use any tactics they chose. Some fired at long range, outside the perimeter of the escorts, usually with a spread of several torpedoes. Some headed straight for the middle of the convoy, firing at close range, picking off ship after ship as each steamed past.

tactics. Many others would follow. The origins of this tactic went back to Dönitz's experience in World War I, when Britain belatedly adopted the convoy system as a defence against individual submarine attacks. The idea was to form a pack of U-boats, and to delay an assault until all were in position to conduct a co-ordinated attack from several directions, confusing the escorts as well as using the sheer number and surprise of the attacking boats to throw the defence into disarray. Whichever tactics were then employed, the general strategy was to attack by night and withdraw by day, with continuous attacks lasting several days, as additional U-boats converged on the scene.

U-47 sent its last radio message at 0454hrs on 7 March 1941 while chasing the westbound convoy OB-293. There is no confirmed explanation for its loss, and it may have been struck by one of its own torpedoes. Its war record shows 31 merchant ships sunk, total tonnage 162,769 GRT, and one battleship, total tonnage 29,616 tonnes (29,150 tons). In addition eight ships were damaged, with a total tonnage of 62,751 GRT.

U-210 (Type VIIC) (1941)

The Type VIIC attack submarine of the Third Reich's U-boat fleet was the most numerous class of submarine ever built, with 507 vessels commissioned. Many of them, including *U-210*, had very brief careers before falling victim to the improved ASW methods of the Allies.

Introduced in 1940, the Type VIIC had the same basic characteristics as the VIIB but numerous improvements of detail, and was slightly larger to make room for additional equipment. New electronic and communication equipment required more space to install, made possible by lengthening the control room by the distance of one half frame forward of, and one half frame aft of, the search periscope. Between 1940 and 1943 the manufacturing time for U-boats was significantly reduced. The shipyards adopted the system of pre-fabrication, but only with the hull

itself. Outfitting was still done as before. Some 19 shipyards assembled between 24 to 26 U-boats per month of Types VIIC, IXC and IXD. Once fitting-out began, each boat's own engineering personnel were involved so that they knew exactly how the machinery was put together.

The naval high command wanted to fit active sonar to new U-boats, and extra space was needed to house this equipment. Little use was made of the sets that were installed, because of the limited range – 4000m (13,123ft) at best – and because its pulses could be picked up from

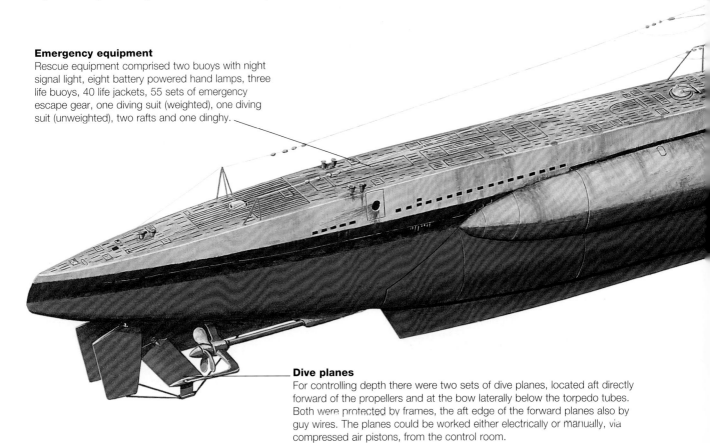

Emergency equipment
Rescue equipment comprised two buoys with night signal light, eight battery powered hand lamps, three life buoys, 40 life jackets, 55 sets of emergency escape gear, one diving suit (weighted), one diving suit (unweighted), two rafts and one dinghy.

Dive planes
For controlling depth there were two sets of dive planes, located aft directly forward of the propellers and at the bow laterally below the torpedo tubes. Both were protected by frames, the aft edge of the forward planes also by guy wires. The planes could be worked either electrically or manually, via compressed air pistons, from the control room.

a much greater distance by enemy craft and used to home in on the transmitting boat. One form was the *Sondergerät für aktive Schallortung* (*S-gerät*) intended to give warning of mines ahead, and fitted to VIIC and some VIIB boats from 11 October 1940. From 1943 it was taken out. The U-boat commanders continued to rely on the well-tried GHG passive arrays. One expert wrote after the war: "The Allies probably did not realize how efficient the German listening equipment was until the summer of 1941 when the

U-570 was captured by the British. They then discovered that German submarines were provided with arrays of 24 3-inch crystal microphones on each bow ... the Germans gave their naval vessels a passive listening ability which may perhaps have surpassed that possessed by the ships of any other country." The additional space on board the VIIC boats was quickly taken up by an ever-greater variety of electronic devices intended to counter the ever-more effective Allied radars.

Wake reduction
During 1940, anti-vibration wires were added to the tops of periscopes to help reduce the wake left by a raised periscope. All the VIICs had this feature.

Armament
For the 88mm (3.4in) gun, 205 rounds of high explosive C/35 shells were carried.

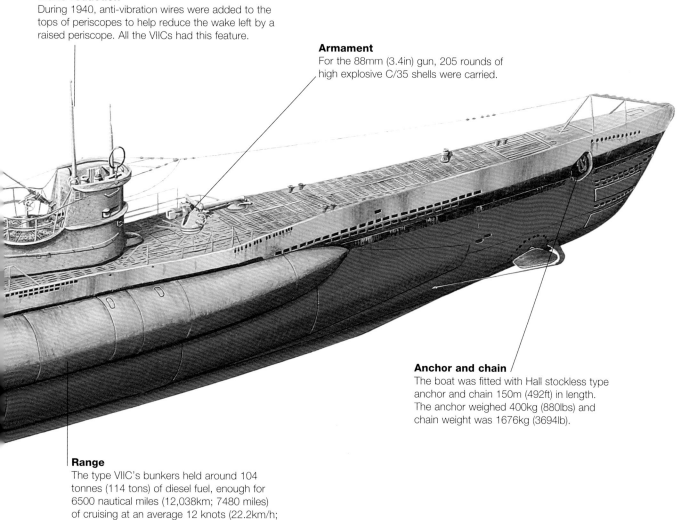

Anchor and chain
The boat was fitted with Hall stockless type anchor and chain 150m (492ft) in length. The anchor weighed 400kg (880lbs) and chain weight was 1676kg (3694lb).

Range
The type VIIC's bunkers held around 104 tonnes (114 tons) of diesel fuel, enough for 6500 nautical miles (12,038km; 7480 miles) of cruising at an average 12 knots (22.2km/h; 13.8 mph) speed. With more than 2500nm (4630km; 2876 miles) to be covered just to arrive on station, fuel had to be carefully conserved.

U-210 was a typical Type VIIC U-boat. Almost all U-boats carried their own emblem, painted on the tower. *U-210*'s was a lobster, with claws extended in attacking mode.

U-210 (Type VIIC)

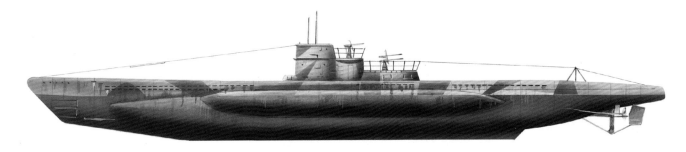

This profile of *U-553* shows adaptation of the VIIC for additional AA protection. The extended platform carries a 4-barrelled 'Flakvierling' 20mm (0.8in) gun.

Laid down on 15 March 1941 at F. Krupp Germaniawerft, Kiel, and launched on 23 December, *U-210* was passed to the *U-Boot Abnahmekommando* (UAK) for testing. Further tests of the boat's operations and systems were made by the *U-Boot Abnahmegruppe* (UAG). Following acceptance by this reception group, it was commissioned on 21 February 1942. A training period followed before *U-210* left Kiel on its first and only war patrol on 18 July 1942, under the command of Korvettenkapitän Rudolf Lemcke, its destination the North Atlantic trade route. Having accomplished its patrol, it was due to join the 9th flotilla at Brest. Ordered first to join the *Pirat* wolfpack, hunting

athwart the standard convoy route, it was then redirected to the *Steinbrinck* pack, about 645km (400 miles) north-east of Newfoundland.

On 6 August the pack encountered Convoy SC 94, a 'slow ship' convoy en route from Sydney, Cape Breton Island, to Liverpool. In patchy fog and with a considerable sea running, *U-210* was spotted at 1125hrs from the Canadian escort destroyer HMCS *Assiniboine*. Believing his boat to be concealed in the fog, Lemcke kept it on the surface but at 1712hrs it was again sighted from *Assiniboine* and promptly dived. A hunt through the fog

Top: VIIC tower conversion for Arctic service, 1942.
Middle: Enlarged tower form of a Type VIIC 'flakboat', 1943.
Bottom: 'Winter garden' two-step platform for AA guns fitted to some Type VIIC boats from 1942.

Specification

Dimensions:	Length: 67.1m (220ft 1in); Beam: 6.2m (20ft 4in); Draught: 4.8m (15ft 9in)
Displacement:	Surfaced – 773 tonnes (761 tons); Submerged – 879 tonnes (865 tons)
Propulsion:	Two GW e.v. 40/46 6-cylinder engines developing 3160hp (2350kW); two BBC GG UB 720/8 electric motors, 740hp (550kW); twin screws
Speed:	Surfaced – 17 knots (31.4km/h; 19.5mph); Submerged – 7.6 knots (14km/h; 8.7mph)
Range:	6500nm (12,038km; 7480 miles) at 12 knots (22.2km/h; 13.8mph)
Armament:	Four bow, one stern 533mm (21in) torpedo tubes, 14 torpedoes; one 88mm (3.5in), two 20mm (0.8in) guns
Complement:	44

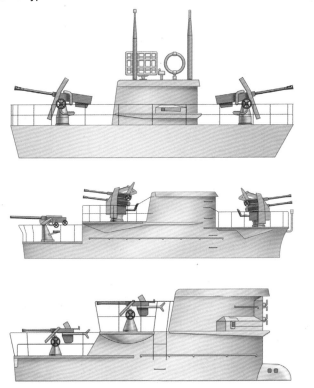

patches followed, and at 1850hrs RDF contact was made at a range of 1180m (3871ft), and *Assiniboine* made for the submarine at full speed. The two vessels reappeared to each other only 200m (656ft) apart. Too near to use its 119mm (4.7in) guns effectively, the destroyer was prepared to ram, while *U-210*, unable to use the exposed deck gun, fired explosive bullets from its 20mm flak gun, starting a fire in the destroyer's forecastle. A shell from *Assiniboine* hit the conning tower, killing Lemcke and three others, but the pressure hull was not breached, and as *U-210* attempted

U-570, captured by the Royal Navy on 27 August 1941, is inspected by Royal Navy crew.

a crash-dive, it was rammed by *Assiniboine* just behind the tower. It went down to 18m (59ft), but was so damaged as to be inoperable. The tanks were blown and it resurfaced, and was immediately rammed again by *Assiniboine*, and sank. In total, 38 of its crew were rescued.

The convoy went on to take a mauling from the surviving U-boats in the area, and 10 ships were sunk on 8–10 August.

Improvements and upgrades

Diving characteristics of Type VIIC, especially in heavy seas, were improved by adding pressure-proof negative buoyancy tanks forward of the port and starboard regulating tanks. Mechanical improvements included a new oil-filter system and an updated electrical control system. One of the two Krupp electrically-driven compressors was replaced by a Junkers diesel-powered compressor in order to reduce electric power consumption. On VIIAs and VIIBs, the main trunk providing air to the diesels was routed up inside the after end of the tower and ventilation holes were located on the sides of the tower walls to let air into the intake trunk. As these admitted water in high seas, the engines could suffer from lack of air. Several modifications were made to the VIIAs and VIIBs to improve the air supply. The VIICs had trunks built up the inside of the tower bulwark and did not have this problem.

Conning tower of a Type VIIC, with wave and spray deflectors.

U-459 (Type XIV) (1941)

U-459, first of the 10 boats of Type XIV, was the *Kriegsmarine's* first purpose-built refuelling and supply submarine, a large boat intended to intensify the Atlantic war by enabling attack vessels to spend longer periods at sea.

Laid down at Deutsche Werke, Kiel, on 22 November 1940, launched on 13 September 1941 and commissioned on 15 November 1941, *U-459* was nicknamed *Milchkuh* ('milch cow') as it was a feeder to other U-boats. It went to the 4th (Training) Flotilla until 31 March 1942, then to the 10th Flotilla at Lorient from April to October 1942 and finally to the 12th Flotilla at Bordeaux from 1 November 1942.

It made six war patrols in all, including one with wolfpack *Eisbär*, 25 August–1 September 1942.

The prime design requirement was maximum space for storing fuel, provisions and ammunition. Tanks between the outer and pressure hulls held 432 tonnes (425 tons) of diesel oil, and four torpedoes were carried in the superstructure. The design was based on the Type IX,

Fuel tanks
The transfer hose was 152m (500ft) long, made up of sections connected by clasp joints, with an internal diameter of 89mm (3.5in). In *U-459* there was an additional 8m (26ft 3in) length of rubber-impregnated linen hose, to which an 8m length of armoured hose was connected to prevent chafing where the hose left the supply boat. Between *U-459* and the combat boat were five 16m (52ft 6in) lengths of non-armoured hose, with a further 8m armoured length where the hose met the U-boat. On the combat boat three further 16m lengths of unarmoured hose were used.

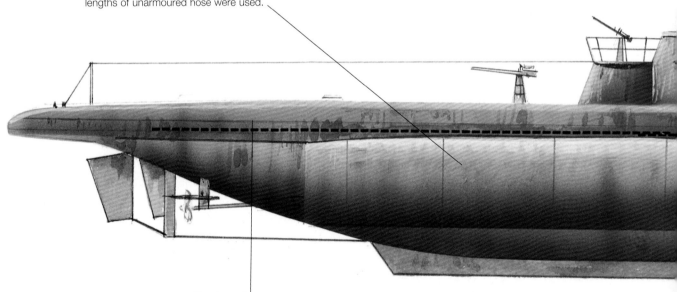

Freeboard
Larger submarines did not necessarily have a high freeboard: there was more of them beneath the surface waterline.

itself a large submarine, but Type XIV had a shorter, deeper and broader hull, bulked out further by a large bulge for the fuel tanks. These tanks increased buoyancy and allowed the pressure hull to be made of steel almost 25.4mm (1in) thick, giving the vessel diving capability to over 150m (492ft). Twin Germania diesel engines and twin SSW electric motors provided the power, and a range of 12,350 nautical miles (22,872km; 14,212 miles) gave it ample operating room. The Type XIV was more capacious inside than the Type IX, but all space was fully utilized. The boats carried lubricating oil, spare torpedoes, gunnery shells, spare parts and had a machine shop for repairs. For the crews they carried drinking water and refrigerated food, and had a bakery that could provide fresh bread. A navy doctor who could perform minor operations was part of the crew, along with extra personnel who could be exchanged for the sick or injured crewmembers of other U-boats.

Rendezvous was made by the U-boat coming to the tanker at a predetermined time and location specified by the U-boat Command Staff headed by Dönitz (BdU) to both vessels, where the U-boat would then cruise around until it found the tanker. As the frequency of air attacks increased, both U-boat and U-tanker would approach the rendezvous area submerged and then surface for an hour or so before sunset to establish

The concept of the U-boat feeder, able to avoid detection until it reached a meeting point, was effective until the German radio codes were broken and their missions ceased to be secret. The system then had to abandoned.

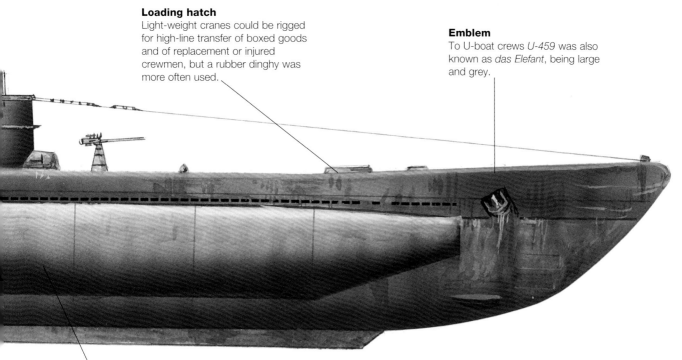

Loading hatch
Light-weight cranes could be rigged for high-line transfer of boxed goods and of replacement or injured crewmen, but a rubber dinghy was more often used.

Emblem
To U-boat crews *U-459* was also known as *das Elefant*, being large and grey.

Internal layout
Compartments from stern to stem were: Workshop; Motor Rooms; Engine Room; Galley; Control Room with Pumps, Magazine and provisions below; Captain's and Officers cabins (port side) – W/T and Hydrophone Room (starboard side); Wardroom (port side, with after Battery Room below) – Petty Officers' Mess (starboard side); Chief Petty Officers' Mess (port side with forward battery below) – Ratings' Mess (starboard side); Bow Compartment. The main provisions store was below the mess room.

The transfer operation, in anything other than a flat calm, was a tricky business. A Type VIIB is being refuelled while another waits.

Specification

Dimensions:	Length: 67.1m (220ft); Beam: 9.4m (30ft 10in); Draught: 6.5m (21ft 4in)
Displacement:	Surfaced – 1688 tonnes (1661 tons); Submerged – 1932 tonnes (1901 tons)
Propulsion:	Two GW supercharged 4-stroke, 6-cylinder diesel engines developing 3160hp (2350kW); two Siemens-Schukert 2GU 345/38-8 double-acting electric motors, 740hp (550kW), twin screws
Speed:	Surfaced – 14.5 knots (26.8km/h; 16.6mph); Submerged – 6.3 knots (11.6km/h; 7.2mph)
Range:	12,350nm (22,872km; 14,212 miles)
Armament:	Two 37mm (1.5in), one 20mm (0.8in) guns
Complement:	53

each other's position. This would be very difficult in bad weather or after dark, and in such cases the U-tanker could transmit a very weak beacon or homing signal, or, more riskily fire recognition signal flares. Although Allied intelligence suspected that U-boats were being refuelled at sea, it was not until the Enigma Shark key was broken consistently in mid-1943 that they were certain. After that, virtually all planned meetings were known in advance, and the rate of successful replenishment rapidly fell.

Refuelling dangers

The refuelling procedure was time-consuming and had to be done on the surface, during which time the boats were especially vulnerable, as it was impossible for a U-tanker to dive instantly if caught while refuelling, since the fuel lines had to be disconnected and stowed away. But with their powerful AA armament, they could hold off an attacking aircraft until cleared to dive. Because they were also slower to submerge than a normal U-boat, it was a standing order that, in the event of air attack, no U-boat could submerge until the tanker had done so. This was so that the U-boats could defend the tanker with their own AA guns until the latter was safely submerged. Although the attack boats

could dive in much less time than the tanker, the grim logic of battle tactics dictated that it was better to lose one standard U-boat than the tanker, whose loss could compromise other submarines on extended patrol.

Between November 1941 and March 1943, 10 supply boats were commissioned. From the new fortified bases,

AA Armament

The Type XIV's only armament was anti-aircraft weapons for self-defence, since their prime enemy was, rightly, expected to be aircraft. Two 37mm (1.5in) cannons were fitted, one forward and one aft of the bridge and a single 20mm (0.8in) on a platform aft. These were upgraded in 1943 after the fifth patrol, with the gun platform behind the conning tower widened and armoured, and a second platform was fitted just aft of the original. The original 20mm cannon on the old gun platform was replaced by a pair of twin 20mm cannon, and the new aft gun platform mounted either a 37mm cannon, or more usually a quadruple 20mm cannon known as a Vierling.

U-459 slowly sinks after the battle with RAF Wellington aircraft, 24 July 1943.

first Saint-Nazaire with the 10th Flotilla, and then Bordeaux (11th Flotilla), *U-459* made five Atlantic patrols between 29 March 1942 and 3 June 1943, making 63 refuelling meetings; on one occasion running so short itself that another 'milch cow', *U-462*, had to refuel it.

On its sixth patrol, *U-459* was attacked on 24 July 1943 by British Wellington aircraft off Cape Ortegal, Spain. One plane, Wellington Q of 172 Squadron, was shot down, crash-landing on the U-boat's deck. The crew cleared the wreckage that included unexploded depth charges with shallow settings. These exploded beneath the boat, seriously damaging it. A second attack from Wellington V of 547 Squadron sealed *U-459*'s fate. Scuttling charges were set. Korvettenkapitän Georg von Wilamowitz-Möllendorf saluted his crew and went down with his boat. In total there were 19 dead and 41 survivors.

By the end of 1943, the Type XIV boats had been virtually eliminated by Allied anti-submarine forces, and in May 1944 work on a planned further 14 was cancelled, together with plans for a larger version to be known as Type XX.

HMS X-5 (1942)

The midget submarine utilized the stealth qualities of a very small undersea craft for launching attacks in unexpected places that normal submarines could not reach. But its operations were hazardous in the extreme and many were unsuccessful.

The accepted definition of a midget submarine is a vessel of less than 150 tonnes (146 tons), with a crew of no more than eight, no on-board living accommodation and operated in conjunction with a mother ship that provides the essential support. Numerous countries, notably Italy, Germany and Japan on the Axis side, and Britain among the Allies, invested in midget submarines. The Italian and British designs, although certainly high risk, were not suicide craft. Their aim was to engage in covert operations where a large vessel would not be able to penetrate. After 1939 the Royal Navy took an interest in the midget submarine, and two prototypes, *X-3* and *X-4*, were built in 1942 and used for training and evaluation at a base at Port Bannatyne on the Scottish island of Bute.

Slim provisions
On board the X-boats food supplies were minimal. Crewmembers survived on Benzedrine tablets and chocolate.

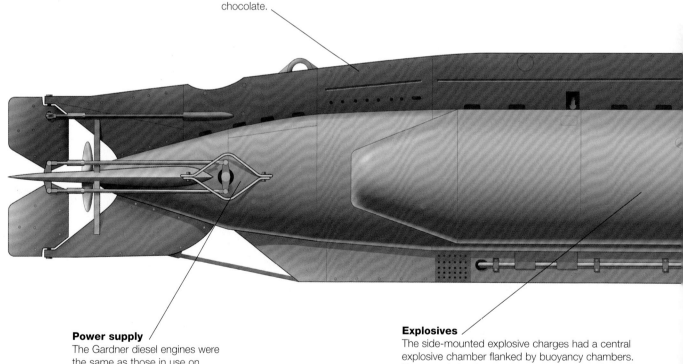

Power supply
The Gardner diesel engines were the same as those in use on London buses.

Explosives
The side-mounted explosive charges had a central explosive chamber flanked by buoyancy chambers. They needed to have pressure-resistant casings with free-flooding ballast chambers so that they would sink as soon as released. The casing proved to be susceptible to leaks from seawater.

Six operational boats, *X-5* to *X-10*, followed, all built by Vickers at Barrow-in-Furness. Resembling scaled-down submarines without conning towers, they packed a control room, engine, diving controls and tanks into a tiny inner space that also contained an airlock compartment to enable a diver to leave and enter. Explosive charges containing two tons of Amatol (a mixture of TNT and ammonium nitrate) were mounted on each side of the hull. These could be detached from inside, placed on the seabed beneath a target ship and detonated by time fuses. Under their own power the X-boats had a range of 500 nautical miles (926km; 575 miles) surfaced, and 82 nautical miles (151km; 94 miles) submerged, but the intention was to tow them to a position close to the target area.

The crew numbered four: commanding officer, pilot, engineer and diver. The diver's function was to cut through cables or nets on which the vessel might snag. Each boat had two crews, a passage crew for the

Though not used in large numbers by the Allied navies, midget submarines operated by both sides scored some significant successes in the course of World War II.

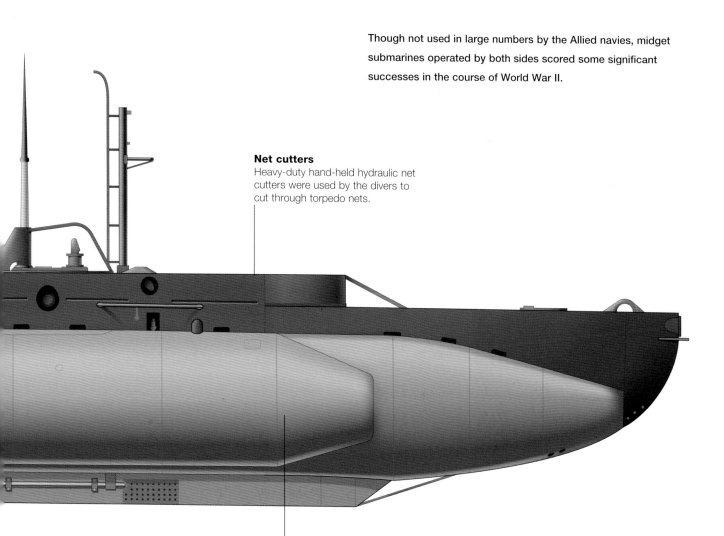

Net cutters
Heavy-duty hand-held hydraulic net cutters were used by the divers to cut through torpedo nets.

Amatol
This explosive is made by mixing TNT (trinitrotoluene) and ammonium nitrate. Although stable and shock-resistant it is highly effective when detonated. From 1943 these charges were replaced by a mixture of torpex and amatol, knows as Amatex.

Sub-Lt K.C.J. Robinson uses the periscope of an X-craft while training in Rothesay Bay, Scotland.

Specification

Dimensions:	Length: 15.7m (51ft 6in); Beam: 1.8m (6ft); Draught: 2.6m (8ft 6in)
Displacement:	Surfaced – 27 tonnes (26.5 tons); Submerged – 30 tonnes (29.5 tons)
Propulsion:	Gardner diesel engine, 42hp (31kW), one Keith Blackman electric motor, 30hp (22kW); single screw
Speed:	Surfaced – 6.5 knots (12km/h; 7.4mph); Submerged – 5.5 knots (10.1km/h; 6.3mph)
Range:	Surfaced – 500nm (926km; 575 miles); Submerged – 82nm (151km; 94 miles) at 2 knots (3.7km/h; 1mph)
Armament:	Two 1944kg (4285lb) charges
Complement:	4

outward/inward voyages and an operation crew for the action. Their equipment was very limited. Electromagnets were fitted to prevent detection by anti-submarine devices on the seabed. They had small, ineffective periscopes, and needed to surface from time to time to gauge their position. Navigation aids were a Browns A gyrocompass and Auto Helmsman, and an AVF6A/602 direction indicator. A four-cylinder Gardner 4LK diesel engine and a 30hp (22kW) electric motor provided power. Discomfort was extreme. The men could not stand upright, and a single narrow exit hatch made a rapid escape for all the crew impossible. Every two hours the towing submarine called the passage crew by telephone – if the connection worked. Its cable was made up in the towrope, and a few contortions of the rope when leaving harbour were enough to ensure that communications would be non-existent for the remainder of the tow.

Operation Source began in September 1943, aimed at the German capital ships based in Norwegian fjords. The six X-boats were towed across the North Sea by conventional submarines. An attempt on 11 September 1943 by *X-8* on the heavy cruiser *Lützow* failed when the explosive charges were penetrated by seawater and had to be jettisoned, resulting in the loss of the X-boat. *X-9* sank with all hands when its towrope parted in the North Sea. *X-10*'s mission to attack *Scharnhorst* was abandoned because of mechanical problems even before it was learned that the battleship had left its anchorage for the open sea, so *X-10* did not reach her target. Soon after slipping there was a major problem with the clutch, which was repaired while the submarine hid in a deserted fjord. On the run into Alten fjord one of the side charges flooded, and severe electrical problems led to a fire and failure of the gyrocompass. The magnetic compass flooded and the periscope also failed.

Mission aborted

Lieutenant Hudspeth realized there was no possibility of making an attack and made his way back to the rendezvous area and HM submarine *Stubborn*. Despite transferring crews (the passage crew from *X-7* were transferred to *X-10*) there were further setbacks in the attempt to tow *X-10* home, and finally, on 3 October, with a gale forecast, orders were received to transfer the passage crew and scuttle *X-10*. All the crew arrived back safely in Britain. *Tirpitz* remained as a prime target for the others.

On 20 September *X-5*, *X-6* and *X-7* were towed to a position close to the battleship in the Kaa Fjord, a branch of the Altenfjord, on the Norwegian coast. *X-6* and *X-7* successfully dropped their charges beneath *Tirpitz*'s hull but were observed, attacked and their crews captured. What happened with *X-5* is not definitely known. The boat did not survive the expedition and may have been sunk by gunfire from *Tirpitz*'s secondary armament or succumbed to mechanical problems before being able to deposit its charges. Detonation of the charges resulted in severe damage to the battleship, keeping it immobilized until April 1944. Two of the X-boat commanders, Lt Donald Cameron (*X-6*) and Lt Basil Place (*X-7*) were awarded the Victoria Cross.

Despite the loss of five out of six X-boats, the operation was considered a success. A further six boats, *X-20* to *X-25*, were built as well as six training craft, *XT-1* to *XT-6*, and played useful roles in the preparation for the D-Day landings in June 1944.

A developed version of the X-boats, *XE-1* to *XE-12*, were also built and *XE-1* to *XE-6* were transported to eastern waters where they cut telephone cables and severely damaged the Japanese cruiser *Takao* in Singapore Harbour in July–August 1945.

Operational risks

The passage crews faced their own hazards. If, for instance, the heavy towrope parted, its weight could drag the craft rapidly to the bottom. On tow, the craft oscillated gently up or down through 30m (100ft) or more, and it was dangerous to tow it submerged in shallow water. Eventually the planesman learned to recognize whether an oscillation was normal or whether it signified that the trim or hydroplanes were wrongly set. Every six hours the midget was brought up to 'guff through', changing the stale air inside by raising the induction mast and running the engine for 10 minutes, or longer if the battery and air bottles had to be recharged.

The X-craft had only a single exit hatch.

Leonardo da Vinci (1942)

This Marconi-class boat was the most successful Italian submarine of World War II, operating on a wide scale in the Mediterranean Sea and in the Atlantic and Indian Oceans, and might have made a daring attack on New York Harbor.

Curio Bernardis was a leading Italian submarine designer of the inter-war period, responsible for numerous classes, including the six-strong Marconi class, of which *Leonardo da Vinci* was the third. Single-hulled, they were large cruising submarines designed for Mediterranean Sea operations. Maximum diving depth was 90m (300ft). Laid down at the CRDA shipyard, Monfalcone, on 19

September 1938 and launched on 16 September 1939, *da Vinci* spent only a few months in the Mediterranean before being deployed to the new BETASOM (*Bordeaux Sommergibile*) Italian base at Bordeaux in August 1940.

The role of the Italian submarines was to patrol the Atlantic south of Lisbon. Italian practice in submarine warfare required the submarine to operate beneath

Attack configuration
Leonardo da Vinci as fitted for the planned New York attack, with the CA-2 in place of the deck gun. The tall fairing around the periscopes was removed to reduce the boat's silhouette. As with many other submarine classes, the Marconi boats showed tower-shape variations as the war went on.

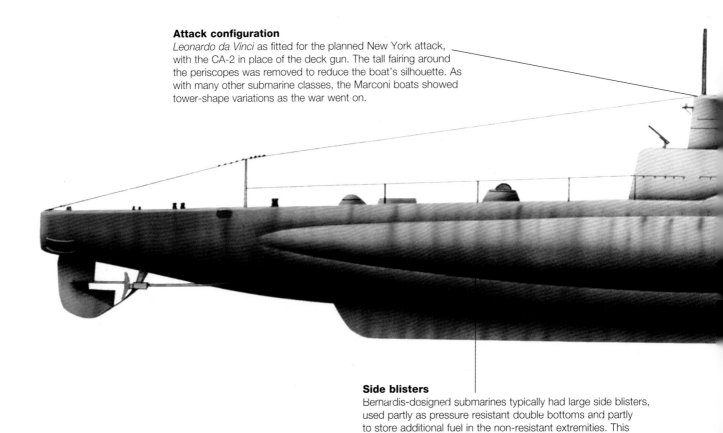

Side blisters
Bernardis-designed submarines typically had large side blisters, used partly as pressure resistant double bottoms and partly to store additional fuel in the non-resistant extremities. This reduced speed, but extended operating range.

the surface while engaging a vessel. The initial torpedo attack would come while submerged, and the attacking boat could rise to the surface to finish off the target if necessary. Longer periscopes were essential to fit this type of submerged warfare, thus a larger conning tower was required on Italian submarines in comparison to the German U-boats. In contrast, German submarines would mostly engage their targets while on the surface, and the U-boats were designed to give as small a silhouette as possible. This partly accounted for the greater profile and larger size of Italian submarines compared to others.

The *Regia Marina* doctrine of attacking below the surface did not presuppose the need to make a quick

retreat after an initial engagement, and Italian boats took longer to complete an emergency dive, which made them more vulnerable to air attack. These differences of tactics and design, combined with the greater speed of the U-boats, made co-ordination of action difficult. As a result Italian boats did not join with the German submarines in wolfpack tactics, but operated as lone raiders, south of a line between Lisbon and the American east coast. Alterations in 1941–42 helped with Atlantic conditions: the conning tower was cut down to a reduced size and the periscope sleeves were lowered to reduce the boat's profile. A consequence of the Italian approach to design, which proved damaging when

Italian submarines were typically larger than German or British wartime submarines. *Leonardo da Vinci* was half as big again as a German Type VIIIC.

'Baby on board'
The CA-2 midget boat had a crew of three. It displaced 13 tonnes (12.8 tons) submerged and was powered by a 28hp (21kW) electric motor. It carried eight 100kg (220lb) and 20 3kg (6.6lb) charges.

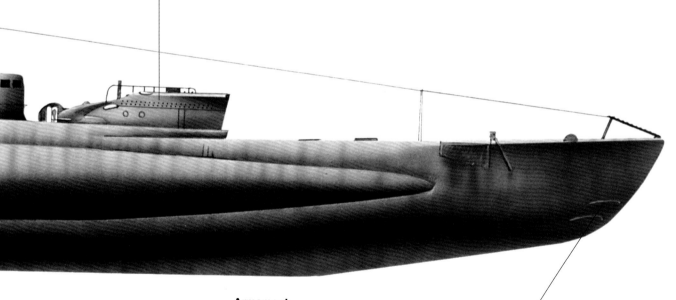

Armament
The Marconi class had four bow and four stern torpedo tubes and carried 12 torpedoes. Italian torpedoes were propelled by heated air and reciprocal engines, which created a wake, and originally fitted with inertial pendulum fuses that exploded on impact. But the Italian scientist Carlo Colossi invented the magnetic pistol detonator that exploded the warhead beneath the target's keel, breaking its back.

Specification

Dimensions:	Length: 76.5m (251ft); Beam: 6.81m (22ft 4in); Draught: 4.72m (15ft 6in)
Displacement:	Surfaced – 1214 tonnes (1195 tons); Submerged – 1510 tonnes (1490 tons)
Propulsion:	Two CRDA diesel engines, 3250hp (2421kW), two Marelli electric motors, 1500hp (1118kW); twin screws
Speed:	Surfaced – 17.8 knots (32.9km/h; 20.4mph); Submerged – 8.2 knots (15.1km/h; 9.4mph)
Range:	Surfaced – 10,500nm (19,446km; 12,083 miles) at 8 knots (14.8km/h; 9.2mph); Submerged – 110nm (203km; 126 miles) at 3 knots (5.5km/h; 3.4mph)
Armament:	Eight 533mm (21in) torpedo tubes; one 100mm (3.9in) gun, four 13.2mm (0.52in) machine guns
Complement:	57

The class leader, *Guglielmo Marconi*, launched at Monfalcone on 27 July 1939. It disappeared in the Atlantic at the end of October 1941.

repairs were needed, was a lack of standardization. While the Germans were able to produce similar vessels with mostly exchangeable parts from different shipyards, Italian submarines had many parts that were specific to a class or building yard, and each class had a relatively small number of boats.

Daring plans

Italy's Decima MAS (Special Operations Unit) under Junio Valerio Borghese devised numerous daring plans for midget submarines. One was to attack the port of New York using a Caproni midget submarine and commando frogmen, who would take their craft up the Hudson River and do as much damage to shipping as possible. *Leonardo da Vinci* was modified at the BETASOM base in Bordeaux, with the deck gun removed and a well and clamps installed to hold the CA-2 midget boat on the transatlantic crossing (the 'pouch' giving it the nickname 'Kangaroo'). The midget came by rail from Italy and tests were carried out in late 1942. Borghese viewed the operation essentially as a stunning psychological blow to the United States. But *Leonardo da Vinci* would be sunk before the raid could be carried out and the scheme was then dropped.

While the New York raid was in preparation, the modified *da Vinci* continued its raiding. In all it made 11 war patrols in the vast area of ocean between Africa and America, with one incursion into the Indian Ocean. These were not entirely on a 'lone wolf' basis as it conducted some operations in concert with *Finzi* and *Tazzoli*, sinking numerous Allied ships. It would seem that the deck gun was reinstalled for this patrol as it sank the Dutch ship *Veerhaven* (4780 tonnes; 5291 tons) by gunfire on 11 November. On 14 March 1943, off the West African coast, it sank the 21,861 tonne (21,517 ton) liner *Empress of Canada*, which had

been converted to a troopship. Unknown to *da Vinci*'s commander, Gianfranco Gazzana-Priaroggia, the vessel was carrying refugees and also Italian prisoners of war. Of the 1800 people on board, 392 were drowned, around half of them being Italians. Rounding the Cape of Good Hope, *da Vinci* sank three ships off the east coast of South Africa. Six weeks later, on 22 May, the submarine sent a radio signal that it was returning to base. This message was intercepted and its position pinpointed by the British. Two convoy escorts, the destroyer HMS *Active* and the frigate HMS *Ness,* were diverted to hunt for the submarine. Subjected to intensive depth-charge attack, *da Vinci* foundered. There were no survivors.

Capitano di Corvetta Gazzana-Priaroggia's record of shipping sunk during World War II – 90,601 gross registered tons – exceeds that of any submarine commander apart from those of Germany.

Equipment limitations

Much of the Italian submarines' equipment was out-dated. They had no adequate mechanical device for the calculation of parameters for effective torpedo firing, particularly in multiple launching. Torpedo ejection was obtained by using compressed air that generated a visible bubble on the surface, liable to betray the submarine's position. Until 1942 no Italian submarines had sonar or similar equipment for the detection of underwater obstacles or vessels, and once below periscope depth they were practically blind. Their capacity for night-fighting was non-existent. In the course of the war improvements were made. Diving speed was increased; the high and bulky conning towers were cut back and the level of equipment was raised, including the provision of a mechanical calculator for torpedo launching.

Leonardo da Vinci at sea. The original massive tower is very noticeable.

Type XXI (1943)

Known as the *Elektroboot*, this was the submarine with which Grand Admiral Dönitz expected to reinvigorate Germany's war at sea and gain control of the Atlantic routes. It was a superb design, but came too late to influence events.

The concept of the Type XXI was elaborated at a conference between Dönitz and U-boat engineers and constructors in Paris in November 1942. To make progress in the war effort the Kriegsmarine needed a U-boat larger and more effective than the VIIC. The ultimate goal was a streamlined, teardrop-shaped, air-independent submarine being designed by Dr Hellmuth Walter, but it was still years away. A stopgap was needed, and the Walter hull form was combined with conventional propulsion, heavy armament and low detectability. This was to be the Type XXI.

Effectively it introduced a new generation of combat submarine. The streamlined outer hull covered a pressure-hull in figure-of-eight cross-section, the upper section of greater diameter than the lower. Instead of a large tower with gun platforms as fairing to an inertial pressure chamber that served as an attack centre, the Type XXI had a streamlined sail, or fairwater, around the shears that supported

The cutaway profile of a Type XXI displays its revolutionary design and systems.

Air intake
Despite its advantages, the snorkel needed to be used with care. The intake pipe drew in air for the crew as well as the engines, letting the entire hull volume act as an air buffer. If the valve was suddenly closed, the diesels could run on for a short time, but would use all internal air, with fatal consequences for the crew. Air supply had to be constantly monitored in order to stop the diesels whenever the valve closed. Eventually this process was automated.

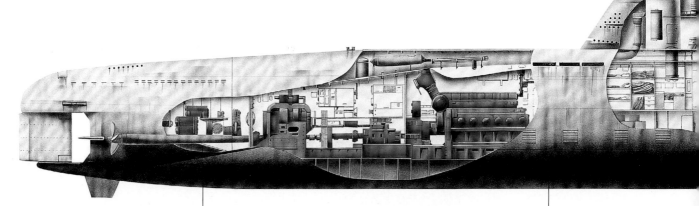

Back-up controls
An emergency steering wheel in the aftermost compartment could operate the single rudder.

Passive/active sonar
In the Type XXI an improved *Gruppenhorchgerät* (GHG) passive sonar system fitted beneath the keel, and a new active system, *Unterwasser-Ortungsgerät Nibelung*, enabled detection and attack of enemy shipping without optical contact – another revolutionary feature.

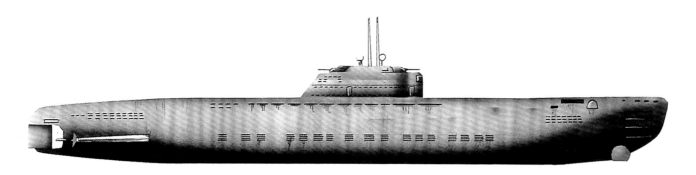

periscopes and other masts and antennae. A key feature was the *Schnorchel* (snorkel) – a double tube with valves at the upper end, which could be extended above water level while the boat was submerged. The tube consisted of an intake and exhaust pipe, allowing outside air to be drawn into the U-boat and exhaust gases to be expelled. The shutoff valve prevented seawater from entering the intake if the mouth of the tube dipped below the surface.

The Type XXIs had a fully streamlined hull and tower and all externally mounted equipment such as the radio

Streamlining of the hull and tower helped to make this the first submarine to travel faster underwater than on the surface.

antennae, hydrophones, direction finder ring and forward diving planes were fully retractable. They had no deck guns and their twin 20mm (0.8in) flak guns were mounted in power-operated fore-and-aft turrets on the tower. The traditional open bridge was discarded in favour of three small openings for the watch officer and two lookouts. They had a superior silent running ability and at 15 knots

Radar
Radar equipment was a FuMB Ant 3 Bali radar detector and antenna and a FuMO 65 Hohentwiel U1 radar with Type F432 D2 transmitter.

Streamlining
All external mountings were retractable when submerged. The 20mm (0.8in) flak guns were in streamlined housings on the tower (actually designed for 30mm/1in cannon).

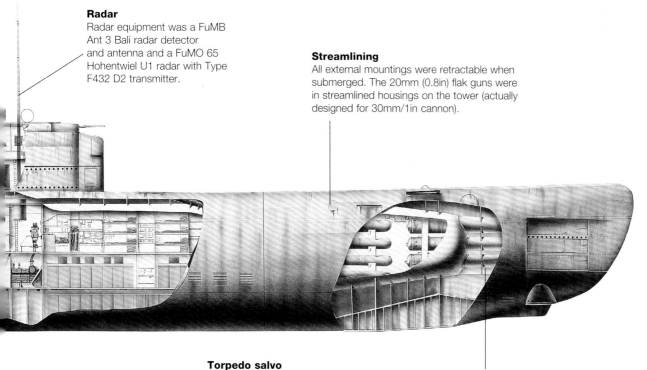

Torpedo salvo
Once a Type XXI had located a convoy, data collected by sonar was to be converted and automatically set in the new LUT (*Lageunabhängiger Torpedo*) torpedoes, which were then fired in spreads of six. This guided torpedo could be fired regardless of the target's bearing and steer an interception course programmed by the torpedo computer. The probability of hits on targets longer than 60m (200ft) was calculated at 95 per cent.

Type XXI

Tugboats attend the hull of a Type XXI. From the condition of the port installations this looks like a late 1943 or early 1944 image.

Specification

Dimensions:	Length: 76.7m (251ft 7in); Beam: 6.6m (21ft 7in); Draught: 6.3m (20ft 8in)
Displacement:	Surfaced – 1621 tonnes (1595 tons); Submerged – 1819 tonnes (1790 tons)
Propulsion:	Two MAN M6V40/46KBB supercharged 6-cylinder diesel engines, 3900hp (2900kW); two SSW GU365/30 double-acting electric motors, 4900hp (3700kW); two SSW GV232/28 silent electric motors; twin screws
Speed:	Surfaced – 15.7 knots (29km/h; 18mph); Submerged – 17.2 knots (31.8km/h; 19.7mph)
Range:	15,500nm (28,706km; 17,837 miles) at 10 knots (18.5km/h; 11.5mph)
Armament:	Six 533mm (21in) torpedo tubes, 23 torpedoes, or 17 torpedoes plus 12 TMC mines; four 20mm (0.8in) flak guns
Complement:	57

(27.7km/h; 17.2mph) were quieter than the US Balao class at 8 knots (14.8km/h; 9.2mph). The pressure hull was formed of a 250mm (1 in) thick steel aluminium alloy with a crush depth reckoned as 340m (1110ft), greater than with any previous submarine. Optimum operating depth was 93m (305ft), but the class could dive to 280m (919ft), again deeper than any other submarine of the time. This was also the first submarine to travel faster submerged than surfaced. Other innovations were incorporated that would be copied in the post-war submarines of the victorious Allied powers, including a semi-automatic hydraulic torpedo reload system that allowed three salvos of six torpedo to be fired in less than 20 minutes. Previous U-boats needed manual reloading and took over 10 minutes to reload a single torpedo.

Crew facilities were also much improved with a deep-freeze for food, a shower compartment and better accommodation. Greater electrical power, with three times the battery capacity of the Type VIIC, gave the class a much wider underwater range, enabling it to traverse the Bay of Biscay at a depth that minimized the risk of detection. It took between three and five hours to recharge the batteries with the snorkel once every two or three days if travelling at a moderate 4–8 knots (7.4–14.8km/h; 4.6–9.2mph), and the Type XXI was thus much less in danger from air attacks that were increasingly responsible for sinking U-boats (over half of all those lost in the war were sunk by aircraft). The four electric motors, two of them designed for silent running, gained it the name of *Elektroboot*. In addition to two main electric motors, there were two crawler motors for quieter operation, which could drive the submarine at 5.5 knots (10.1km/h; 6.3mph) for 320 nautical miles (592km; 368 miles), an unprecedented underwater endurance.

New type

In summer 1943 U-boat construction was switched from Type VIIs to Type XXI and the smaller Type XXIII. Prefabrication and welding of eight separate sections were used to speed up building time to a hoped-for six months. Up to 32 factories at inland sites were involved in building sections and components, delivered by canal and river barges to 11 fitting-out yards, with the completed sections assembled into finished vessels at three yards – Blohm & Voss in Hamburg, A.G. Weser in Bremen and F. Schichau in Danzig. At Bremen the Valentin bunker, a huge bombproof complex intended to function as a 13-stage submarine assembly line, was built but not finished in time to deliver any completed submarines.

Between 1943 and 1945 118 U-boats of Type XXI were ordered. It was hoped that delivery of new boats would start in April 1944, with 152 in operation by the end of

Type XXI hulls under construction at A.G. Weser, Bremen, following air raids in early 1945.

October. The first was not however commissioned until 28 July (*U-2501*) and a further 30 were commissioned by 1 November. Mechanical problems, difficulties in crew training and bombing raids on factories all contributed to a lengthy interval between apparent completion and actual availability for service. By 1 January 1945 62 Type XXI were nominally available, but few were ready for battle action and only five or six had been out at sea. The type had been cleared for volume construction without a prototype being built and the problems normally fixed on a prototype were multiplied down the production line. Sectional construction, although greatly time saving, caused problems with delivered sections failing to meet within the 2mm (.08in) tolerance required. Incorporation of snorkels into the design caused delays, and the use of new and insufficiently tested hydraulic control systems, including working of the periscopes and anti-aircraft guns, also proved problematic.

To the end, Dönitz hoped to operate the Type XXI from bases in northern Norway. At the time of the German surrender, 10 of the class had been deployed to Norway and three to Denmark's Baltic coast. Between December 1944 and May 1945 17 completed or almost-completed Type XXIs were destroyed in yards. As a result, only four were combat-ready at the time of Germany's surrender, and only *U-2511* and *U-3008* undertook any offensive patrols. Neither sank anything although on the day of surrender, 4 May, *U-2511* made a demonstration run at the British cruiser *Suffolk*, which did not even notice the U-boat's presence.

Battery manufacture

The batteries of the Type XXI were 62 cell 2x21 MAL 740 (5400Ah). Between the years 1905 and 1945 the *Akkumulatoren Fabrik Aktiengesellschaft Berlin-Hagen* (AFA, but known as VARTA Batterie AG since 1962) was the sole manufacturer of batteries for the U-boats of the Kriegsmarine. AFA's main plant was in the city of Hagen on the south-east edge of the Ruhr valley. Opened in 1887, within 10 years it became one of the world's largest battery and accumulator works. During World War II, the Hagen plant was unable to produce sufficient quantities to meet the needs of the Kriegsmarine, and AFA set up new battery plants near Hanover, Posen and Vienna, which began production in 1940, 1943 and 1944 respectively.

USS Ray (1943)

A long-lived veteran of warfare in the Pacific, the Gato-class USS *Ray* went through eight war patrols and was given a new post-war role as a radar picket submarine.

Although originally planned before the outbreak of war as fleet boats, the U.S. Navy's Gato class turned out to be well-suited to the different kind of naval war that developed in the Pacific, requiring commanders to learn the skills of fast attack by single boats or groups, sometimes operating on a scale similar to that of the German wolfpacks.

Construction began on 11 September 1940 with USS *Drum*, at Portsmouth, New Hampshire, which was also the first to be commissioned on 1 November 1941. Diving depth was 90m (300ft). The Gato-class was the first to be fitted with air-conditioning from the start. Engine power was either Fairbanks-Morse or General Motors diesels. Many detail modifications were made in the course of the war, usually in order to accommodate radar, direction finding and sonar equipment.

USS *Ray* (SS-271) was laid down in the wartime yard set up at Manitowoc on Lake Michigan on 20 July 1942, launched on 28 February 1943 and commissioned into

After the experiments with the V-boats, the US Navy understood the basic requirements of a fleet submarine. While many variations and improvements were made, responding to wartime conditions, there were few drastic changes.

Lookout platform

The fairwater has been cut away directly under the SD radar mast, leaving a short lip-extension for an aft lookout platform. 'Fairwater' refers to the support structure and plating attached to the main deck and enclosing a free flooding area around the horizontal cylinder of the conning tower, a separate pressure vessel directly above the control room of the submarine. Use of the term 'conning tower' to refer to the combined conning tower and fairwater structure is common but technically inaccurate.

Torpedo Data Computer

Ray was fitted with a Torpedo Data Computer (TDC) linked to the targeting systems, allowing continuous data updates and automatically setting courses right up to the moment of firing. Mark III was the standard, replaced by Mk IV from 1943 on new and refitted boats. As radar became available, it was also linked to the TDC.

Access point

The tower's after end had a watertight access door for the gun crew. This proved to be a liability as several boats had them unseated during depth charge attacks. Moving the gun to the forward position removed the need for the door and in the spring of 1943 it was omitted on Gatos under construction, and the concave aft end was changed to an outward-dished convex one.

Deck gun

The deck gun was twice increased in size, first to 101mm (4in) in late 1943, then to 127mm (5in) from late 1944, reflecting the increasing surface activity in destroying small vessels like sampans and trawlers. Fortunately the original specification provided for a gun emplacement robust enough to hold a 127mm (5in) gun.

Rate of fire

With the ammunition magazine located under the galley and crew's mess aft of the control room, a long passing chain was needed to get shells up to the gun in the forward spot, slowing down firing rates. Eventually, watertight ammunition lockers were placed in the fairwater under the forward gun platform.

service on 27 July 1943. After shakedown and training, it was despatched via canals, the Mississippi River and Panama Canal systems to Brisbane, Australia, arriving on 30 October 1943. *Ray* was among the most active of US submarines in the Pacific, conducting eight war patrols, mostly in the Timor, Java and South China Seas, and

Specification

Dimensions:	Length: 95.02m (311ft 9in); Beam: 8.31m (27ft 3in); Draught: 5.18m (17ft)
Displacement:	Surfaced – 1549 tonnes (1525 tons); Submerged – 2463 tonnes (2424 tons)
Propulsion:	4 Fairbanks-Morse 38D8-1/8 9-cylinder opposed diesel engines; 4 GE electric motors giving 5400hp (4000kW) surfaced, 2740hp (2040kW) submerged; twin screws
Speed:	Surfaced – 21 knots (38.8km/h; 24.1mph); Submerged – 9 knots (16.6km/h; 10.3mph)
Range:	11,000nm (20,372km; 12,658 miles)
Armament:	10 533mm (21in) torpedo tubes, one 76mm (3in) deck gun, Bofors 40mm and Oerlikon 20mm (0.8in) AA cannon
Complement:	107

USS *Ray* on sea trials in Lake Michigan, February 1943.

scoring many successes, sinking a variety of Japanese transports and tankers. On its sixth patrol it inflicted severe damage on the heavy cruiser *Kumano* on 6 November 1944, forcing it to enter a period of extensive repairs (it was subsequently sunk by air attack while undergoing repair) and sinking another smaller warship eight days later. Apart from attacks, *Ray* also picked up 22 downed airmen and escaped prisoners in four rescues. *Ray* was awarded seven battle stars and a US Navy Unit Citation for its sixth patrol. The boat was also awarded the Philippine Republic Presidential Unit Citation for World War II service.

Cold War role

Ray was decommissioned from service on 2 February 1947 and laid up in the Atlantic Reserve Fleet, New London Group, Connecticut. In December 1950 it was towed to Philadelphia Naval Shipyard to be converted into a radar picket submarine. By this time, the Cold War with the Soviet Union was hardening, and air defence of American carrier battle groups on potential strike missions near the Russian landmass generated a requirement for submarine radar pickets to give advance warning of air attacks. This gave rise to the MIGRAINE programme of converting former fleet submarines in 1948. *Ray* and five other Manitowoc-built Gato-class boats were chosen for the MIGRAINE III conversion. Picket boats refitted in the two earlier phases were seriously cramped, and the MIGRAINE III design involved cutting the boats in two and inserting a 7.5m (24ft) plug to provide additional room for an expanded combat information centre (CIC) and electronic spaces forward of the main control room. Even so, the boats lost their after torpedo tubes to give more berthing space. They were fitted with a larger, streamlined sail, with BPS-2 search radar mounted aft of the periscopes and other masts. An AN/BPS-3 height-finder radar on a pedestal just behind the sail and an AN/URN-3 TACAN beacon on the afterdeck completed the installation. All were converted at the Philadelphia Navy Yard between 1951 and 1953, giving the US Navy a total of 10 radar picket submarines, designated SSRs, to act as front line in Cold War conditions.

Reclassified as SSR-271 on 3 January 1951, and recommissioned on 13 August 1952, in its new role *Ray* conducted several training exercises and served two tours of duty with the US 6th Fleet. Overhauled at Charleston Navy Yard, South Carolina, in April–November 1955, it continued in fleet exercises, typically lying 50 to 100 nautical miles (93–185km; 57–115 miles) in front of carrier battlegroups. The overall effectiveness of the radar pickets was, however, hampered by their relatively modest surface speeds, particularly when task-group course changes required rapid repositioning. With the successful introduction of carrier-borne early warning aircraft in 1958, the SSR/SSRN mission was phased out. *Ray* was decommissioned for the final time at Charleston Navy Yard. Placed in reserve on 30 September 1958, it was stricken on 1 April 1960 and subsequently sold for scrap.

Changing USS *Ray*'s profile

The original large fairwater of the Gatos provided a smooth hydrodynamic water flow around the conning tower while submerged and a relatively spacious covered navigation bridge while surfaced. But it also offered a large visual target. Almost immediately after the war began, an effort began to reduce the boats' profile. First, the bulwark around the so-called 'Cigarette Deck' aft of the periscope shears was cut away. This was followed in 1943 by the removal of the plating around the periscopes. Finally the covered navigation bridge at the forward end of the fairwater was cut down and lowered. The new configuration provided platforms for the mounting of additional anti-aircraft guns, and locations for additional radar masts and auxiliary antennas. Three heavy I-beams rose up vertically on either side of the conning tower, then turned 90° inwards to provide structural support for the periscopes and platforms for lookouts. Once the plating was removed from around these beams, the visual effect gave rise to the Gatos' nickname of 'Covered Wagons'.

Ray moving at slow speed, approaching Mare Island Naval Base, California, on 9 March 1945.

I-400 (1943)

The multi-hulled *Sen-Toku* I-400 class were the largest submarines built by any country before the appearance of nuclear-powered SSBNs, and with by far the greatest power and longest range. Envisaged for strategic roles, they were never actually deployed on an operational mission.

Admiral Isoroku Yamamoto, Commander-in-Chief of the Imperial Combined Fleet, was sponsor of the class. His aim was to have a group of submarines capable of mounting attacks on the western or eastern coasts of the United States, and the squadron was originally meant to number 18. Work started in January 1943, but after Yamamoto was shot down and killed in April 1943, the number was scaled

back to five, of which only three, *I-400*, built at Kure, and *I-401* and *I-402*, built at Sasebo, were completed.

Known as *Sensuikan toku* (special or secret submarine), unlike other Japanese aircraft-carrying submarines they were attack rather than scouting vessels, with an operating range sufficient to make three round trips across the Pacific, or to circumnavigate the globe. Within the partial

Profile and plan of the I-400 class. It struck awe into American observers in 1945, but the Japanese war effort would have been better served by more conventional submarines in greater numbers.

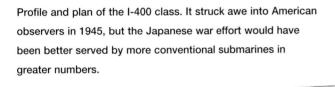

Kitchen galley
The galley was in the starboard hull, fitted with giant steam kettles for preparing rice for the 157-strong crew.

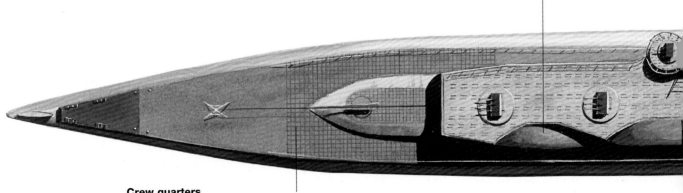

Crew quarters
Accommodation was situated towards the stern.

double hull were two parallel cylindrical pressure hulls. To accommodate a hangar for three specially-designed Aichi M6A Seiran bombers, the conning tower was offset to port, which made for steering difficulties – to proceed on a straight course the helmsman had to steer 7° to starboard. A compressed-air 26m (85ft) catapult on the forward deck launched the aircraft, loaded with a 800kg (1800lb) bomb. The fighters, with their wings folded in, were rolled out through a heavy hydraulic door onto the catapult. All three could be launched within 45 minutes, or only 15 minutes if the floats were not fitted – although this meant the plane would be ditched on return. After completing their mission, they would land in the sea and be picked up and loaded

back by a collapsible hydraulic crane. Great ingenuity went into the folding and collapsible equipment, including the retrieval crane.

The three I-400s were fitted with Mk3 Model 1 air search radar, Mk2 Model 2 surface search radar and an E27 radar detector. During a repair-refit in May 1945, I-400 had a German snorkel system fitted, enabling the vessel to remain just below the surface at periscope depth while recharging the batteries. Day and night periscopes also of German origin were fitted. An anechoic coating made from a mixture of gum, asbestos and adhesives, based on German technology, was applied to the hulls from the waterline to the bilge keel. This was intended to absorb or diffuse

Crane boom
The crane was capable of lifting approximately 4.6 tonnes (4.5 tons). It was raised mechanically to a height of 8m (26ft) and operated by a motor inside the boat. The boom extended out to a length of 11.8m (39ft).

Submarine-launched attack floatplane
The key assembly points of the aircraft were marked with fluorescent paint so that they could be assembled in darkness.

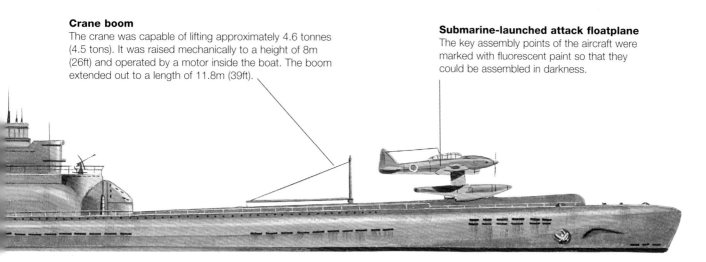

Deck layout
The upper section with the bridge deck was canted out on the port side, with the pressurized conning tower alongside. The AA placings were to starboard and port of the centreline.

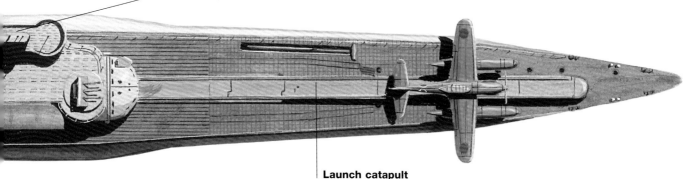

Launch catapult
The Seirans were launched from a 26m (85ft) Type 4 No. 2 Model 10 compressed-air catapult, rising at a shallow angle from the hangar door.

One of the two surrendered I-400s arrives in Tokyo Bay, manned by a US Navy prize crew, 30 August 1945.

Specification

Dimensions:	Length: 122m (400ft); Beam: 12m (39ft 4in); Draught: 7m (23ft)
Displacement:	Surfaced – 5306 tonnes (5223 tons); Submerged – 6670 tonnes (6560 tons)
Propulsion:	Four diesel engines developing 7700hp (6720kW); two electric motors, 4200hp (3360kW); twin screws
Speed:	Surfaced – 18.7 knots (34.6km/h; 21.5 mph); Submerged – 12 knots (22.2km/h; 13.8mph)
Range:	37,500nm (69,450km; 43,154 miles) at 14 knots (25.9km/h; 16.1mph)
Armament:	Eight 533mm (21in) torpedo tubes, 20 Type 95 torpedoes; one 140mm (5.4in) gun; four 25mm (1in) AA cannon
Complement:	144 (157 including aircraft crews)

enemy sonar pulses and dampen reverberations from the boat's own machinery, helping it to remain undetected as it traversed the globe. Dive time for the class was 58 seconds, almost double that of an American submarine. Provision for the large crew was poor, with no air conditioning, insufficient bunk accommodation and primitive non-flush toilets. A 140mm (5.4in) deck gun was fitted aft of the bridge superstructure along with four 25mm (1in) Type 96 triple-mount anti-aircraft cannon. These were fitted in pairs forward and aft of the tower, on the superstructure platform, with a single-mounted cannon on a pedestal mount aft of the bridge.

In 1944–45 an attack on the Panama Canal locks from the Pacific coast by Submarine Squadron 1, formed of the only two operational I-400 boats plus the reconnaissance aircraft-carrying fleet submarines *I-13* and *I-14*, was devised and carefully prepared. The Seiran bombers were to fly without floats, originally with the intention of ditching on return, although this was altered to a kamikaze-type attack, with the bomb fixed to the aircraft. American advances in the Pacific put paid to the scheme. With the fall of Okinawa in July 1945 and the imminent threat of land invasion, the Panama attack was abandoned in favour of attacking a

I-400 and *I-401* alongside the submarine tender USS *Proteus*, 31 August 1945.

Harder-hitting munitions

The Japanese fleet had the most effective torpedoes available during World War II. The Type 95 (smaller submarine version of the Type 93 'long lance', an American name not used by the Japanese) developed from 1928, used pure oxygen to burn kerosene, instead of the compressed air and alcohol used in other nation's torpedoes. This gave them a range of up to 12km (7.5 miles), about double that of their Allied counterparts, and also reduced their wake, making them harder to notice and avoid. The Type 95 also had by far the largest warhead of any submarine torpedo, initially 405kg (893lb), increased to 550kg (1210lb) late in the war. The Type 95 used a simple contact exploder that was far more reliable than its American counterpart, the Mark 14, until the latter was improved in late 1943.

concentration of US carriers at the Ulithi Atoll base. This too was planned as a suicide mission for the bomber pilots. Japan's surrender in August pre-empted the operation.

Surrender and discovery

The Americans never learned of the existence of the *I-400* class submarines until the Japanese surrendered. Work on *I-404* at Kuré Naval Arsenal was halted on 4 June 1945, by which time the submarine was almost complete. After severe damage in air raids on 28 July 1945, it was scuttled. The wreck was salvaged for scrap in 1952. The surviving craft were studied by the United States Navy at Sasebo, Japan. The Russians too wanted to examine these remarkable submarines, but before they got a chance the US Navy launched Operation Road's End to sink *I-402*, which had been converted to a tanker, off Nagasaki, near the Gotō Islands, in April 1946. Despite protests from Russia, both I-400 and *I-401* were transferred to Hawaii for further examination before being sunk as targets in May–June 1946. In 2005 the remains of *I-401* were discovered on the ocean floor off Hawaii and in 2013 the wreck of *I-400* was found on the ocean floor off the southwest coast of Oahu.

USS Piper (1944)

The Balao class was the most numerous in the US submarine force, with 120 boats commissioned. Designed in 1941–42, the lead boat commissioned in February 1943, these submarines were purpose-built for taking the fight to the enemy, with food, fuel, and weapons sufficient for long-range independent patrols.

The Balao class was short on major novelties. Its difference from its predecessors was a matter of improvements. By this time the US Navy knew it had the right sort of submarines to prosecute the war and that what it needed was more, but even better, versions of the same (as well as better torpedoes). The Balao hull was made of thicker steel, 22.2mm (.874in) compared to the Gatos' 14.3mm (.56in), enabling it to dive to over 140m (459ft), well below the level

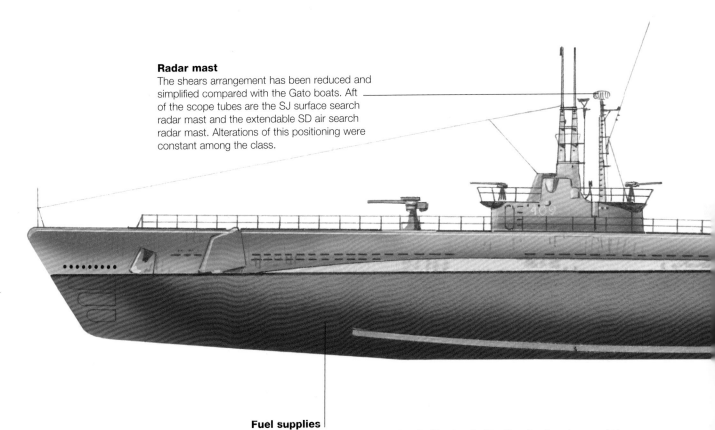

Radar mast
The shears arrangement has been reduced and simplified compared with the Gato boats. Aft of the scope tubes are the SJ surface search radar mast and the extendable SD air search radar mast. Alterations of this positioning were constant among the class.

Fuel supplies
Up to 495,000 litres (110,000 gallons) of bunker fuel for the diesel engines could be carried. Raw diesel was pumped through a centrifugal purifying system and held in a day tank with 2700-litre (600 gallon) capacity, from which fuel was fed to the engines. Since refined diesel was not always available during the war, this allowed the boat to store bunker fuel from any source and clean it up as needed to run the engines.

of possible depth charge attacks. A high tensile titanium-manganese steel alloy was used to make the hull plates rather than mild steel as formerly used.

The process of development continued through the production run, with a significant improvement being the adoption of a heavy-duty slow-speed electric motor to replace the older high-speed motors and their noisy reduction gears. This was ready in time to be installed on new boats commissioned from July 1944 onwards. New fire-resistant materials – including asbestos – were also used for insulation and fireproofing. Six torpedo tubes were mounted forward and four aft. The thicker, heavier hull obviated the need for lead ballast. During their lifetime the Balao class introduced new sophisticated electronic gear for detecting targets, an improved Torpedo Data Computer (TDC) for working out and setting torpedo firing angles, new Mark 18 electric torpedoes and a Bathythermograph for detecting thermoclines (cold water layers) under which the boat could slip to deflect enemy active sonar, making it hard to detect. These technological advances

Though American fleet submarines did serve as fleet escorts and scouts, especially to carrier groups, they also had a 'hunter-killer' role in seeking out and destroying Japanese naval craft. Smaller vessels were usually sunk by gunfire.

Armament
Some Balao class submarines acquired a second Mk 17 127mm (5in) deck gun from late 1943, as torpedo-worthy targets were becoming scarce.

Power supply
All Balao submarines were diesel-electric with engines from Fairbanks-Morse or General Motors. *Piper* was driven by four Fairbanks-Morse Model 38D8-1/8 10-cylinder opposed diesel engines driving electric generators that powered two low-speed Elliott electric motors.

Specification

Dimensions:	Length: 95m (311ft 8in); Beam: 8.3m (27ft 3in); Draught: 5.1m (16ft 8in)
Displacement:	Surfaced – 1550 tonnes (1526 tons); Submerged – 2440 tonnes (2401 tons)
Propulsion:	Diesel-electric: Four Fairbanks-Morse 38D8-1/8 10-cylinder opposed piston engines, 5400hp (4.0MW) driving generators; two low-speed direct-drive Elliott motors, 2740hp (2.0MW); twin screws
Speed:	Surfaced – 20.25 knots (37.5km/h; 23.2mph); Submerged – 8.75 knots (16.2km/h; 10mph)
Range:	11,000nm (20,372km; 12 658 miles) at 10 knots (18.5km/h; 11.5mph)
Armament:	10 533mm (21in) torpedo tubes, 24 torpedoes; one 127mm (5in) deck gun, one 40mm (1.6in) and one 20mm (0.8in) gun
Complement:	81

Sister ships – USS *Piper* and *Threadfin* were launched on the same day, 26 June 1944, at Portsmouth Navy Yard, Maine.

gave the class a level of reliability, battle effectiveness and survivability exceeding the capacity of any previous submarine. Internally virtually identical to the late production Gatos, the Balao design displayed a substantial change to the external appearance. The tower, fairwater and periscope shears were built from the start in the cut-down form that was being retrofitted to the Gatos.

Efficient production line

Such was the efficiency of the American submarine production line by 1944 that *Piper* (SS-409), 94th boat of the Balao class, was laid down at Portsmouth Navy Yard, Kittery, Maine, on 15 March, launched on 26 June and commissioned on 23 August, less than six months after laying-down. It was built and launched simultaneously with USS *Threadfin* (SS-410). *Piper*'s first mission on 25 January 1945 was as leader of a five-boat wolfpack clearing the sea off Honshu in preparation for carrier strikes, followed by a similar patrol in the Sea of Okhotsk in May–June. *Piper* made three war patrols before the Japanese capitulation. During its war service, it was responsible for sinking more than 6200 tonnes (6000 tons) of Japanese shipping, and earned four battle stars for participating in the assault on and occupation of Iwo Jima, 15 February–16 March 1945; the Fifth Fleet raids against Honshu and the Nansei Shoto on 15–16 and 25 February 1945, and 1 March 1945; the assault on and occupation of Okinawa Gunto, 17–22 March 1945; and Third Fleet operations against Japan, 11–13 August 1945. Lieutenant Commander Edward L. Beach, its new commander, wrote: "The Commanding Officer may be pardoned, surely, for feeling a little disappointment at the fact that, after 11 War Patrols in subordinate capacities, he finally achieved command, and entered one of the last areas still considered potentially productive with a ship and crew trained to a high condition of readiness, only to have the war end 10 hours after he arrived in the area."

From 15 October 1945 *Piper* spent five years based at New London, Connecticut. From 2 May 1950, it undertook a tour of duty with the Sixth Fleet in the Mediterranean,

and on returning to the USA it spent six weeks at Guantanamo Bay, Cuba, on special exercises. In June 1951, *Piper* entered the Charleston Naval Shipyard for 'Guppy' conversion, which gave it the streamlined 'new look' and snorkel gear, then returned to New London. Throughout the 1950s it was on active service in the Atlantic Ocean and the Caribbean and Mediterranean Seas. From 1 July 1957 to June 1958 it was flagship of the Submarine Force, Atlantic Fleet.

In early 1961 *Piper* became the first snorkel submarine to make its 10,000th dive. The boat remained in service during the 1960s, but by 22 March 1967 the main storage battery had deteriorated to the extent that *Piper* was restricted to surface operations. At this time it had made 13,724 dives, a record for commissioned submarines.

On 15 June 1967, *Piper* was reclassified as auxiliary submarine AGSS-409, and the next day was placed 'out of commission, special', as Naval Reserve Training submarine at Detroit, Michigan. It was struck from the Navy List on 1 July 1970 and sold for scrap in June 1971.

Design tweaks

For the masts and periscope shears, the original arrangement for both the government and Electric Boat designs had (forward to aft) the two tapered cone-shaped periscope support shears, followed by a thin mast for the SJ surface search radar and then by a thin mast for the SD air search radar. There were minor differences in how the periscopes were braced against vibration, but both designs were nearly identical. About halfway through their production run, Electric Boat altered their design, moving the SJ radar mast forward of the periscopes, then soon altered it again by enlarging the SD radar mast. Late in the war, many Balaos had the SD air search radar moved slightly aft onto a thickened and taller mast. As a result of these re-arrangements, along with variations in the gun layout, at any given time no two Balaos looked exactly alike.

Piper's tower, shears and mast before post-war conversion. The scene is Halifax, Nova Scotia, on 15 May 1948.

USS Tench (1944)

The submarines of the Tench class were a developed version of the previous Gato and Balao classes, fitted with improved interior machinery and ballast tank arrangements. A total of 29 were completed for the United States during or immediately following World War II, and most never made a war patrol.

USS *Tench* (SS-417) was laid down at the Portsmouth Navy Yard, Kittery, Maine, on 1 April 1944, launched on 7 July and commissioned on 7 October in the same year. Only 10 submarines of the class were commissioned in time to see service in the Pacific during World War II. The pressure hull was of 21mm (0.85in) high-tensile steel, as with the Balao class. There were eight waterproof

compartments in addition to the conning tower. They were equipped with four main and one auxiliary diesel engines, the main engines connected to two low-speed direct drive electric motors. Two 126-cell battery sets were fitted.

Submerged endurance was 48 hours at 2 knots (3.7km/h; 2.3mph). Cruising range was 16,000 nautical miles (29,632km; 18,412 miles) on the surface at 10 knots

Sargo battery
Two 126-cell Sargo batteries were carried in forward and after compartments. Designed by the Bureau of Steam Engineering, they were named for USS *Sargo* whose commissioning C.O., Lieutenant E. E. Yeomans, suggested the design. Cells had two concentric hard rubber cases with a layer of soft rubber between them. This helped to prevent leakage of sulphuric acid in the event of depth charging or ramming. The Sargo battery was the standard design for US submarines to the end of the war.

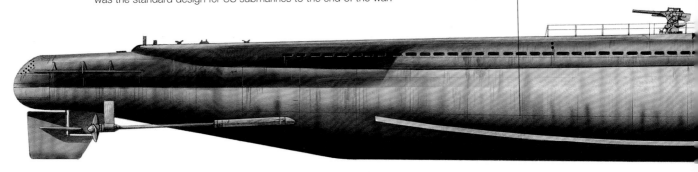

The Tench class had a low superstructure and hull profile, and streamlined lines that gave it a good surface speed.

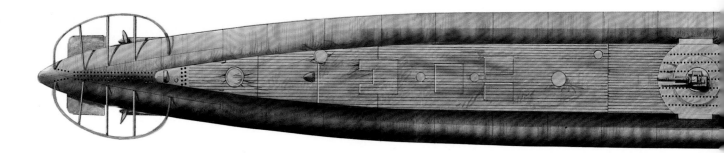

(18.5km/h; 11.5mph). The principal development from the Balao class was a rearrangement of the ballast tanks and venting pipes in the interest of safety, although it also enabled the class to carry four additional torpedoes in the forward torpedo room, making a total of 28. As with later Balao-class boats, all the Tench class had low-speed double-armature electric motors providing direct drive to the propeller shafts, with the diesel engines acting as power generators. This diesel-electric system was both more reliable and quieter in operation than the reduction gear arrangement previously used.

Deployed to Pearl Harbor, Tench made three wartime patrols, sinking four Japanese ships and several small craft. Its first patrol was as a member of a 'co-ordinated attack group', modelled on the German wolfpack, with USS Sea Devil, Balao and Grouper. The four submarines rotated patrol/attack, weather-reporting, photographic-reconnaissance and lifeguard duties. This last was becoming more important in the final stages of the war – picking up downed US airmen from the sea: the Japanese Navy and merchant fleet had been virtually annihilated by now. On 11 June 1945, during an inconclusive surface

LF loop antenna
This was mounted between the periscopes, although later Tench-class boats had it mounted on a bracket aft of the SJ mast.

Dive planes
Forward diving planes were stowed ready-tilted in dive position so that when extended they would immediately force the bow down. Diving to periscope depth could be achieved in 30–40 seconds.

Guppy 1A refit programme (1951)
The profile shows Tench in wartime form. Under Guppy IA, the pointed fleet bow was retained and the motors, already slow-speed type, were not modernized, although the auxiliary diesel generator was replaced by air-conditioning equipment. With the Guppy project, the tower ceased to hold a control station and came to be known as the sail (US) or fin (Britain).

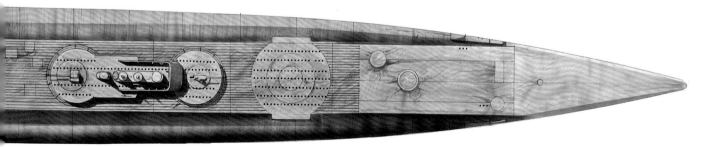

Fairwater
The fairwater has been minimized: the extent of the lip on the after gun platform is so great as to require a support stanchion.

Ballast tanks
Re-planning of the ballast tanks also allowed space for an additional four torpedoes compared with the Balao and Gato boats.

USS Tench

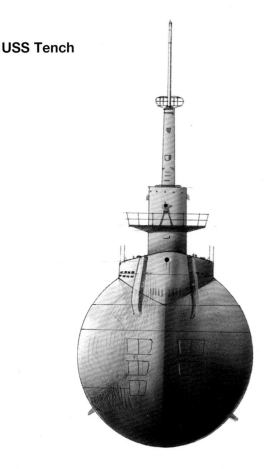

Below the surfaced waterline, the hull takes on an almost spherical shape.

Specification

Dimensions:	Length: 95m (311ft 8in); Beam: 8m (27ft 4in); Draught: 5.18m (17ft)
Displacement:	Surfaced – 1600 tonnes (1570 tons); Submerged – 2455 tonnes (2416 tons)
Propulsion:	Diesel-electric, four Fairbanks-Morse 38D8-1/8 10-cylinder opposed piston engines, 5400hp (4023kW); two low-speed direct-drive GE motors, 2740hp (2041kW); twin screws
Speed:	Surfaced – 20.25 knots (37.5km/h; 23.3 mph); Submerged – 8.75 knots (16.2km/h; 10mph)
Range:	11,000nm (20,372km; 12,658 miles) at 10 knots (18.5km/h; 11.5mph)
Armament:	10 530mm (21in) torpedo tubes, 28 torpedoes; one 127mm (5in) deck gun
Complement:	81

engagement with a Japanese destroyer, *Tench* narrowly avoided being hit by one of its own Mark 14 torpedoes which had made a wide erratic swing. As the US Navy drew ever closer to the Japanese home islands, *Tench* was involved in tricky and dangerous offshore attacks on coastal shipping. The submarine was awarded three battle stars for support in the Iwo Jima and Okinawa Gunto assault operations in March 1945.

Tench-class USS *Torsk* is credited with firing the last torpedoes and sinking the last Japanese combatant ships of the war, Coast Defence Vessels No. 13 and No. 47, on 14 August 1945. Had the war continued, the Tench class would have been very large. Six (from SS-429 to SS-434) were cancelled in July 1944, two more (SS-427 and 428) in August 1945 and a further 105 were cancelled in January 1946 (SS-491 to 562 and 437 to 474). Following its return to New London on 6 October 1945, *Tench* itself was decommissioned in March 1946 and laid up in the Atlantic Reserve Fleet.

Modernization and upgrade

From October 1950, along with nine Balao-class boats, *Tench* was modernized under Project Guppy (Greater Underwater Propulsion Programme), set up to enhance the capacities of the existing fleet. From June 1946, the programme passed through seven phases until 1963. It began with the intensive examination and testing of two Type XXI U-boats, *U-2513* and *U-3008*, but further refinements were soon being added. USS *Odax* and *Pomodon*, Tench-class boats commissioned in 1945, were adapted under Guppy I in 1947 and 24 boats were refitted under Guppy II. In Guppy I, deck guns were taken off, the bridge and shears structure adapted to reduce drag, capstans and deck cleats were made retractable and the bow was redesigned from the sharp 'fleet bow' to a rounded 'Guppy bow'. Battery power was greatly increased in order to provide power for new sonar and radar equipment. Guppy II included reconstruction of the sail. A submarine sail might now support 12 or 13 separate antennas for range and direction finding, communications at different frequencies and radar for both surface and air search. *Tench* was refitted in 1951 under the Guppy 1A programme, a less comprehensive and lower-cost procedure, which retained the former battery wells with new

In harbour in October 1945, *Tench's* battle honours are displayed on the flag.

batteries, and relocated the sonar room from the forward torpedo room to beneath the galley. With its reconstructed sail, and no deck gun, the post-Guppy *Tench* had a very different appearance to its previous form.

In January 1951 *Tench* was recommissioned at Norfolk, Virginia, in the 6th Submarine Squadron (Subron 6), serving on the US East Coast and in the Caribbean Sea, with one deployment to the Mediterranean in 1952. In 1955 it was transferred to Subron 2 at New London, Connecticut, where its role was chiefly in training and wargame exercises, both in local waters and on wider deployments in the Eastern Atlantic and Mediterranean. *Tench* ran aground twice: on 14 January 1955 off Cape Henry lighthouse, Virginia; and on 4 October 1959 in Portsmouth Harbour, England, but was refloated without damage. On 1 October 1969 the boat was reclassified as AGSS-417, a general auxiliary submarine, and was placed on reserve. On 8 May 1970 *Tench* was decommissioned, but remained in the reserve fleet until 16 August 1973, when it was stricken, and subsequently sold to the Peruvian Navy as a source of spare parts for its other ex-Tench class boats.

Tench and Type XXI comparisons

It is interesting to compare the features of the Tench class with those of Germany's Type XXI. Both represented the culmination of their respective navies' World War II submarine development. The Type XXI, although a quickly-conceived stopgap between the Type VII and Type IX and the super-submarine envisaged by Hellmuth Walter, incorporated a whole range of new ideas, equipment and performance characteristics, including the snorkel. Production systems had to be revised or new ones set up. By contrast the Tench class was a relatively modest progression on its Gato and Balao predecessors. But it moved smoothly and rapidly into action via an established production line while introduction of the Type XXIs was held up partly by their own new (and untried) features that crews had to master.

Tench after undergoing Guppy 1A conversion.

The Nuclear Age

A revolutionary change in the naval world was introduced in 1954 with the nuclear submarine. The nature of superpower rivalry and offensive capacity during the Cold War period, 1948–89, was altered by the development of the submarine as a ballistic missile platform, offering a 'second strike' capacity to hit back in the event of any attack. From around 1990, though, the international situation became much more fluid. Regional conflicts and rivalries, most notably in the Middle East, but also in Afghanistan, the western Pacific and the India–Pakistan border all threatened stability. A new generation of high-performance, multi-role boats with an emphasis on co-ordinated sea-air-land operation was introduced.

Opposite: US Navy sailors stand topside as their boat, the Los Angeles class *USS Dallas* (SSN 700), arrives for a port visit at Souda Bay, Crete.

USS Nautilus (1954)

To some experts, *Nautilus* was the first true submarine – not a surface ship that could submerge for limited periods, but a vessel capable of staying underwater for lengthy periods without needing to draw any sustenance from the surface.

Once the construction of the compact reactor became technically feasible, its application to submarines was only a matter of time, although it did not seem like that to the proposers who had to persuade the naval authorities and the US Congress. The naval reactors programme had been running since 1948. Design of a nuclear-powered propulsion plant was undertaken at Naval Reactors Branch

of the Atomic Energy Commission, under the leadership of Captain Hyman G. Rickover, USN. The brief was a daunting one: atomic research was still very new and there were no blueprints to work from. Existing nuclear reactors were very large and this one had to fit with its steam turbines within a vessel of 8.5m (28ft) beam. No-one had yet tried to connect an atomic reactor to a propulsion device. By March

Steel plate
The hull is formed of HY-42 steel plate, of 290 MPa (2704 ton/sq ft) yield strength. The improved HY-75 steel used on later boats was not available until the mid-1950s.

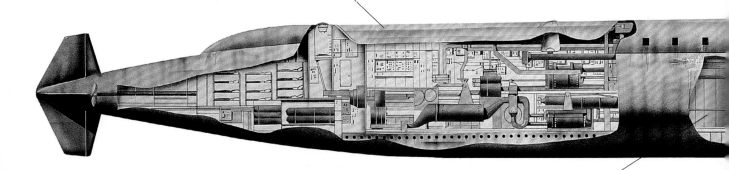

Nuclear reactor
The reactor compartment, with the reactor, primary coolant circuit and steam generators, was not accessible when the reactor was operating.

1953 a viable compact pressurized water reactor had been constructed at the National Reactor Testing Station in Idaho, designated as the S1W (Submarine Platform, 1st Generation, Westinghouse). Successful installation and simulation testing led to the S2W reactor, also built by the Westinghouse Corporation, being fitted to *Nautilus*.

In July of 1951, Congress authorized construction of the world's first nuclear powered submarine. On 12 December, the Navy Department announced that it would be the sixth ship of the fleet to bear the name *Nautilus*, and the keel was laid by President Harry S. Truman at the Electric Boat Shipyard in Groton, Connecticut, on 14 June 1952. It was launched on

21 January 1954, and commissioned on 30 September of that year as SSN-571. Apart from its nuclear drive, *Nautilus* was modelled on the Tang class of diesel-electric drive submarines, although with greater dimensions to allow for the atomic reactor. Engine and reactor rooms occupied almost half the boat. Information on *Nautilus*'s operational depth does not appear to have been released, but the Tang class could dive to 210m (689ft), allowing it to take advantage of deeper ocean conditions to evade sonar detection as well as to manoeuvre more safely at moderate depths.

Nautilus is inseparably linked with Rickover, later a US Admiral, and known as 'father of the nuclear navy'.

Nautilus's hull design followed previous models, though a new form was already under test with USS *Albacore* from 1953, and would be influential in subsequent submarines.

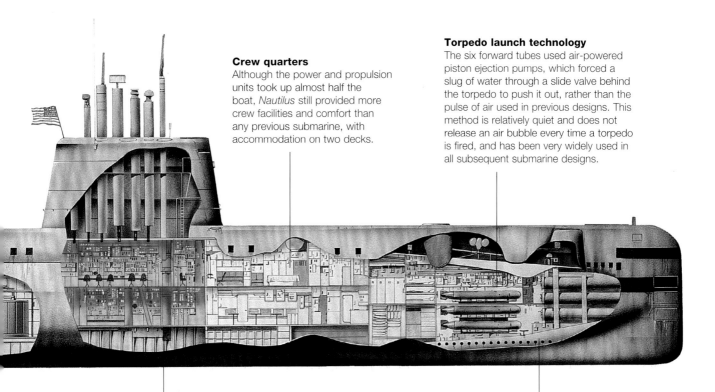

Crew quarters
Although the power and propulsion units took up almost half the boat, *Nautilus* still provided more crew facilities and comfort than any previous submarine, with accommodation on two decks.

Torpedo launch technology
The six forward tubes used air-powered piston ejection pumps, which forced a slug of water through a slide valve behind the torpedo to push it out, rather than the pulse of air used in previous designs. This method is relatively quiet and does not release an air bubble every time a torpedo is fired, and has been very widely used in all subsequent submarine designs.

Control room
This includes navigation equipment, steering, diving valve controls and operators of the diving planes.

Sonar array
Nautilus had a BQR-4 passive sonar system with 48 vertical stave hydrophones mounted in the forefoot of the bow. But the boat's own noise precluded effective use of sonar at speeds above 7 knots (12.9km/h; 8mph).

USS Nautilus

The US Navy's eighth nuclear submarine, USS *Skate* (SSN-578), emulated *Nautilus's* sub-Arctic transit, but actually surfaced very close to the North Pole, on 11 August 1958.

Specification

Dimensions:	Length: 97m (323ft 6in); Beam: 8.4m (27ft 6in); Draught: 6.6m (21ft 9in)
Displacement:	Surfaced – 3589 tonnes (3533 tons); Submerged – 4168 tonnes (4102 tons)
Propulsion:	One S2W pressurized water-cooled reactor, geared steam turbines; 13,400hp (10MW); 2 screws
Speed:	Surfaced – 22 knots (40.7km/h; 25.3mph); Submerged – 25 knots (46.2km/h; 28.7mph)
Range:	Unlimited
Armament:	Six 533mm (21in) torpedo tubes
Complement:	105

A brilliant, driven man, he closely supervised the design and construction not only of *Nautilus*, completing it years before most people expected, but also of its successors until 1982. On 17 January 1955 *Nautilus* went to sea for the first time and in the next two years covered distances unthinkable for a conventional submarine, breaking all previous records for underwater speed and distance. After more than two years of operation and evaluation, *Nautilus* was refuelled in April 1957. On the first core it had steamed a total of 62,562 nautical miles (115,864km; 71,995 miles), more than half of which was submerged.

Arctic adventure

On 3 August 1958 in 'Project Sunshine' *Nautilus* became the first vessel to pass over the North Pole, using an inertial navigation system developed by North American Aviation. This Arctic mission was no mere 'flag-waving' display, but a major technological challenge that took three attempts to achieve. While submerged, there could be no radio communications or navigational aid from the outside world as the submarine would not be in sight of stars for navigation or within terrestrial radio range. In addition there were no sea charts for the Arctic. On its first attempt in August of 1957, *Nautilus* became lost due to failures of its navigational equipment and ultimately had to turn back. At that time, it was equipped with relatively primitive navigational aids, only a gyrocompass and magnetic compass, both of which are unreliable near the Poles. A new N6A-1 inertial guidance system navigation system was installed, originally created by North American Aviation for the Navaho cruise missile. There were serious doubts about its capability on the *Nautilus* as it was designed to support missiles moving at very fast speeds for brief periods of time, whereas a submarine moves slowly for long periods. In fact, the inertial guidance system turned out to be a reliable navigational tool, and in April 1958 *Nautilus* again attempted the polar traverse. Due to shallow waters and thick ice conditions it failed to find a safe route through the Chukchi Sea to enter the Arctic Ocean. On its third attempt in August 1958, a safe passage was found near Point Barrow, Alaska, allowing *Nautilus* to complete the voyage below the icecap.

After a major overhaul and second replacement of the fuel core in 1959 at Portsmouth Naval Shipyard in Maine, in 1960 it was assigned to the Sixth Fleet. *Nautilus* served with US naval units in the Atlantic and Mediterranean. By the

Radioactive health & safety

Rickover's insistence on stringent quality control and safety procedures was stamped into the US Navy's design and handling of nuclear ships. The design philosophy employed with *Nautilus* and subsequent U.S. nuclear submarines is that personnel stationed outside the nuclear propulsion plant should be subject to lower amounts of radiation than would be encountered from natural sources on shore. This was made possible by a combination of low natural radioactivity materials used in the ship construction, shielding techniques used on the reactor and a lower exposure to cosmic background radiation while under the ocean. Although US nuclear submarines have had their share of mishaps and disasters, there has been no incidence of an accident releasing fissionable materials into the sea or the atmosphere.

Nautilus at New York City, 25 August 1958, on its return from under the Arctic icecap.

mid-1960s, a range of more advanced nuclear submarines was in operation and *Nautilus* spent its final active years as a training boat. It was decommissioned at Mare Island Navy Yard, California, on 3 March 1980, by which time it had travelled 513,550 nautical miles (951,094km; 590,982 miles) and made 2507 dives. Named as a 'historic ship', it was converted as a public museum craft and towed to Groton, Connecticut. On 1 April 1986 it was opened to the public as part of the Submarine Force Museum.

Project 641 (Foxtrot Class)
(1958)

The Project 641 boats were the Soviet Navy's largest conventionally powered submarines and the last to be constructed with old-style hulls, although the sail was of streamlined design. Incorporating numerous novel features, they also served with other navies.

Project 641 was intended to provide a more up-to-date patrol/attack boat than the Whiskey class of 1949 and the subsequent 1952 Zulu class, both World War II derivatives, and the resultant design, noted as Foxtrot by NATO, fulfilled the objective. Design work was undertaken by the TsKB-18 (Rubin) bureau under the supervision of P. P. Pustintsev. All were constructed by the Sudomekh Division of the Admiralty Shipyards at St Petersburg (formerly Leningrad), with the first of the class laid down in 1957 and commissioned in 1958. Construction continued until 1983, and in total 58 were built for the Soviet Navy, plus a further 20 or so for other countries. The Foxtrot, its hull built of newly developed AK-25 high tensile steel, had a greater underwater speed and went deeper than the Zulu. These classes marked a shift in Soviet strategic thinking, dropping the previous strategy of small and mid-size submarines with

Project 641 submarines were involved in the Cuban missile crisis of October 1962. The last one was not decommissioned from the Russian fleet until 2003.

UHF antenna
For two-way communication the boat came to snorkel depth of 7m (23ft) and raised this telescopic mast antenna to communicate on higher frequencies than is possible from underwater.

Torpedoes
There was no spare torpedo storage for the 406mm (16in) aft tubes and the four torpedoes had to be replaced in dock or from a supply tender.

limited range, seen as defensive weapons for guarding the sea approaches of the Soviet Union. Now, with improved communications and other technology – and American nuclear submarines already a reality – the focus was on large attack submarines with long range and endurance to use as offensive weapons in deep water.

Foxtrot operated at a depth of 250m (820ft), could dive to over 300m (984ft) and was capable of reaching 16.8 knots (31.1km/h; 19.3mph). Its hydroplanes enabled the Foxtrot to dive and surface quite horizontally. Angled at more than 30°, however, it lost control. The class was powered by three Kolomna diesel engines and three electric motors, driving three propeller shafts. These made the boats relatively noisy, and their submerged speed of 15 knots (27.7km/h; 17.2mph) did not allow for rapid chasing or shadowing. Two of the three decks in the central section

Right: The bow antenna and the starboard-positioned UHF mast gave the class a distinctive forward appearance.

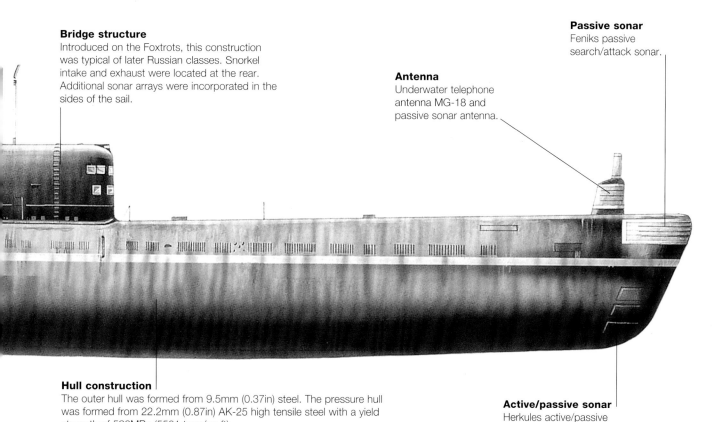

Bridge structure
Introduced on the Foxtrots, this construction was typical of later Russian classes. Snorkel intake and exhaust were located at the rear. Additional sonar arrays were incorporated in the sides of the sail.

Antenna
Underwater telephone antenna MG-18 and passive sonar antenna.

Passive sonar
Feniks passive search/attack sonar.

Hull construction
The outer hull was formed from 9.5mm (0.37in) steel. The pressure hull was formed from 22.2mm (0.87in) AK-25 high tensile steel with a yield strength of 590MPa (5501 tons/sq ft).

Active/passive sonar
Herkules active/passive sonar.

Project 641 (Foxtrot Class)

The Cuban Navy had five Foxtrot units, one of which appears in this aerial view.

Specification

Dimensions:	Length: 91.5m (300ft 2in); Beam: 8m (26ft 3in); Draught: 6.1m (20ft)
Displacement:	Surfaced – 1983 tonnes (1952 tons); Submerged – 2515 tonnes (2475 tons)
Propulsion:	3 Kolomna 2D42M 2000hp (1500kW) diesels, two 1350hp (1010kW) and one 2700hp (2000kW) electric motors; triple screws
Speed:	Surfaced – 16 knots (29.6km/h; 18.4mph); Submerged – 15 knots (27.7km/h; 17.2mph)
Range:	surfaced – 20,000nm (37,040km; 23,015 miles) at 8 knots (14.8km/h; 9.2mph)
Armament:	10 533mm (21in) torpedo tubes, 22 torpedoes
Complement:	80

dedicated to batteries gave it an underwater endurance of 10 days, but the weight of the batteries cost the Foxtrot around 2 knots (3.7km/h; 2.3mph).

Diesel powered

In the mid-1960s, the two stroke/cycle 37D engines installed in around 40 Foxtrots were supplanted in new construction with the four-stroke/cycle Kolomna 30/38 1D42 – based on a pre-World War II design, but a well-proven engine, connected to the propeller shafts through a single-stage gear system that reduced the maximum engine speed of 715rpm to a shaft speed of 500rpm. Turbo-charging, using exhaust gases to pre-compress air entering the cylinders and so boost power output, was applied to some Foxtrot diesels. The class carried a maximum of 22 533mm (21in) torpedoes that could be conventional or nuclear tipped anti-submarine/anti-ship types, fired from 10 launch tubes, six in the bow and four in the stern, from a depth down to 100m (328ft). An additional 44 AMD-1000 mines could also be carried, placed via the torpedo tubes.

The Foxtrot class played an important role in the Soviet Navy for more than 20 years, as a submarine that could be and was deployed almost anywhere as units of the

Northern and the Pacific fleets. Foxtrot submarines were involved in the extremely tense encounters that took place during the Cuban missile crisis of 16–28 October 1962. Four of the class were deployed to Cuban waters on 1 October. Although they did not have combat orders, all (unknown to the Americans) were carrying torpedoes with nuclear warheads. A Zulu-class boat, *B-75*, armed with two nuclear warheads, was also in the Atlantic under instruction to protect Soviet shipping between Russia and Cuba. Aware of the presence of Russian submarines in the North Atlantic, on 23 October the Pentagon ordered U.S. Navy units to track them and 'induce' them to surface and identify themselves. This involved the use of small-size practice depth charges. Three Foxtrots, *B-36*, *B-59* and *B-130*, were forced to the surface either by depth charges or through battery exhaustion. *B-59*, on 27 October, had been out of contact with its base for some days and its officers, believing that war might have already broken out, readied its nuclear-armed torpedoes to strike the nearby US carrier *Randolph*.

Foxtrot from above. Note the open navigation deck on top of the sail.

Assent of the three senior officers was needed to fire: only one, Vasili Arkhipov, refused to concur in an action that would have tipped the world into a nuclear war.

Foxtrots were built until 1983, by which time the design was obsolescent. Submarines of the class were also sold to India (eight), Libya (six), Cuba (three) and Poland (two). At least two were lost in accidents: *B-37* by a torpedo explosion in 1962, and *B-33* sank at Vladivostok in 1991. Between 1995 and 2000 the Russians retired their Foxtrots and the last Indian unit was withdrawn in 2010. The last of the type known to be operational was a Ukrainian unit, the one-time Soviet *B-435*, taken over by the Russians at Odessa on 22 March 2014, but not reincorporated into the Russian Navy. At least six members of the class are on exhibition as museum ships, the best preserved being at Kaliningrad on the Russian Baltic coast.

Tracking Foxtrots

The USA's Sound Surveillance System (SOSUS) station, operational since September 1954, found the Foxtrots hard to track, as to conserve fuel on long patrols they snorkelled on only one outboard diesel-driven shaft line. This created an off-axis thrust that had to be compensated for by an off-set rudder angle, significantly disturbing the inflow to that propeller and producing high levels of low-frequency noise (cavitation), quite different to their surfaced sound. SOSUS initiated the long-running American programme, later implemented by submarines, to obtain and record the sound 'signatures' of all Russian naval vessels, particularly nuclear submarines.

A Soviet Navy Foxtrot surfaces in the Mediterranean, close to the Sicilian coast.

Project 659 (Echo Class)
(1960)

The two Echo classes of guided the missile submarine carried an evolving range of armament and underwent a change of role in the course of some 35 years of fleet service.

The Echo class originated as Soviet Russia's first five guided-missile (SSGN) submarines, designated Project 659 by the Russian Navy and Echo I by NATO. Designed by the Rubin Central Marine Designs Bureau (TsKB-18) at Leningrad (St Petersburg), built at Komsomolsk on the Amur Peninsula and commissioned between June 1961

and July 1963, they were fitted with six launchers for P-5 Pyatyorka (SS-N-3C 'Shaddock') cruise missiles intended for land targets, and all were deployed with the Pacific Fleet. The launchers were placed above the pressure hull and reports suggested that they seriously interfered with the handling and manoeuvrability of the submarine. In addition,

The profile shows an Echo I submarine with two launchers in the open position.

Armament
The P-6 was the first practical anti-ship missile to be deployed on a submarine. Between 1977 and 1983 10 Echo IIs were fitted with the Kasatka-B satellite-guided target system and the P-500 Bazalt missile.

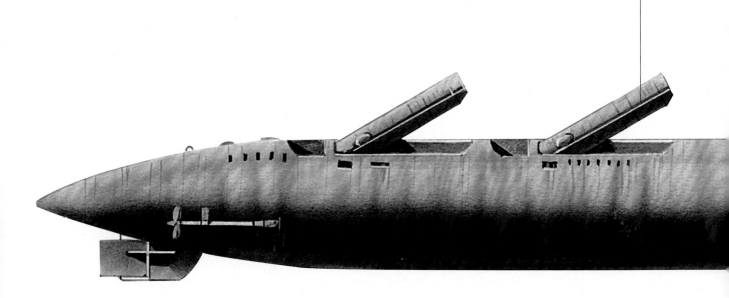

the vessel had to surface in order to fire the missiles, and fire control and guidance systems were inadequate.

After the introduction in 1967 of the Yankee-class SSGNs, which had far more sophisticated communication and navigation systems, the cruise missiles were removed from the Echo I boats between 1969 and 1974, and they were converted to SSNs. For the role of attack submarines the hulls were streamlined and plated, and they were equipped with the same sonar system as the Project 627A November class: MG-200 Arktika-M active search sonar, MG-10 Feniks-M passive search sonar and Luch sonar system for detection of mines and underwater obstacles. Leningrad fire control was installed, with RLK-101 Nakat

surface search radar and the Pluton 627 navigation system. Operating depth was 300m (984ft), although they could go down to 500m (1640ft).

The 29 Echo II boats, Project 675, were built at Severodvinsk and Komsomolsk between 1962 and 1967 for anti-ship warfare, with aircraft carriers particularly in mind. At 4m (13ft) longer than Echo I, they were fitted with four launchers for eight P-6 (SS-N-3a Shaddock A) anti-ship cruise missiles, which as with Echo I could only be fired from a surfaced position. In order to effect guidance of a fired missile, the boat had to remain surfaced until mid-course correction and final target selection had been made. In total, 14 boats were modified from 1970 to carry

UHF mast
For submergence the UHF mast aft of the sail could be folded back into a deck recess between the second set of missile tubes.

Antenna
On the surface, the forward end of the sail was rotated 180° and opened out to form an antenna to track the Shaddock missile in flight. This led to the nickname of *Raskladishka* ('folding bed') and the NATO designation of 'Front Door'.

Launchers
The forward part of the hull was lengthened by 4m (13ft) to make space for the two additional launchers.

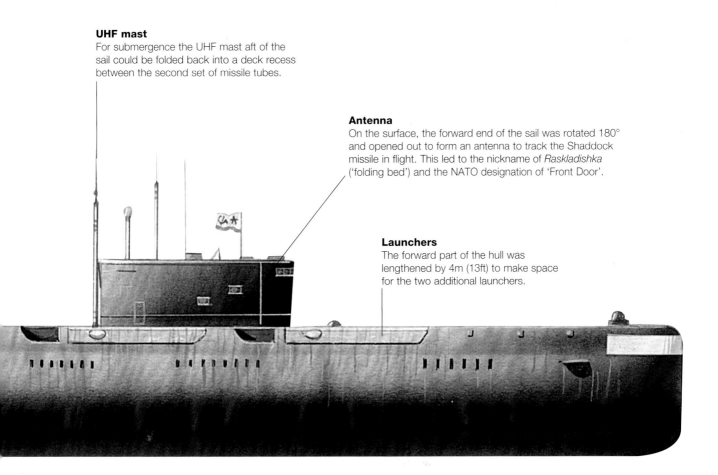

Project 659 (Echo Class)

One of the 29 Echo II anti-ship submarines surfaces in a swell.

Specification

Dimensions:	Length: 115m (377ft 2in); Beam: 9m (29ft 6in); Draught: 7.5m (24ft 6in)
Displacement:	Surfaced – 4486 tonnes (4415 tons); Submerged – 5852 tonnes (5760 tons)
Propulsion:	Two VM-A pressurized-water nuclear reactors each 70,000hp (52MW), powering two steam turbines delivering a total of 30,000hp (8MW); auxiliary diesel engine; two screws
Speed:	Surfaced – 20 knots (37km/h; 23mph); Submerged – 23 knots (42.5km/h; 26.4mph)
Range:	Unlimited
Armament:	Six 533mm (21in) and two 406mm (16in) torpedo tubes (bow), four 406mm (16in) torpedo tubes (stern). Eight P-6 (SS-N-3) cruise missiles
Complement:	90

the P-500 Bazalt (SS-N-12 Sandbox) anti-ship cruise missile. This had a range of 550km (340 miles) and three were further upgraded with the P-1000 Vulkan (GRAU 3M70) with a 700km (430 mile) range. These missiles could be controlled in-flight from a Tupolev T-95 Bear D maritime reconnaissance and guidance plane, allowing the submarine to dive once the launches had been effected. The class was divided between the Northern and Pacific Fleets, and some of the Echo-II submarines were reported to have been rebuilt to be able to carry midget submarines.

Underwater collision

On 20 June 1970, *K-108* (Echo II) was being tailed by USS *Tautog* (SSN-639) in the Sea of Okhotsk when the Soviet submarine made a U-turn on its tracker and they collided at a depth of 45m (148ft). The outer hull of *K-108* was damaged in the area of compartments VIII and IX, and *Tautog*'s sail was damaged and flooded, but there were no fatalities. Both the US and USSR denied that the incident had occurred.

The Echo class was one of the first generation of Soviet nuclear submarines, and at least four had serious internal accidents. On 21 August 1980 *K-122* lost power about 137km (85 miles) off the east coast of Okinawa,

understood to be the result of a fire in the propulsion spaces that cost the lives of nine men. *K-122* was withdrawn from active service in 1985. On 10 August 1985 Echo II *K-431* (ex-*K-31*) had a reactor explosion while refuelling in the shipyard at Chazhma Bay, Sea of

An Echo II under way on the surface, location unknown.

Soviet R&D bureaucracy

All aspects of planning and construction of submarines for the Soviet Navy were controlled by the First Main Production Directorate of the Ministry of Shipbuilding Industry. It devolved the design of ballistic missile boats to Central Design Bureau (TsKB 16), known as the Volna Bureau from 1966 to 1974, after which year it was incorporated into the Malakhit Naval Machine-Building Bureau (TsKB 143) and to Central Design Bureau (TsKB 18), known from October 1966 until September 1989 as the Rubin Leningrad Design and Installation Bureau of Naval Equipment. This latter bureau was the prime one for missile-armed nuclear submarine design, starting from 1956 with Project 658 (Hotel class) and Project 659 (Echo I).

Japan, killing 10. In another serious incident, on 25–27 June 1989 a leak was discovered in the primary circuit (linking reactor and turbine) on Echo II *K-192*. To top up the coolant the crew diverted water from the submarine's fresh water tanks and contaminated water from the leak was pumped out into the sea. Support ships provided further water supplies. On 26 June, the crew of *K-192* made an attempt to close the leak, and in order to accomplish this the supply of coolant from Northern Fleet service ship *Amur* was shut off, and the temperature in the reactor increased to danger point. Renewed supply of cold coolant led to the cracking of the overheated fuel assemblies and water came into contact with the uranium fuel. Subsequently, water was taken in directly from the sea and pumped out into it again. The amount of radioactive water released from *K-192* into the sea is not known.

By the early 1980s the Echo I and II were becoming obsolete. All of Echo I were decommissioned by 1989, and the Echo II boats were decommissioned between 1989 and 1995.

Sturgeon Class (1966)

This class of nuclear-powered SSNs formed the core of the US Navy's attack and espionage submarine fleet in the later stages of the Cold War, carrying a range of tactical missiles, special mission gear and detection equipment.

In the early 1960s American submarine development focused on improvements in quiet running, better sonar system integration, and formal tactical and operational management. Beginning with the Thresher/Permit class, successive SSN designs demonstrated a willingness to prioritize quietness over other operational capabilities such as speed and diving performance. In the progression from *Skipjack* to *Thresher* to the Sturgeon class in 1967, significant improvements in quieting with each generation were considered worth the loss of several knots in top speed, in order to have a submarine fleet whose capacity for surveillance and surprise attack was unmatched by any other. Originally conceived as a modest upgrade to the Permit class, the Sturgeon class were built for anti-submarine warfare in the late 1960s and 1970s. Using the same propulsion system as their smaller predecessors

of the Skipjack and Permit classes, the larger Sturgeons possessed greater combat capabilities. The sail-mounted dive planes were strengthened and made rotatable to a vertical position for breaking through the ice when surfacing in Arctic regions.

Ordered in November 1961, laid down at General Dynamics, Quincy, Massachusetts, on 10 August 1963, launched on 26 February 1966 and commissioned on 3 March 1967, *Sturgeon* (SSN-637) inaugurated a 37-strong class, ending with USS *Russell* (SSN-687) in 1975. *Sturgeon*'s size allowed for improved quieting,

Though armed with anti-submarine torpedoes, the Sturgeon class's undisclosed prime function was intelligence gathering and other covert operations.

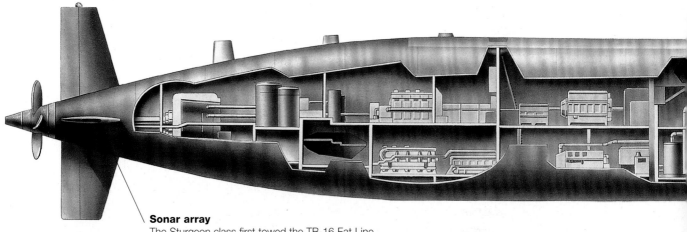

Sonar array
The Sturgeon class first towed the TB-16 Fat Line sonar array: a 630kg (1400lb) acoustic detector array, 8.6cm (3.5in) in diameter and 73m (240ft) long, attached to a 731m (2400ft) coaxial cable of 9.4mm (0.37in) diameter, weighing 202.5kg (450lb). Later the TB-23 Thin Line array, with greater sensor capacity, was used.

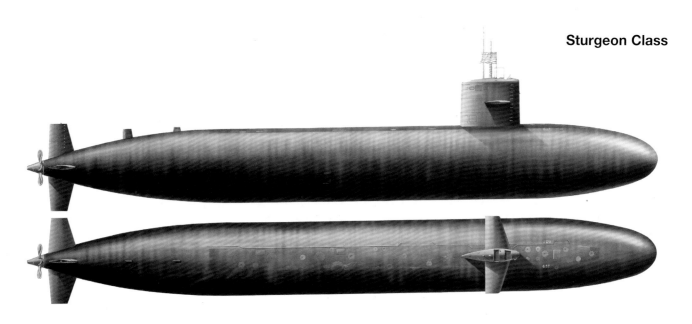

The submarine's sleek lines were intended to minimize disturbance of the water it traversed, though these were still the early days of 'stealth' design.

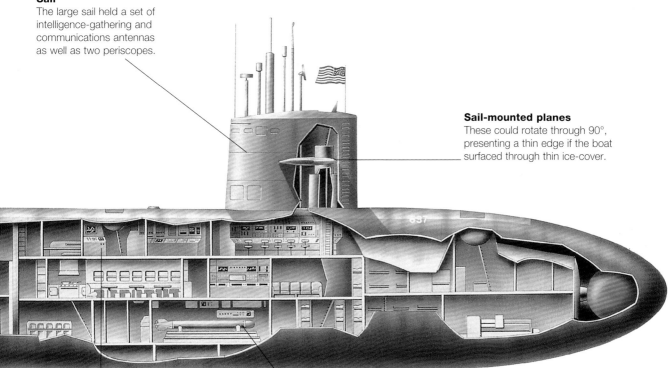

Sail
The large sail held a set of intelligence-gathering and communications antennas as well as two periscopes.

Sail-mounted planes
These could rotate through 90°, presenting a thin edge if the boat surfaced through thin ice-cover.

Internal layout
The five-compartment arrangement of the Permit-class hull was retained in the design of *Sturgeon*: bow compartment with diesel generator, operations compartment with torpedo room beneath, reactor compartment, auxiliary machinery room no. 2 and engine room.

Armament
Outwards-canted torpedo tubes. Up to 21 reload weapons were carried, including both Mk 48 and Mk 48 ADCAP torpedoes, four sub-Harpoon missiles, up to eight Tomahawk missiles and a maximum of four SUBROC ASW missiles.

Sturgeon Class

Sturgeon-class USS *Billfish* (SSN 676) surfaces at the North Pole, 30 March 1987. Note the vertically-turned diving planes on the sail.

Specification

Dimensions:	Length: 89m (292ft 3in); Beam: 9.7m (31ft 8in); Draught: 8.8m (28ft 10in)
Displacement:	surfaced – 3698 tonnes (3640 tons); submerged – 4714 tonnes (4640 tons)
Propulsion:	One S5W pressurized water reactor, two S5W steam turbines; single screw
Speed:	Surfaced – 15 knots (27.7km/h; 17.2mph); Submerged – 25 knots (46.2km/h; 28.7mph)
Range:	Unlimited
Armament:	Four 533mm (21in) torpedo tubes; Harpoon and Tomahawk missiles, torpedoes or mines
Complement:	109

and also the installation of a more advanced acoustic and SIGINT (signals intelligence) sensor suite. Originally this was the WLR-6 Waterboys system, replaced during the 1980s by Sea Nymph, described as an "advanced automatic modular signals exploitation system designed for continuous acquisition, identification, recording, analysis and exploitation of electromagnetic systems". All Sturgeon-class boats had the basic framework and throughout their careers were used in the covert intelligence-gathering operation known as 'Holystone', which involved stealthy penetration of Soviet waters, even harbours, to monitor ship movements and communications.

With this class the submarine force adopted LOFAR (LOw Frequency Analysis and Ranging) signal processing as a tool for both detection and classification, finding it highly effective for improving acoustic signal-to-noise ratios. Using LOFAR, the sonar focused only on those low frequency tonals where a submarine's source levels are highest, and could detect that narrow component of the submarine's overall sound spectrum at much greater ranges than before. Experimental spectrum analyzers like the BQQ-3 were replaced in the early 1970s by digital systems and were deployed on all the 637s, which were also used for early experiments with towed arrays. One of the first and most important uses for these systems was the creation and maintenance of a library of Soviet submarine signatures. Each class of submarine, and individual vessels within classes, generated their own unique blend of narrow- and broadband sound at varying levels. Knowledge of these signatures was fundamental to the effective use of LOFAR, and submarines were uniquely able to collect and maintain this database of other submarine's signatures.

Attack boat

The Sturgeon class were equipped to carry the Harpoon missile, the Tomahawk cruise missile and a mixed load of torpedoes, including Mk 14 Mod 6, Mk 37 and Mk 37TS, Mk 48 and Mk 48 ADCAP. Bow positioning of the BQQ-2 active and BQQ-7 passive sonar sphere required the Mk 63 torpedo tubes that were positioned immediately aft of the array to be canted some 15° outwards. They could also carry Mk 57 deep-water mines and Mk 60 CAPTOR mines. From 1965 until around 1980 some of the class were equipped with a SUBROC (UUM-44A) nuclear-tipped rocket-propelled ballistic missile, launched from a 533mm

(21in) tube, with a range of 48km (30 miles). Clearing the surface, it ignited before following its course to dive on to its target. It required the Mk 113 fire-control system.

Beginning with SSN-678 *Archerfish*, 10 units of the class were lengthened by a 3m (10ft) plug in order to experiment with new propulsion systems and increase mission capabilities. USS *Parche* was lengthened by 30m (100ft) to carry special search-and-recovery equipment. Between 1982 and 1991 six boats were modified to carry the SEAL Dry Deck Shelter (DDS), a 30-tonne (33-ton) launch hangar that attached to the weapon-shipping hatch and could be used to service undersea or surface operations. SSN 678-680, 682, 684, 686 were listed as 'DDS Capable' – either permanently fitted with the DDS or trained to use them. In this configuration they were primarily tasked with the covert insertion of Special Forces troops from an attached DDS.

USS *Sturgeon* was struck from the Naval Register on 1 August 1994, and dismantled by NPSSRP (Nuclear Powered Ship and Submarine Recycling Program) at Puget Sound Naval Shipyard, Bremerton, in 1995. Its sail and some of its equipment were later installed at the Naval Undersea Museum at Keyport, Washington. Last of the class to be withdrawn was USS *Parche* in 2005.

Covert tracking operations

Another capability provided for the first time on a large scale by the 637s was an enhanced ability to covertly track another vessel, approaching it from astern and maintaining a position within its 'sound baffles'. Apart from its quiet running, the Sturgeon class's large spherical bow sonar array gave its crew a wider angle view in both azimuth and elevation of its target than did a Skipjack or a Skate, enabling them to develop routine tactics for covert tracking operations that could be implemented on a force-wide basis. Target screw noise could be distinguished from that of the ship's own machinery and ambient sea return. This required quite close – and dangerous – proximity to the other craft and rapid response to its speed and movements.

USS *Queenfish* (SSN-651), commissioned 6 December 1966, made three tours to map the Arctic seabed, apart from other missions.

HMS Resolution (1966)

The Resolution class was the Royal Navy's first ballistic missile submarine, and HMS *Resolution* fired the RN's first nuclear-capable Polaris missile on 15 February 1968, taking over the nuclear deterrent role from the Royal Air Force.

With the introduction of the Resolution class of SSBN, the role of maintaining Britain's force of nuclear deterrence passed from the Air Force to the Navy. Four nuclear-powered submarines were ordered, with HMS *Resolution* as class leader. Laid down at the Vickers-Armstrong yard at Barrow-in-Furness on 26 February 1964 and launched on 15 September 1966, *Resolution* was commissioned on 2 October 1967. Its cost was given as £40,240,000.

The designated missile was the American Polaris, and American contribution to the design was evident. Bow

and stern sections were constructed separately, and the American-designed missile compartment inserted between them. The design has been called a lengthened modification of the British Valiant class of first-generation SSNs that entered service in the mid-1960s, but resemblances to the US Navy's Lafayette class of SSBN were also clear. The Resolution boats had the distinctive whale-like hull adopted by the RN for the Valiants, with hydroplanes fitted to the bows rather than sail-mounted in US style. Other specifically British features included the 'rafting' of the main machinery,

Resolution's form is typical of the ballistic missile submarine, with the sail set well forward and the missile compartments in the widest section.

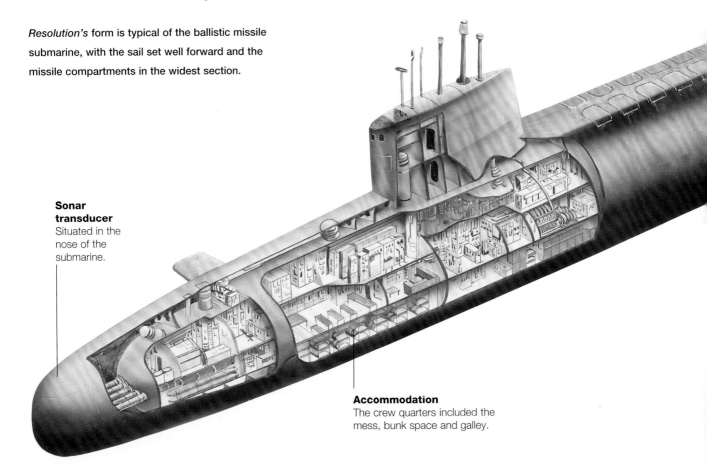

Sonar transducer
Situated in the nose of the submarine.

Accommodation
The crew quarters included the mess, bunk space and galley.

an automated hovering system, welded hull valves and
the machinery-loading hatch. Like the Valiant class it had
the Rolls-Royce PWR I Core 1 pressurized water reactor,
powering English Electric turbines.

A total of 16 UGM-27 Polaris A-3 were carried. Britain
contributed 8 per cent of the missile's research and
development costs, and denied speculation that the Nassau
Agreement permitted the addition of electronic overrides
in the control system to give the United States a veto over
its use. The British Ferranti DCB Fire Control system was
installed. The Polaris warheads were also designed and
built in Britain and initially comprised a modified version
of the WE177 device. This was replaced from 1982 by
the Chevaline warhead, which was designed to address
concerns about the increasing vulnerability of the Polaris

Rudder
The two-level rudder gave a
distinctive tail-end look when
the boat was surfaced.

Main turbine
'Rafting' of the machinery to minimize
contact with the hull was a British idea.
The US Navy was sceptical for some
years before being won over to what is
now a standard practice.

Reactor compartment
PWR1 was the first reactor plant designed and
manufactured by Rolls-Royce for the British
nuclear submarine programme. The first core,
based on an American design, was fitted to the
Valiant and Resolution classes.

Armament
Polaris was a US-developed two-stage solid fuel
rocket 9.4m (31ft) long, with a diameter of 1.4m (4ft
6in). Three versions were produced between 1960
and 1971, when phasing out began. Version A-1
carried a one-megaton nuclear warhead 2200km (1400
miles). A-2 had the same warhead, but a range of
2700km (1670 miles). A-3 could carry three 200-kiloton
warheads a distance of 4500km (2800 miles), and was
adapted by the UK for the A-3TK Chevaline system,
fitted with decoy warheads and electronic jammers for
penetrating ballistic-missile defences.

A Royal Air Force Sea King helicopter winches a crewmember up from the deck of HMS *Resolution*.

Specification

Dimensions:	Length: 129.5m (425ft); Beam: 10.1m (33ft); Draught: 9.1m (30ft)
Displacement:	Surfaced – 7620 tonnes (7500 tons); Submerged – 8535 tonnes (8400 tons)
Propulsion:	One Vickers-RR PWR1 pressurized water reactor, steam turbines, 27,500hp (20.5MW); single screw
Speed:	Surfaced – 20 knots (37km/h; 23mph); Submerged – 25 knots (46.2km/h; 28.7mph)
Range:	Unlimited
Armament:	16 Polaris A3TK SBM; six 533mm (21in) torpedo tubes
Complement:	154

system, in particular its inability to penetrate an anti-ballistic missile screen. Chevaline was fitted with multiple decoys, chaff and other countermeasures. *Resolution* was upgraded to carry Chevaline in 1984.

First patrols

Its operational patrols began on 15 June 1968, with the class based with the 10th Submarine Squadron at Faslane, Scotland. In the following year the Royal Air Force's V-bombers were withdrawn from the nuclear role. *Resolution* was followed by HMS *Renown*, launched in February 1967, *Repulse* in November 1967 and *Revenge* in March 1968. By 13 December 1969 all four Resolution-class submarines had been accepted for service. As with other SSBNs, each boat had two crews, 'Port' and 'Starboard', serving on alternate missions. In order to maintain the deterrent effect, at least one member of the class was intended to be on patrol on a secret route at any given time.

Noise problems with *Resolution* resulted in a visit to the naval base at Rosyth in 1986/87 for special treatment. The Resolution class, like all other British nuclear-powered submarines, were subject to a programme of regular

The missile control station on HMS *Resolution*.

Tigerfish hit and miss

The Tigerfish torpedo as carried by the Resolution class had an unfortunate history. Mod 0 was introduced as an ASW torpedo. On service trials in 1973 only about 40 per cent functioned as intended. The torpedo tended to dip, breaking the guidance wires. It failed provisional fleet acceptance trials in 1979, but was issued to the fleet from 1980. Mod 1 passed trials in 1978 and was issued to the fleet the following year. However, in a 1982 test, two out of five Mod 1 torpedoes fired at a target hulk failed to function because of bad batteries and none hit the target. This unreliability led to vintage Mark 8 torpedoes being used by HMS *Conqueror* to sink the Argentinian cruiser *General Belgrano* in 1982. A 'Consolidation Programme' during the mid-1980s improved reliability to 80 per cent, and torpedoes built to the new standards were designated as Mod 2, with existing Mark 24 torpedoes modified to this standard by 1987. The Royal Navy had removed all Tigerfish from service as of February 2004.

inspections, set in hand as a precautionary measure following the discovery of a technical defect in one of the Royal Navy's hunter-killer submarines. HMS *Renown* required a five-year refit between 1987 and 1992, and there was concern about whether a Polaris submarine was always on patrol. Britain's Ministry of Defence issued an assurance in 1991 that the operation of the strategic deterrent was being continued uninterrupted, with at least one SSBN remaining on patrol. *Resolution* was noted as being in sustained use throughout this period, including conducting the longest Polaris patrol at 108 days, in 1991.

Resolution was de-commissioned on 22 October 1994 after 69 patrols, and laid up at Rosyth Naval Dockyard in Scotland. Disposal of decommissioned nuclear submarines, especially of radioactive waste, is a continuing problem for the navies that own them. Britain has 27 such submarines, now forming part of the Ministry of Defence's Submarine Dismantling Project, whose stated aim is to deliver a safe, environmentally responsible and cost-effective solution, beginning in 2016 with seven vessels at the Rosyth naval base. The Polaris era ended at a ceremony on 28 August 1996 at Faslane to mark the decommissioning of the last Resolution-class submarine, HMS *Repulse*.

Project 671 *Shchuka* (Victor Class) (1967)

To the Soviet Navy, it was Project 671, denoted *Shchuka* ('Pike'). To NATO recorders it was the Victor class. Built between 1967 and 1992, the final Victor III was contemporary with the USA's Sturgeon class, significantly faster and with comparable stealth characteristics.

The Project 671 brief, given to the Malakhit Central Design Bureau (TsKB 143), was for a new class to engage hostile ballistic missile submarines and anti-submarine task forces, and protect friendly vessels and convoys from attacks. A total of 48 were built in three phases. Victor I featured an advanced teardrop hull design for high underwater speeds, used also in Victor II and III. A total of 15 units were built. The Project 671 boats were retrofitted to handle the TEST-68 wire-guided torpedo weapons under the designation Project 671B

Towed sonar array
This was the first Soviet submarine to carry a Barrakuda towed passive sonar array, mounted in the pod. Its lengthened hull was largely to provide more processing room for the additional sonar data.

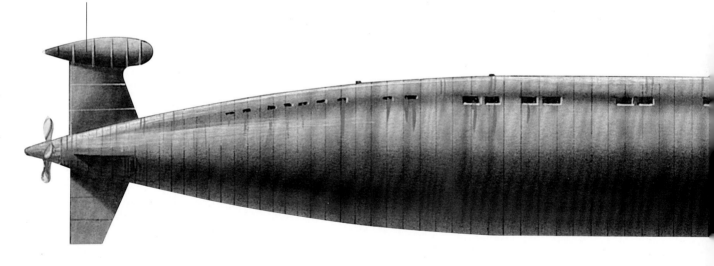

Profile of Victor III. The distinctive sonar pod was detachable, and not all Victor IIIs carried it.

(sometimes referred to as Project 671V). Two were subsequently equipped with the Kolos non-acoustic detection system and redesignated as Project 671K.

Victor II

The Victor II version was enlarged to provide additional weapons capabilities and improved fire-control system. The new generation of 650mm (25.3in) heavy torpedoes were longer than earlier models, and required power assistance for handling in the torpedo room. The hull of the Victor II class was divided into eight compartments: torpedo room and accumulators; accommodation and mess rooms; control room; reactor; turbines; turbo generators; living accommodation and diesel generators; steering system and electric motor. A total of seven units of this type were built. While the Project 671RT class was building, intelligence supplied from the Walker spy ring in the USA emphasized the vulnerability of

Soviet submarines due to their high noise levels, and construction was curtailed pending an improved design.

Victor III

This was Project 671RTM, Victor III, whose first unit was launched at the Admiralty Shipyard in Leningrad (now St Petersburg) in 1976. In 1978 the Komsomolsk yard joined in production, building two boats per year. A total of 26 Victor III class boats were built between 1976 and 1985. In the new design, the hull was lengthened by nearly 6m (20ft) forward of the sail to make room for rafting and sound insulation of the turbine machinery. The Victor III's were visually identifiable by the distinctive pod mounted above the upper rudder, later identified as a hydrodynamic housing for a passive sonar array that could be towed to gather data and then reeled back in. The extra volume also provided for additional electronic equipment required to process the data from the towed array and two new

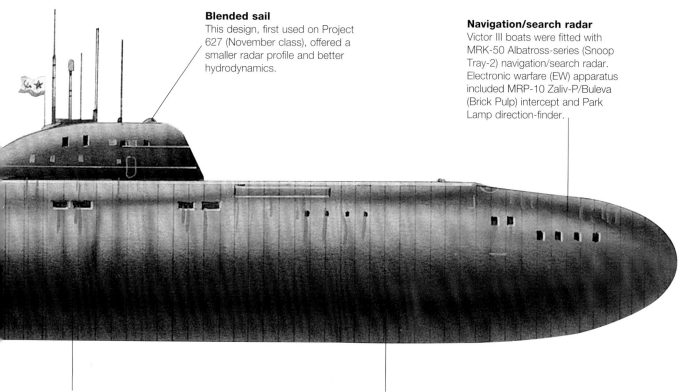

Blended sail
This design, first used on Project 627 (November class), offered a smaller radar profile and better hydrodynamics.

Navigation/search radar
Victor III boats were fitted with MRK-50 Albatross-series (Snoop Tray-2) navigation/search radar. Electronic warfare (EW) apparatus included MRP-10 Zaliv-P/Buleva (Brick Pulp) intercept and Park Lamp direction-finder.

Hull construction
The outer hull was formed from light alloys with an anechoic coating. Victor III was a very quiet submarine.

Armament
Victor-class boats had two of their 533mm (21in) tubes fitted with 406mm (20in) ASW torpedo liners for self-defence use.

Project 671 *Shchuka* (Victor Class)

A 1997 photograph of a Victor III, with bow diving planes extended.

flank arrays. There were also improvements in electronics, navigation systems and radio and satellite communication systems. Victor II and Victor III were equipped with radio buoys allowing the submarine to maintain communications while submerged. All Victors were double-hulled. The outer hull, made partly from light alloys, was coated with anti-hydroacoustic materials to reduce the possibility of detection.

At high speed underwater or on the surface, the bow hydroplanes could retract into the hull. Victor III inaugurated a series of ever-quieter Russian submarines and was considered by US Navy technicians as the equivalent to the USS Sturgeon class SSN in quietness. All Victor submarines were powered by two pressurized water reactors, model OK-300 with a VM-4P type reactor core generating 31,000hp (75MW). In addition to the main propulsion they could move at low speed driven by two electric 'creep' units.

A further five, Project 671RTMK, were built at the Admiralty Yard, equipped with the Kolos non-acoustic

sensor suite and commissioned between November 1987 and September 1992. Some Project 671RTMs were upgraded to this configuration, and all units of this variant were fitted for new S-10 Granat (SS-N-21) strategic cruise missiles. Project 671RTMK also incorporated for the first time a fully integrated submarine combat direction and fire control command system. The Viking system, said to be based on that developed for the Norwegian Ula-class submarines (1987), ran on computers allegedly obtained from the Toshiba Corporation of Japan.

A single unit of the class had a 10m (33ft) fairing mounted forward of the sail for S-10 Granat missile tests. Some Victor III boats were permanently assigned to ASW duties, loaded with the RPK-7 (SS-N-16) missile that were fired from the 650mm (25.3in) tubes, while others were armed with the new P-100 anti-ship missile. All Victor-class boats had two of their 533mm (21in) tubes fitted with 406mm (20in) ASW torpedo liners for self-defence. Victor III could carry six 650mm (25.3in) and up to 18 533mm (21in) torpedoes.

Specification (Victor III)

Dimensions:	Length: 107m (351ft); Beam: 10.8m (35ft 5in); Draught: 7.2m (23ft 6in)
Displacement:	Surfaced – 5283 tonnes (5200 tons); Submerged – 7366 tonnes (7250 tons)
Propulsion:	Two OK-300 VM-4 pressurized water reactors, steam turbines developing 31,000hp (75MW); single screw
Speed:	Surfaced – 18 knots (33.3km/h; 20.7 mph); Submerged – 30 knots (55.5km/h; 34.5mph)
Range:	Unlimited
Armament:	Two 650mm (25.3in) and six 533mm (21in) bow tubes; RPK-7 anti-submarine missiles, S-10 Granat missiles, total 24 weapons; 36 mines as alternative to missiles
Complement:	115

Something of the enormous propulsive power of a nuclear-driven submarine can be gathered from this Victor III image.

Reactor accidents

On 10 August 1985 one of two reactors on the K-314 Victor I-class submarine was being refuelled at Chazhma Bay, near Vladivostok. A crane used to reposition the reactor lid failed, triggering a nuclear reaction that caused a thermal explosion that ruptured both the aft bulkhead and the pressure hull. The freshly loaded core was thrown out of the reactor. The official casualty figures were 10 killed, 10 cases of acute radiation sickness and 39 other cases of radiation sickness. In a very different episode in February 1996 a British Sea King helicopter airlifted a sick crewman from a Victor III that had been on patrol off the Faslane ballistic missile submarine base, following an urgent call for help.

On 21 March 1984 USS *Kitty Hawk* (CV-63) was struck during night operations by a surfacing Soviet Victor I in the southern Sea of Japan, approximately 160km (100 miles) from mainland Japan, sustaining a minor hole below the waterline. The submarine was towed by a Soviet salvage vessel to the Vladivostok naval base.

All Victor Is and IIs had been decommissioned by 1996. The last Victor III known to be active was *Tambov*, commissioned in 1994 and with the Northern Fleet in 2004. Any survivors of the class are likely to be out of service. The Victor-class vessels are being dismantled under the Russian–Japanese Star of Hope programme for the dismantlement of decommissioned nuclear submarines in Russia's Far East, first adopted in 2003. Japan had allocated 20 billion yen (about $171 million) for the project. In the dismantling process spent nuclear fuel is removed from the submarine's reactors and sent to storage, the hull is cut into three sections and the bow and stern sections are removed and dismantled. The reactor section is sealed and transferred to storage.

HMS Swiftsure (1971)

This was the lead ship of a six-strong British hunter-killer class, showing a number of significant design changes from its predecessors. The class took part in several campaigns, including the Falklands War of 1982 and the NATO strikes against Serbia in 1999.

From its first generation of nuclear submarines in the 1960s, the British Royal Navy's submarine arm was based on two types, the SSN hunter-killer, intended to be fast and tactically-armed; and the SSBN missile-carrier, intended for long-range sub-surface cruising and armed with ballistic missiles. The Swiftsure class formed the second generation of SSNs. Laid down on 6 June 1969 at the Vickers Yard at Barrow-in-Furness, HMS *Swiftsure* was launched on 7 September 1971 and commissioned on 17 April 1973. Its cost was noted as £37.1 million. With *Swiftsure* a hull

form shorter and fuller than that of the preceding Valiant class was introduced, in order to provide more interior space and create a stronger pressure hull for operation at greater depths and speeds. The fin was smaller and the retractable diving planes were located below the surface waterline. They were also considerably quieter than previous British nuclear submarines. Like previous classes, including the Resolution class, the Swiftsures were equipped with Paxman auxiliary diesel engines, in their case two Ventura 16YJAZ, each of 896hp (615kW).

Skew-blade propeller
Swiftsure was the only submarine of its class to have a propeller rather than a propulsor. It had a large skew-blade propeller, perhaps intended for comparative tests of mobility and speed.

Core Z
A longer-lasting reactor core known as Core Z, ready in the mid-1970s, was retrofitted to Swiftsure-class submarines.

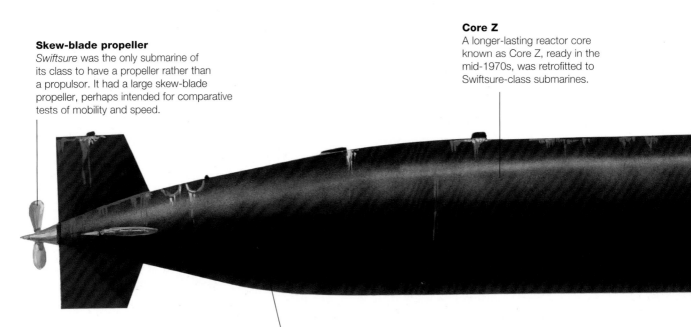

Ballast tanks
On surface travel the stern ballast tanks had to be kept flooded to maintain trim, lowering the boat in the water and making the bridge, lower in height than on the preceding Valiant class, more exposed to spray and waves.

In October 1973 *Swiftsure* carried out torpedo-firing trials off Gibraltar, at varying speeds and depths down to 300m (984ft). In 1976 HMS *Sovereign* of the same class demonstrated the Royal Navy's ability to conduct ASW operations under the ice pack when it undertook a trip to the North Pole, the operational aspects being combined with a successful set of scientific experiments. Through the 1970s and 1980s the Swiftsure class carried out a sequence of covert operations, shadowing Soviet vessels and groups in the Norwegian Sea and other northern waters. In late 1977 *Swiftsure* was sent to the Barents Sea to gather information on the acoustic signature of the Russian aircraft carrier *Kiev*, a tricky covert operation

conducted within the Soviet Northern Fleet's home waters during a Russian naval exercise. Submarines with optical periscopes had only dim red interior lighting when it was dark above the surface, as the light at the bottom of the periscope had to be least as dark as that at the top. With only an hour's daylight each day *Swiftsure* had only red lighting for almost two months.

Occasionally roles were reversed with the snooper pursued. In July 1980 HMS *Spartan* found itself shadowed by a Russian Lira class and only with difficulty shook off the pursuit. Having informed the Northwood control base in England, it was ordered to track the Lira to gather as much information as possible, but, given the Lira's 45-knot

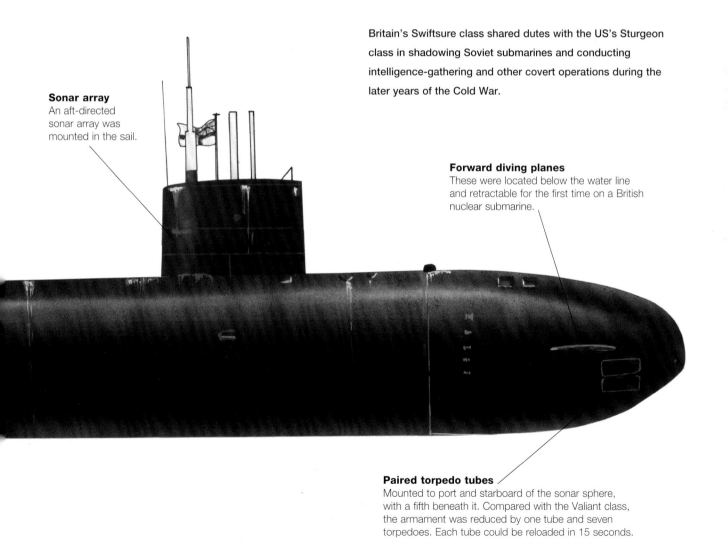

Britain's Swiftsure class shared dutes with the US's Sturgeon class in shadowing Soviet submarines and conducting intelligence-gathering and other covert operations during the later years of the Cold War.

Sonar array
An aft-directed sonar array was mounted in the sail.

Forward diving planes
These were located below the water line and retractable for the first time on a British nuclear submarine.

Paired torpedo tubes
Mounted to port and starboard of the sonar sphere, with a fifth beneath it. Compared with the Valiant class, the armament was reduced by one tube and seven torpedoes. Each tube could be reloaded in 15 seconds.

(83.3km/h; 51.7mph) speed compared to the 30-knot (55.5km/h; 34.5mph) maximum of the Swiftsures, this proved impossible. *Spartan* and *Splendid* were involved in the 1982 Falklands war, engaged in reconnaissance and enforcing the maritime exclusion zone around the islands.

The class were used both in the ASW screening role for task forces, and in the independent anti-ship and ASW roles. Their sonar fit was basically the same as that of the

Specification

Dimensions:	Length: 82.9m (272ft); Beam: 9.8m (32ft 2in); Draught: 8.5m (28ft)
Displacement:	Surfaced – 4471 tonnes (4400 tons); Submerged – 4979 tonnes (4900 tons)
Propulsion:	One RR Mk 1 pressurized water reactor, two GEC steam turbines, 15,000hp (11,175kW); single screw
Speed:	Surfaced – 20 knots (37km/h; 23mph); Submerged – 30 knots (55.5km/h; 34.5mph)
Range:	Unlimited
Armament:	Five 533mm (21in) torpedo tubes; Tomahawk and Sub Harpoon SSMs
Complement:	116

Swiftsure-class HMS *Sceptre*, close to the Faslane submarine base on the River Clyde.

Valiant class, and all had the Type 2020 fitted as the Type 2001 replacement during normal refits. The armament was reduced by one tube and seven torpedoes, but this reduction was balanced by the fact that it could take as little as 15 seconds to reload individual tubes. Apart from *Swiftsure*, the other class members were the first British submarines to be propulsor-driven. The reason for fitting a propeller on *Swiftsure* has never been disclosed, as a prototype propulsor had already been tested on HMS *Churchill*. Emergency power on all six was provided by the same 112-cell electric battery and associated diesel generator and electric motor as fitted in the Valiant and Churchill classes.

Class upgrade

The Swiftsure & Trafalgar (S&T) Class Update was a two-phase incremental programme to counter obsolescence of the sonar system and to enhance the military capability of the in-service attack submarines. The Initial Phase (Stages 1 & 2) was successfully completed in June 1996. This phase resolved sonar obsolescence, introduced enhanced sonar capability (Sonars 2074 & 2082), integrated the new submarine command system (SMCS) and delivered an incremental improvement in weapon system effectiveness to the remaining

Swiftsure target acquisition

From 2004 the surviving Swiftsure-class boats carried the new Spearfish torpedoes produced by BAE Systems, a sophisticated wire-guided weapon comparable to the Mk 48 ADCAP, which can reach the general vicinity of a target and then conduct a covert passive search. The high-capacity guide wire system, specifically designed to match the Spearfish's manoeuvre and speed envelope, provides two-way data exchange between it and the launch submarine, maximizing the submarine's organic sensor and combat control capabilities. At close range the Spearfish uses active sonar to classify and home in on its target. High-power transmissions and signal processing enable it to accurately discriminate targets from background noise and give it high resistance to acoustic countermeasures and/or evasive manoeuvres. If it fails to hit the target on its first attack, it automatically selects a viable re-attack mode.

Swiftsure class HMS *Splendid* and Trafalgar-class HMS *Turbulent* surfaced together at the North Pole in May 1988, demonstrating their ice-breaking abilities at a time when Canada was considering the acquisition of nuclear submarines.

Swiftsure-class and older Trafalgar-class submarines. The Final Phase (Stages 3 & 4) were to enhance the operational effectiveness of the four newest Trafalgar-class submarines, principally by the introduction of a new integrated sonar suite (Sonar 2076), an upgraded Tactical Weapon System (TWS) and a number of signature reduction measures.

Swiftsure was decommissioned in 1992 after cracks were found in its reactor during a refit: a problem encountered also with the Trafalgar class and other early members of the Swiftsure class. Damage to the pressure hull in depth trials was also suggested as a reason for the boat's premature retirement. A hull life of at least 25 years had been predicated. Others of the class lasted longer: HMS *Superb* served for 32 years, from 1976 to 2008, and HMS *Sceptre* was the Royal Navy's oldest seagoing vessel when it was retired in 2010.

USS Los Angeles (1974)

USS *Los Angeles* (SSN-688) was the lead ship of the Los Angeles class. Defined as fast attack submarines and escorts for carrier battle groups, they are in fact versatile craft that have undertaken a variety of combat, escort and intelligence-gathering missions over the years.

Los Angeles was laid down at the Newport News Shipbuilding Company, Virginia, on 8 January 1972. Launched on 6 April 1974, it was commissioned on 13 November 1976. It set the pattern for the following 30 boats. Internally the hull is divided into two main watertight compartments. The forward section houses all the living spaces, weapons systems, control centres and sonar/ fire control equipment. The after compartment houses the nuclear reactor and the ship's propulsion equipment. The class is equipped with a 26MW nuclear pressurized water

reactor, model GE PWR S6G, developed and supplied by General Electric, with a fuel cell life of around 10 years. The Magnatek auxiliary prop motor develops 324hp (242kW).

Of the 62 Los Angeles class, SSNs 688–718 were built to the original design. From SSN-719, commissioned in July 1985, 12 vertical launch tubes for Tomahawk

The cutaway shows just how much equipment has to be packed into a hull 110m (362ft) long and 10m (32ft) wide, along with 133 personnel.

Air and water processing
Atmosphere control equipment replenishes oxygen used by the crew, and removes carbon dioxide and other atmosphere contaminants. Two distilling plants convert salt water to fresh for drinking, washing and the propulsion plant.

Decoy canisters
Noise-making decoy canisters can be ejected as part of anti-detection measures.

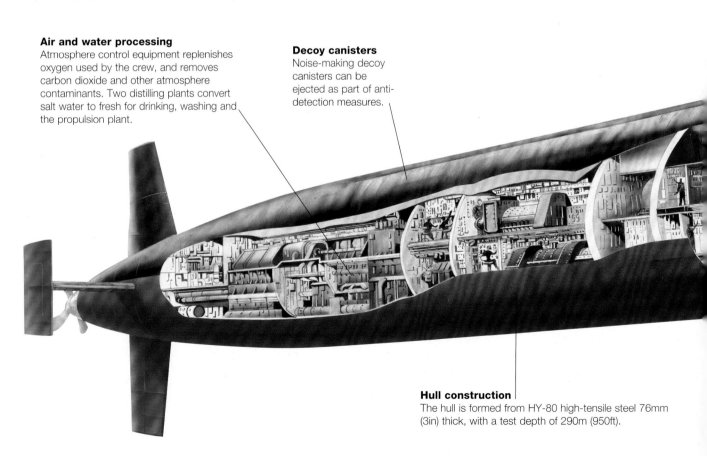

Hull construction
The hull is formed from HY-80 high-tensile steel 76mm (3in) thick, with a test depth of 290m (950ft).

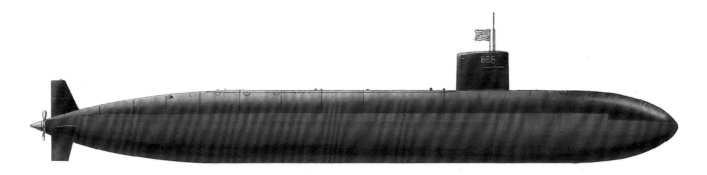

Bridge
In the forward top portion of the sail is the bridge. When the submarine is on the surface, the Officer of the Deck shifts his watch from the control room to here.

In the 1990s, construction cost of a Los Angeles-class submarine was $900,000,000. Extension of its service life by 12 years is estimated to cost $200,000,000.

Nose cone
This is made of composite materials that allow external sounds to penetrate to the sonar sphere.

Data handling
Sonar processing and analysis room.

Mess deck
Mess and berthing deck, plus galley. Hot meals are prepared four times a day, in line with the six-hour watches.

Armament
Torpedo and missile storage room holding 24 weapons, also housing controls for the vertical cruise missile launch tubes.

USS *Los Angeles* spreads its wake as it heads out to sea with the coast of Oahu, Hawaii, in the background.

Specification

Dimensions:	Length: 110.3m (362ft); Beam: 10m (32ft 10in); Draught: 9.9m (32ft 6in)
Displacement:	Surfaced – 6180 tonnes (6082 tons); Submerged – 7038 tonnes (6927 tons)
Propulsion:	One GE S6G pressurized water reactor, two turbines, 35,000hp (26MW) single shaft; auxiliary Magnetek motor
Speed:	Surfaced – 20 knots (37km/h; 23mph); Submerged – 33 knots (61.1km/h; 37.9mph)
Range:	Unlimited
Armament:	Four 533mm (21in) torpedo tubes; Tomahawk Land Attack missiles, Harpoon SSM
Complement:	133

cruise missiles were fitted. The last 23, SSN 751 to 773, commissioned between 1988 and 1996, sometimes referred to as 688I (for Improved boats), are configured for under-ice operations, with forward diving planes moved from the sail to the bow, and the sail strengthened for ice breaking. They are also quieter, incorporate an advanced BSY-1 sonar suite combat system and the ability to lay Mobile Mark 67 and Captor Mark 60 mines.

Currently, operational vessels in the class are being upgraded with the Lockheed Martin AN/BQQ-10(V4) sonar processing system, under the Acoustic-Rapid Commercial-Off-the-Shelf Insertion (A-RCI) programme. A-RCI is a sonar system that integrates and improves towed array, hull and sphere arrays, wide aperture and high-frequency arrays, and other ship sensor processing, by means of rapid insertion of new commercial off-the-shelf-based hardware and software, such as commercial blade servers. A-RCI is an open-architecture sonar system that offers an advantage in acoustic detection of threat submarines, using legacy sonar sensors. The programme regularly refreshes central processors with COTS technology and software, enabling onboard data-handling and computing power to grow at nearly the same rate as commercial industry, and facilitates regular updates to submarine sonar-processing software and hardware with minimal disruption to patrol schedules.

The electronic support measures (ESM) include a BRD-7 direction finding system, the WLR-1H and WLR-8(v)2 interceptors and the WLR-10 radar warner. Northrop Grumman AN/WLY-1 acoustic interception and countermeasures system has replaced the former WLR-9A/12 system. The surface search, navigation and fire control radar is the Sperry Marine BPS 15 A/16, incorporating a video processor, touchscreen radar controls and a hydraulically driven raise-and-rotate mechanism.

Tomahawk missiles

The class is armed with both the land-attack and anti-ship version of the Tomahawk missile from Raytheon. The land-attack Tomahawk has a range of 2500km (1550 miles). A TAINS (Tercom Aided Inertial Navigation System) guides the missile towards the target, flying at subsonic speed at an altitude of 20m (65ft) to 100m (330ft). Block III improvements include an improved propulsion system and Navstar Global Positioning System (GPS) guidance capability. Tomahawk can be fitted with a nuclear warhead, although these are not normally carried on the Los Angeles class. The anti-ship version is equipped with inertial guidance and an active radar and anti-radiation homing head. Its range is up to 450km (280 miles). The class also carry the Harpoon anti-ship missile, which uses active radar homing to deliver a 225kg (495lb) warhead. Four 533mm (21in) torpedo tubes are located midships, with a Mark 117 torpedo fire control system. Altogether there is capacity for 26 tube-launched weapons.

USS *Los Angeles* made its first operational deployment, to the Mediterranean Sea, in 1977. In the following year it transferred to the Pacific Fleet at Pearl Harbor, and thereafter remained in the Pacific. Altogether it conducted 17 deployments in the Pacific. In 1999 it was modified to carry a Dry Deck Shelter (DDS). *Los Angeles* gained eight Meritorious Unit Citations and a Navy Unit Citation in a career lasting more than 35 years, from 1974 until withdrawal in February 2010. It was finally decommissioned on 23 January 2010 in the port of Los Angeles. As of early 2016, 39 of the class remain active, based at Groton, Norfolk, San Diego, Pearl Harbor and Guam.

Ears under the water

The Los Angeles class submarines have always possessed a comprehensive and state-of-the-art suite of sonars: TB-23/29 thin line passive towed array (being replaced by the Lockheed Martin TB-29A, the first array to use advanced towed array integrated product team (TAIPT) telemetry. This is a commercial off-the-shelf (COTS)-based telemetry architecture. Also carried are BQG 5D wide aperture flank array, BQQ 5D/E low frequency passive and active search and attack sonar, Ametek BQS 15 close-range, high-frequency active sonar also used for ice detection, MIDAS (Mine and Ice Detection Avoidance) System high frequency active sonar and Raytheon SADS-TG active detection sonar. A Near-term Mine Reconnaissance System (NMRS) is being installed. The NMRS is a fibre-optic controlled vehicle that is equipped with AQS 14 side-scan sonar. The launch and recovery of the reconnaissance vehicle is via a torpedo tube.

Crew members of Los Angeles class USS *Oklahoma City* (SSN-723) at the control centre during the course of an exercise.

Project 705 Lira (Alfa Class)
(1977)

In 1971, the Soviet Union completed the world's first titanium-hulled submarine, which was also the fastest. A revolutionary design in almost every way, including a new kind of compact nuclear reactor, it was the precursor of a bold new class of attack submarines.

The design team for Project 705 at the Malakhit Design Bureau (TsKB-143) was led by Mikhail G. Rusanov. It was a double-hull design, with the inner hull able to withstand the enormous pressures that would be faced by extreme operating depths, and a lighter outer hull optimized for speed, manoeuvrability and acoustic stealth. Numbered K-162 (K-222 from 1978), codenamed Papa by NATO,

it was the prototype of Project 705, the Lira ('Lyre') class submarine, commenced in 1974 and known to NATO as Alfa. Since the prime aim of Project 705 was to achieve very high speed, other considerations were adapted to make this possible. A smaller, more streamlined hull was designed with a profile of unique form, the sail blending smoothly into the hull. The inner hull was built to function at depths stated

Propeller pods
The single screw was adopted for Project 705 almost simultaneously with the Project 671 (Victor II) second-generation SSN design. To provide these submarines with emergency propulsion and, in suitable circumstances, low-speed and ultra-quiet manoeuvres, both classes were fitted with small two-blade propeller 'pods' on their horizontal stern surfaces.

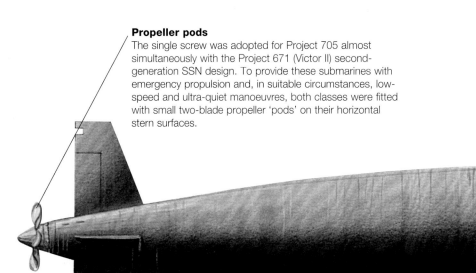

Titanium hull
This material gave a 30 per cent lower mass, a 25 per cent lesser displacement and a 10 per cent increase in speed compared to steel plate.

as in excess of 670m (2200ft), with some sources putting its crush-depth deeper than 1100m (3600ft).

Both hulls were formed of titanium alloy, far exceeding steel in its lightness, tensile strength and resistance to corrosion, enabling the pressure hull to be stronger without increasing displacement, allowing the greater diving depth and also increasing resistance to explosive shock at lesser depths. In addition the alloy was non-magnetic, minimizing the likelihood of magnetic anomaly detection (MAD). Construction presented new problems, as the bending, shaping and welding of titanium alloy plates is far more difficult than with steel. According

to some reports the shed in which the Lira boats were built was filled with inert argon gas and the workers wore moon-suits while welding the hull plates. The inner pressure hull was divided into six main compartments, of which the central one was for the crew's daily use, the others being packed with weapons, sensors, nuclear propulsion and other machinery. The command and living section was a pressure vessel in itself, which would have greatly increased the crew's survivability if the boat were disabled. The Liras also had a crew escape module that could take all the personnel safely to the surface if the vessel should have to be abandoned.

The Project 705 submarines were the fastest, deepest-diving, and most highly-automated submarines of their time.

Escape chamber
The sail contained an escape chamber above the control room that could hold the entire crew – another unique feature of the class.

Control integration
This was the first submarine to have integrated combat information and control systems, providing integration of navigation, tactical handling and weapons deployment.

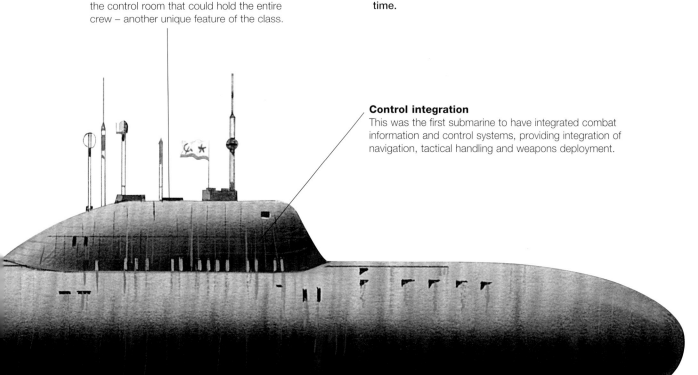

Automated procedures
Only two central compartments, for control and living space, were manned. In the other four compartments procedures were automated. The original proposals envisaged a crew of only 18.

Armament
In addition to SET 65A and SAET 60 torpedoes, the submarine could carry the RPK-2 Vyuga (Blizzard) ASW missile, given the NATO designation SS-N-15 Starfish. This was a ballistic missile capable of carrying a 200kt nuclear warhead, similar to the US Navy's SUBROC. Its range was 45km (28 miles).

Project 705 Lira (Alfa Class)

Two power plants were developed independently, BM-40A by OKB Gidropress in Leningrad and OK-550 by the OKBM design bureau in Nizhniy Novgorod, both of essentially the same type, using a eutectic lead-bismuth solution for the primary cooling stage, and both producing 155MW of power. These reactors could operate for 20 years or more without requiring to be refuelled, after which they could be replaced. The OK-550 plant was used on the prototype boat, but on the 705Ks, the BM-40A plant was

Images of the Liras are quite rare. The fine streamlining of the sail is evident in this aerial view.

installed, as the OK-550 had suffered a dangerous failure during sea trials on K-222, when the liquid metal coolant spilled from the reactor containment vessel into the bilge. While more reliable, BM-40A was much more demanding in maintenance than pressurized water reactors. The lead-bismuth mixture has a very high boiling point (1679°C) and the reactor is not kept under pressure as is the case with water-cooled reactors. But it must be kept constantly heated above 125°C or the metal solution will solidify, making it impossible to restart the reactor.

Nuclear reactors

At the Bolshaya Lopatka base a special facility was constructed to supply superheated steam to the vessels when the reactors were shut down, but this external method of heating proved to be unsatisfactory, and from the early 1980s the reactors of all the operational Lira submarines had to be kept constantly running. This led to extra wear on the reactors and required that the vessels be constantly manned. It also made repairs or alterations to the power plant difficult.

By 1985, the Soviet Navy had at least six operational Lira-class boats. They were so different to any previous Russian (or other) submarine that it took almost 10 years

Specification

Dimensions:	Length: 81m (265ft 9in); Beam: 9.5m (31ft); Draught: 8m (26ft 3in)
Displacement:	Surfaced – 2845 tonnes (2800 tons); Submerged – 3739 tonnes (3680 tons)
Propulsion:	BM-40A liquid-metal reactor, 2 steam turbines, single screw
Speed:	Surfaced – 20 knots (37km/h; 23mph); Submerged – 42 knots+ (77.7km/h+; 48.3mph+)
Range:	Unlimited
Armament:	Six 533mm (21in) torpedo tubes; 18 torpedoes or 21 RPK-2 Vyuga missiles or 36 mines
Complement:	31

A section of the sail top could be opened to provide a cockpit with wind/water screen for surface observations.

Innovation and automation

The submarine's relatively small size, displacing only 3739 tonnes (3680 tons) – as opposed to more than double that for the Victor class – meant that the crew numbers had to be greatly decreased, requiring a high level of innovation and automation to allow for a crew of only 31. The Liras were manned by a specially selected all officer and warrant officer complement, and all systems were run from a single control room with just eight men on each watch. With such a small crew and their limited access to sensitive components, no maintenance work was required while at sea other than emergency repairs. The concentration of control in one room was found to reduce reaction time in simulated combat situations, leading to faster decision making and enhanced combat effectiveness.

for the US Navy to appreciate their remarkable and highly advanced qualities. As alert high-speed interceptors they were not used on screening missions or patrol duties. Kept in port in a state of readiness, when a target was detected they would set out and move at speed to the target's last known location. The fastest submarines yet built, they could reach a top 'burst speed' of 45 knots (83km/h; 51.7mph). Pursuit and detection – and potential destruction – was their task, aided not only by speed but by the highest levels of automation yet seen in a submarine. These included the Akkord combat information and control system, using data from other systems, displaying information on control terminals, with recommendations for specific action, and the Sargan weapon control system. The Okean automated hydroacoustic sonar provided target data to these systems. Sozh navigation radar and Boksit course control systems were integrated, while the Ritm system controlled operation of all machinery aboard, without requiring crew intervention.

The difficulty of maintaining the liquid-metal reactors, and the very high costs of construction, meant that the class number was held at seven, despite its abilities. All were decommissioned by 1990.

USS Ohio (1979)

The *Ohio* class remains the basis of America's strategic nuclear deterrent until the 2030s. The largest submarines built for the US Navy, all 18 have undergone substantial modification and updating programmes in the early 21st century.

USS *Ohio*, the class leader, was laid down as SSBN-726 at the General Dynamics Electric Boat Yard, Groton, Connecticut, on 10 April 1976 and launched on 7 April 1979. The largest submarine yet built for the US Navy, it was commissioned on 11 November 1981 as SSBN-726 and equipped with 24 Trident C-4 ballistic missiles with multiple independently targeted warheads, set in parallel rows of 12. The class is powered by the S8G pressurized water reactor, providing steam to two geared turbines. Its core requires refuelling every

nine years. A 325hp (242kW) Magnatek auxiliary prop motor is fitted, and auxiliary power also comes from a Fairbanks-Morse 38 8-1/8 two-stroke opposed-piston diesel engine.

Ohio made its first full operational cruise in October 1982. From June 1993 to June 1994 it was overhauled at Puget Sound Naval Shipyard, receiving extensive upgrades to sonar, fire control and navigation systems, before resuming regular patrols in January 1995. Exhaustive engineering analysis was already being made, resulting in the service life

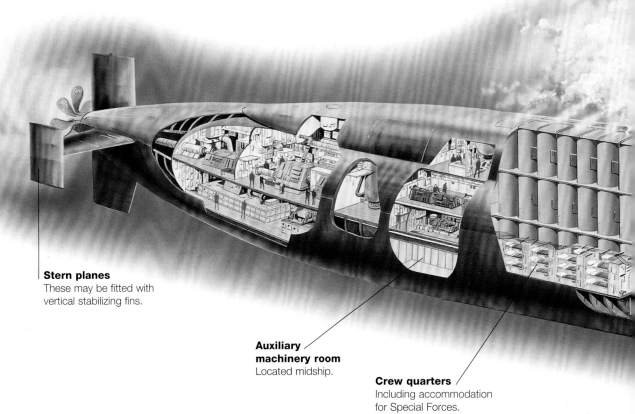

Stern planes
These may be fitted with vertical stabilizing fins.

Auxiliary machinery room
Located midship.

Crew quarters
Including accommodation for Special Forces.

The Ohio class's massive hull was formed of five major compartments, with four operating levels.

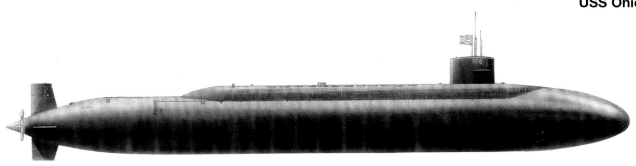

of the US Navy 'boomer' (ballistic missile submarine) force being extended by 12 years to a total active service of 42 years. From the ninth boat, USS *Tennessee*, the class has carried the Trident II D5 SLBM, capable of carrying up to 12 MIRVs (multiple independent re-entry vehicles), and older boats have been retrofitted. The dimensions of the three-stage solid fuel Trident II missile are 13.6m (44ft 7in) long with a diameter of 211cm (6ft 11in), and a weight of

The paint scheme for the Ohio class has varied between a combination of red (below the surfaced waterline) and black (above the waterline) – see cutaway; and all-black, as above.

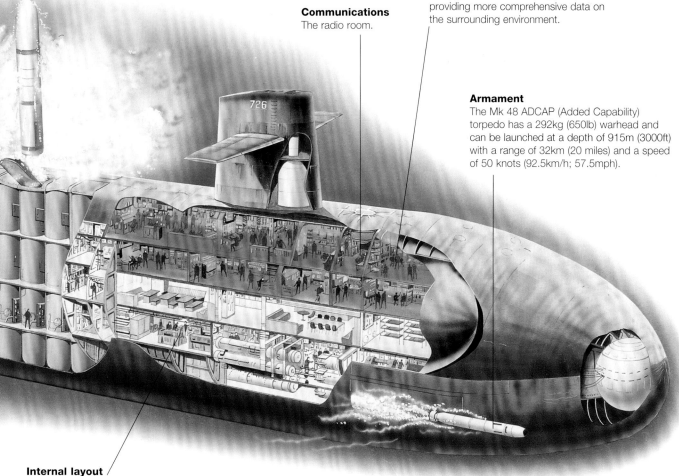

Communications
The radio room.

Sonar room
Under A-RCI the system can be upgraded by improving processing without changing the sensors. It integrates the boat's sonar arrays, running more advanced algorithms and providing more comprehensive data on the surrounding environment.

Armament
The Mk 48 ADCAP (Added Capability) torpedo has a 292kg (650lb) warhead and can be launched at a depth of 915m (3000ft) with a range of 32km (20 miles) and a speed of 50 knots (92.5km/h; 57.5mph).

Internal layout
Level 1: Navigation centre; Level 2: Missile control room;
Level 3: Crew mess deck; Level 4: Auxiliary diesel engine.

59 tonnes (58 tons). The U.S. Navy gives the range as greater than 7360km (4575 miles), but it could be up to 12,000km (7460 miles) depending on the payload mix. The Sperry Univac Mark 98 control system controls the missiles via an inertial navigation system, supported by stellar navigation. Four 533mm (21in) torpedo tubes with a Mk 118 digital fire control system are fitted.

Following the START II arms limitation treaty of June 1992, which limited the number of ballistic missiles carried

USS *Rhode Island* (SSBN 740) is manoeuvred by tugs to a mooring jetty at the Kings Bay submarine base in Georgia.

by US and Russian submarines, four, including *Ohio*, have been altered from SSBN to SSGN. USS *Ohio* began conversion in November 2002, and work was completed in January 2006. As SSGNs, the boats carry up to 154 Tomahawk TLAM (land attack) or Tactical Tomahawk (block IV) missiles and are capable of conducting special operations missions. They can accommodate Northrop Grumman advanced SEAL delivery systems (ASDS), 102 special operations troops and a mission control centre. Each has had its two forward-most missile tubes converted into ASDS capable lock-out chambers. All carry highly sophisticated countermeasures systems including AN/WLY-1 from Northrop Grumman, providing automatic response against torpedo attack. Conversion of all four was completed in 2008, effectively forming two Ohio classes with separate roles.

Missile launch tubes

On the four SSGNs, General Dynamics Advanced Information Systems installed a new fire control system for the Tomahawk weapon. Northrop Grumman Electronic Systems adapted the missile launch tubes. The missiles are loaded in seven-shot Multiple-All-Up-Round Canisters (MACs). The tubes can also accommodate additional stowage canisters for special operations forces' equipment,

Specification

Dimensions:	Length: 170.7m (560ft); Beam: 12.8m (42ft); Draught: 11.1m (36ft 5in)
Displacement:	Surfaced – 16,764 tonnes (16,499 tons); Submerged – 18,750 tonnes (18,450 tons)
Propulsion:	One S8G pressurized water reactor, two steam turbines developing 60,000hp (45MW), single screw
Speed:	Surfaced – 24 knots (44.4km/h; 27.6mph); Submerged – 28 knots (52km/h; 32.2mph)
Range:	Unlimited
Armament:	Four 533mm (21in) torpedo tubes. SSBN: 24 Trident C4 SLBMs; SSGN: 152 Tomahawk cruise missiles
Complement:	155

Cutaway profile of an Ohio-class SSBN, with red and black paint scheme.

food and other items to extend the submarines' ability to give forward support to combatant units. The design takes account of potential future payloads, including new types of missile and unmanned aerial and undersea vehicles. For ASW countermeasures, the class is equipped with eight launchers for the Mk 2 torpedo decoy. Electronic warfare equipment is the WLR-10 threat warning system and the WLR-8(V) surveillance receiver from GTE of Massachusetts. This uses seven YIG-tuned and vector-tuned superheterodyne receivers to operate from 50MHz up to J-band. An acoustic interception and countermeasures system, AN/WLY-1 from Northrop Grumman, has been developed to provide automatic response against torpedo attack. Surface search, navigation and fire control radar is BPS 15A I/J-band radar. The sonar suite includes IBM BQQ 6 passive search sonar, Raytheon BQS 13, BQS 15

active and passive high-frequency sonar, BQR 15 passive towed array from Western Electric and the active BQR 19 navigation sonar from Raytheon.

The Ohio submarines are upgraded with the Lockheed Martin AN/BQQ-10 (V4) sonar processing system under the US Navy's Acoustic-Rapid Commercial-off-the-Shelf Insertion (A-RCI) programme. A total of 14 Ohio-class SSBNs were on the active list in January 2016, with the four SSGN conversions also still in service. Preliminary work has been in hand since 2007 for a replacement class, with specification documents completed in late 2014. These submarines will have reactor cores that need no refuelling in the hull's lifetime, and are also expected to have electric rather than mechanical drive to the propulsion gear. The first batch will be armed with Trident II D5LE (Life Extension) missiles. Detailed design work is expected to begin in 2017, with the first patrol scheduled for 2031. As many as 12 new vessels will replace the 14 existing Trident-equipped Ohio-class boats.

War in a box

Despite their great size, which limits their access to shallow coastal waters, the Ohio-class SSGNs are equipped to provide complete operational management and support for localized military operations, the so-called 'war in a box' capacity. Within a wider perspective, they have the armament and operational ability to negate the anti-access/area denial capability of an opposing force. Cruise missiles, unmanned aerial and undersea vehicles (for which a retrieval module can be fitted) can be deployed. Anti-access and area denial (A2/AD) are strategies focused on preventing a technically developed opponent from operating military forces near, into or within a contested region. A2/AD is a high-technology arena in which counter-counter-measures are always being sought, and submarines will continue to play a key role.

USS *Ohio* as converted to SSGN, carrying two Dry Deck Shelter (DDS) modules.

Project 941 Akula (Typhoon Class) (1981)

The largest submarines yet to be constructed, with multiple pressurized hulls, the six vessels of the Typhoon class deployed Russia's ballistic missile deterrent until the 2000s. These submarines did not have to submerge or go to sea to launch their long-range missiles. They were able to do so tied up at the dock.

In the late 1970s the Rubin Design Bureau was working on Project 941 Akula ('Shark'), an SSBN intended to carry 20 long-range missiles, each with up to 10 MIRV nuclear warheads – a total of 200 nuclear weapons. This was comparable with the American Ohio class, but the Soviet RSM-52 (SS-N-20) missiles were much heavier than the American Tridents, and the submarine had to be built to a suitably large scale to carry and launch them. Given the reporting name Typhoon by NATO, it is the largest submarine yet to be constructed. The design included features for travelling under ice and ice breaking through ice cover up to 3m (9ft 10in) thick. The new-design stern fin had horizontal hydroplanes fitted behind the screws, and the bow horizontal hydroplanes are retractable into the hull.

Presure hulls

In the main body, two pressure hulls lie parallel with a third, smaller pressure hull above them, producing the bulge just below the sail; and two other pressure hulls for torpedoes and steering gear. Two OK-650 pressurized-water reactors, 254,800hp (190MW) each, supply steam to two VV-type turbogear assemblies, 49,600hp (37MW) each; and four 4288hp (3,200kW) turbogenerators. Emergency propulsion comes from two DG-750 1072hp (800kW) diesel generators. Maximum diving depth is

The outer casing over the *Akula*'s sail and pressure hulls is believed to be capable of breaking through ice up to 3m (13ft) thick.

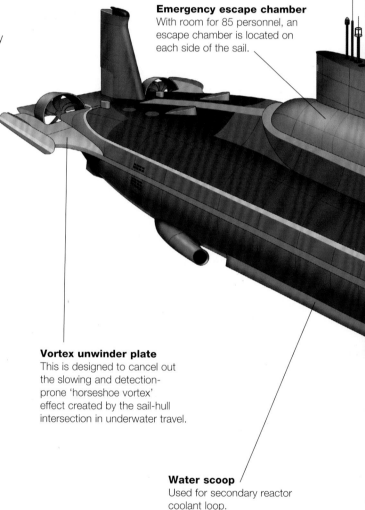

Emergency escape chamber
With room for 85 personnel, an escape chamber is located on each side of the sail.

Vortex unwinder plate
This is designed to cancel out the slowing and detection-prone 'horseshoe vortex' effect created by the sail-hull intersection in underwater travel.

Water scoop
Used for secondary reactor coolant loop.

400m (1312ft). The Typhoons could spend at least 120 consecutive days submerged. The class was built specifically for operations with the Soviet Northern Fleet in the Arctic ice pack. The reinforced sail, advanced stern fin with horizontal hydroplane fitted aft of the screws and retractable bow hydroplanes allow the submarine to break through areas of thin ice within the Arctic ice shelf. One consequence of the great size was crew facilities much superior to those on most submarines. Even a small sauna was installed.

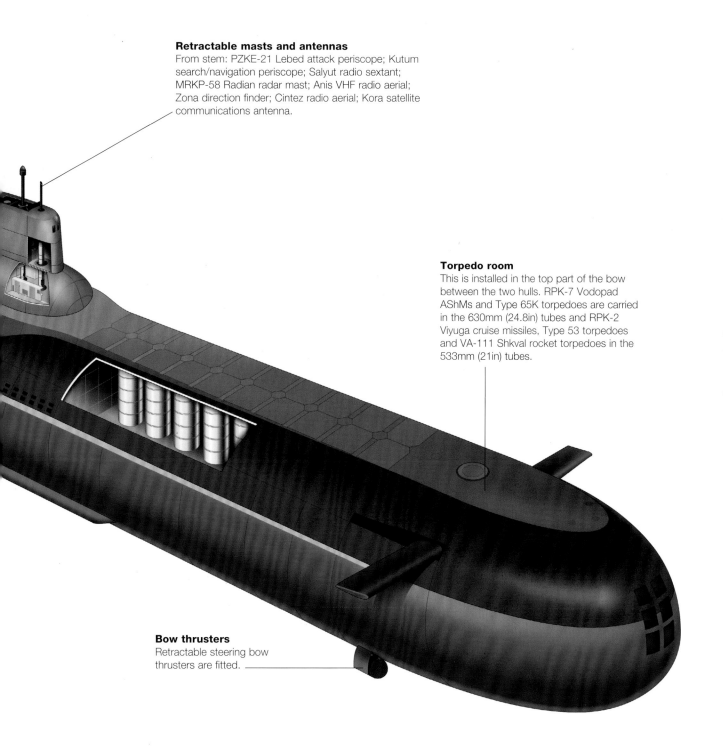

Retractable masts and antennas
From stem: PZKE-21 Lebed attack periscope; Kutum search/navigation periscope; Salyut radio sextant; MRKP-58 Radian radar mast; Anis VHF radio aerial; Zona direction finder; Cintez radio aerial; Kora satellite communications antenna.

Torpedo room
This is installed in the top part of the bow between the two hulls. RPK-7 Vodopad AShMs and Type 65K torpedoes are carried in the 630mm (24.8in) tubes and RPK-2 Viyuga cruise missiles, Type 53 torpedoes and VA-111 Shkval rocket torpedoes in the 533mm (21in) tubes.

Bow thrusters
Retractable steering bow thrusters are fitted.

Project 941 Akula (Typhoon Class)

Specification

Dimensions:	Length: 170m (557ft 9in); Beam: 24m (78ft 8in); Draught: 12.5m (41ft)
Displacement:	Surfaced – 25,400 tonnes (24,994 tons); Submerged – 48,000 tonnes (47,240 tons)
Propulsion:	Two OK-750 pressurized water reactors each 190MW, two VV-type steam turbines, each 49,600hp (37MW); twin screws
Speed:	Surfaced – 22 knots (40.7km/h; 25.3mph); Submerged – 27 knots (50km/h; 31mph)
Range:	Unlimited
Armament:	20 RSM-56 ballistic missiles; four 650mm (25.4in) and two 533mm (21in) torpedo tubes
Complement:	160

Black was the standard colour of the Project 941 submarines. The closed doors of the torpedo tubes can be seen.

Northern Fleet

The first unit was laid down in 1976 at Severodvinsk and commissioned in 1980, achieving operational status in 1981. Six more were constructed between 1981–89, entering service to form part of the 1st Flotilla of Atomic Submarines within the Western Theatre of the Northern Fleet at the Siberian base of Nyerpicha. Construction of a seventh vessel was abandoned in 1990. This was the first SSBN to have launch tubes installed forward of the sail. Its 20 RSM-52 intercontinental three-stage solid propellant ballistic missiles were each capable of holding nuclear warheads with an explosive force of 100 kilotons. It is also fitted with four 650mm (24.4in), two 533mm (21in) torpedo tubes and eight Igla (Needle) anti-aircraft missile systems.

Sophisticated Type 53-65 torpedoes are carried. To arm the Typhoons, design of a fifth-generation SLBM, the R-39 Taifun (SS-N-20), began in 1973. The R-39 allowed the submarine to fire from within the Arctic Circle and still hit a target anywhere within continental USA. In 2005, the Typhoon *Dmitriy Donskoy* made flight tests of a three-stage solid fuel SLBM, the RSM-56 Bulava (SS-NX-30).

The Russian Navy cancelled a modernization programme of the class in March 2012, stating that modernizing one Typhoon would be as expensive as building two new Borei-class submarines. Three have been scrapped, with two decommissioned on reserve. The R-39 missile was eliminated in September 2012. Current deployment is limited to *Dmitriy Donskoy*, still the world's largest

submarine. In late 2015 it was engaged in exercises in the White Sea and unconfirmed reports suggested it was then deployed to patrol off the Syrian coast. It is believed to be armed with 20 RSM-56 Bulava (NATO-code SS-N-30) intercontinental ballistic missiles with a reported range of 10,000km (6200 miles), and each carrying from six to 10 MIRV nuclear warheads.

Replacement class for the Typhoons is the Borei ('North Wind') class SSBN of which three were operational in 2015, with a further three under construction. Its submerged displacement of 24,384 tonnes (24,000 tons) ranks it as the world's second biggest submarine. It carries the RSM-56 Bulava SLBMs and has six 533mm (21in) torpedo tubes that can launch RPK-2 Viyuga cruise missiles.

Upgrades and refits

Project 941 *Akula* should not be confused with the submarines of Project 971 *Shchuka-B* ('Snow Leopard') of 1985, which NATO codenamed *Akula*. The lead unit of Project 941, TK-208, spent 10 years in refit between 1992 and 2002. It had been

intended that the boats would be retrofitted with improved R-39M (SS-N-28) missiles. This was supplanted by the new Bark missile (SS-N-28), which was 2cm (0.78in) wider than the R-39M, and the submarine's launchers had to be remade at a cost of 10 billion roubles. While under test, the Bark project was abandoned in favour of the new Bulava missile. Further refitting had to be done to *TK-208*, which was finally re-launched in mid-October 2002 under the name *Dmitriy Donskoy* from the Sevmash shipyard in Severodvinsk after its decade-long refit.

A port view of an Akula-class SSBN under way.

Västergötland (1987)

The Royal Swedish Navy's Västergötland (Type A 17) class was designed to carry out a variety of roles to provide defence against invasion including anti-surface warfare, mining, surveillance, anti-submarine warfare and insertion of Special Forces.

Four SSK boats of the A-17 or Västergötland class were commissioned between 1987 and 1989: *Västergötland* (November 1987), *Hälsingland* (October 1988), *Södermanland* (April 1989) and *Östergötland*

(January 1990). The type was conceived with a single hull of toughened high-strength steel, with X-type after control surfaces combining rudder and hydroplane functions, and a Pilkington Optronics CK 38 search

Periscope
The search periscope was a Pilkington Optronics CK 38 optronic periscope enhanced with night vision capability.

Hull construction
Västergötland is a single-hull design using toughened high-tensile steel.

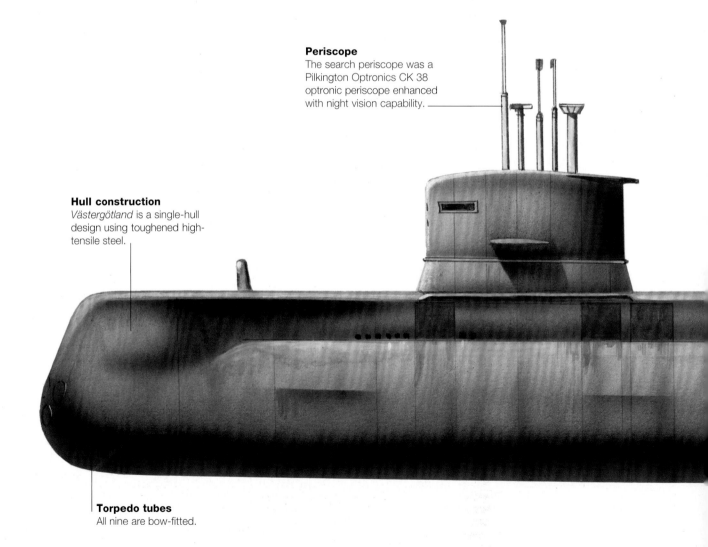

Torpedo tubes
All nine are bow-fitted.

periscope enhanced with night vision capability. They were assembled by Kockums at Malmö, who built the central section, while bow and stern sections came from Karlskronavarvet at Karlskrona. Operations in the shallow, acoustically tricky waters of the Baltic require special consideration of quietening features, and the boats are coated with an anechoic layer to reduce their reflection of active sonar pulses. The two-deck single-hull design features two watertight compartments divided by a central watertight bulkhead. The pressure hull is

of circular cross-section ending in truncated cones. Fore and aft the hull extends into ballast tanks. The forward compartment houses accommodation, stores, communications room and control room on the upper level. On the lower deck is weapons handling, with nine torpedo tubes: six of 533mm (21in) with 12 torpedoes, and three of 400mm (15.6in) with six weapons; the forward battery section and auxiliary machinery.

The torpedo tubes are located in the bow. All are used for wire-guided torpedoes, the larger-diameter tubes

Sweden retains its own submarine-building capacity and as part of a high-level technological package can offer an AIP (air-independent propulsion) system for sustained sub-surface operations.

Shallow water mobility
The X-formation stern control surfaces combine the functions of rudder and dive planes, assisting mobility in shallow waters and among reefs.

Sensor
The original sensor system was a CSU-92 integrated ASDIC suite.

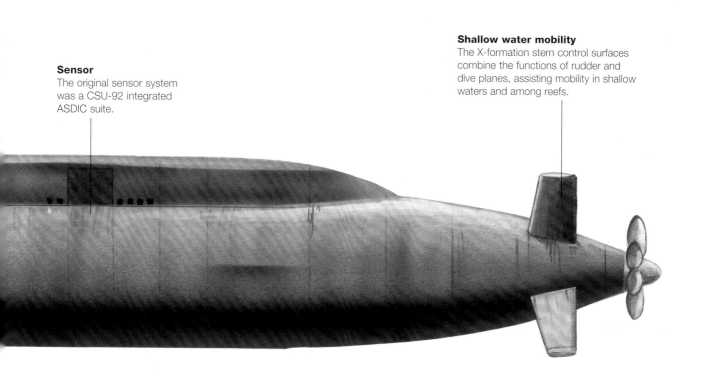

Västergötland

Västergötland at sea. The submarine is designed for a number of roles, including anti-submarine warfare and surveillance.

Specification

Dimensions:	Length: 48.5m (159ft 1in); Beam: 6.1m (20ft); Draught: 5.6m (18ft 4in)
Displacement:	Surfaced – 1087 tonnes (1070 tons); Submerged – 1161 tonnes (1143 tons)
Propulsion:	Diesel-electric, two Hedemora V12A/15 diesel engines, each 1300hp (968kW); one Jeumont-Schneider electric motor; single screw
Speed:	Surfaced – 11 knots (20.3km/h; 12.6mph); Submerged – 20 knots (37km/h; 23mph)
Range:	Undisclosed
Armament:	Six 533mm (21in) and three 400mm (15.6in) torpedo tubes; 18 torpedoes or 22 mines
Complement:	28

firing swim-out FFV Type 613 passive-homing anti-ship weapons carrying a 240kg (528lb) warhead to a range of 20km (12.4 miles) at 45 knots (83.3km/h; 51.7 mph), and the smaller-diameter tubes firing FFV Type 431/451 active/passive-homing antisubmarine weapons carrying a 45kg (99lb) warhead to a range of 20km (12.4 miles) at 25 knots (46.2km/h; 28.7mph). The Bofors Underwater Systems Type 613 torpedoes are fired from the 533mm tubes. The Type 613 is a heavyweight anti-surface ship torpedo with wire guidance and passive homing, delivering a warhead of 240kg (529lb). Launch is by swim-out discharge, the speed is 40 knots (74km/h; 46mph) and the range is also 20km (12.5 miles).

Refit and relaunch

The first two boats were retired early due to defence cuts, sold to Singapore in 2005 and refitted with AIP engines and climatization for service in high-salinity tropical waters before delivery as the Archer class. *Södermanland* and *Östergötland* were retained after undergoing a mid-life refit and are known as the Södermanland class. *Södermanland* began refit at Kockums in late 2000 and was relaunched on 8 September 2003 for six months of sea trials before returning to service in mid-2004. Improvements included installation of Air Independent Propulsion (Stirling Mk 3 AIP), requiring the insertion of a 12m (39ft 4in) section in the pressure hull; installation of a diver's pressurized lock-out in the base of the sail to facilitate special forces operations; and installation of a new climate control system incorporating cooling equipment featuring freon compressors. The climate control measures were intended to enable international operations in waters warmer than the Baltic Sea. Following a similar refit, *Östergötland* returned to service in 2005. As the Södermanland class, the boats were considered by experts at the time to be the quietest and most effective 'conventional' submarines in service anywhere. They continue to perform a variety of anti-invasion roles including attack, mining, surveillance, anti-submarine and placing of Special Forces.

Production and manufacturing politics

In 2011 Kockums, builder of Swedish submarines, was sold by the Swedish Government to the German Thyssen-Krupp Corporation. This deal later produced political, military and financial problems. ThyssenKrupp also own the Howaldtswerke (HdW) submarine builders in Germany and wished to rationalize production between their yards. This would have meant that Sweden's desired new A26 submarines would not be built in Sweden. In addition the Swedish government was unhappy over Singapore's purchase of two HdW Type 218SG submarines as successors to the Swedish-built Archer (ex-Västergötland) class. On 29 June 2014 it was announced that the Swedish company Saab had repurchased Kockums for $50.4 million, assuring a continuance of Sweden's home production of its own submarines and of its presence in the international marketplace.

Södermanland, refitted with AIP. The observation post on the sail offers minimal space forward of the thermal-imaging, non-hull penetrating periscope.

Immediately aft of the watertight bulkhead is a cylindrical tank section with a passage aft and an escape lock, which connects to a rescue vehicle or bell. The after section houses the electrical control centre with the aft battery section, diesel generators and propulsion motor on the deck below. Manoeuvrability is exercised through an X-configuration rudder/after hydroplane design. The refitted boats carry a comprehensive range of sensors, including periscopes, Terma radar, the American EDO RSS AR-700-S5 ESM and a wide range of ATLAS Elektronik sonars, including the CSU-83. Sonar arrays are mounted on and under the casing. The boats are equipped with an Ericsson IPS-17 weapons control system developed from the NIBS system fitted in the Näcken class (1978).

Sweden's two Södermanland class boats remain in service, based at the Karlskrona naval headquarters. Saab has a $1 billion contract for the construction of two new submarines, Type A 26, for delivery by 2022.

Zeeleeuw (1987)

As NATO allies, both the Americans and the British encouraged the Dutch government to build larger conventionally-powered submarines, filling a gap between the smaller boats being built in Germany and the large nuclear submarines.

The Royal Netherlands Navy possesses four submarines, all of the Walrus class. Developed by the Nederlandse Verenigde Scheepsbouw company and built by the Rotterdam Dry Dock company, this was a sophisticated submarine. *Zeeleeuw,* second boat of the class, was laid down on 24 September 1981, launched on 20 June 1987 and commissioned on 25 April 1990, earlier than *Walrus,* whose construction had been delayed by a fire.

The new submarines were required to carry out open-ocean missions, collect intelligence, conduct coastal reconnaissance, lay sea mines and put ashore Special Forces from the Netherlands Marine Corps. The design brief was a challenging one, including diving to 300m (980ft), a range of 10,000 nautical miles (18,520km; 11,507 miles), extreme quiet running, high manoeuvrability, a high level of automation to keep crew numbers down,

The Walrus class: compact but effective, with great attention paid to minimising detectability, and with a service life extended into the 2020s.

Sonar
A connection clip for a GEC Avionics Type 2026 towed sonar array can be attached to one of the upper fins of the X-rudder gear.

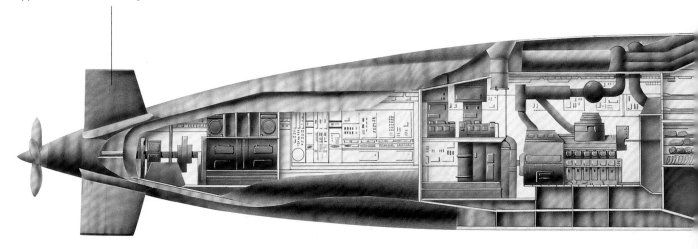

versatility in weapon capacity and sophisticated detection and fire control systems. Unusually, much of the design work was done without the use of computers.

The X-rudder configuration, combining rudders and diving planes, was decided on to maximize manoeuvring ability, and an advanced autopilot system was developed. French MAREI high-tensile steel was used in hull fabrication. The number of regulators and weld joints in the hull were also reduced to improve its pressure resistance at deep levels. Snorkel tubes were fitted, and in 1996 a new snort diffuser was fitted to *Zeeleeuw*'s sail, and subsequently to the others in the class. Problems arose with the inboard closing valves, intended to prevent water from entering the exhaust when the boat is submerged. For safety, both inboard and outboard valves were fitted, designed to withstand the full hydrostatic pressure at maximum diving depth. The closing valves showed signs of micro-fractures and all four boats were temporarily withdrawn from active service. *Zeeleeuw* resumed service with new valves in February 2001.

Howaldtswerke-Deutsche Werft, the German shipbuilding company, was contracted in June 2009 to install the second-generation Thyssen-Krupp tower escape system HABETaS in the Walrus class. It has been tested (unmanned) at depths up to 540m (1770ft). In a joint Dutch–

Snorkel
Original snorkel air-feed and exhaust system for the diesel motors. A new diffuser system was fitted in 1996, extending aft from the upper part of the sail.

HD optics
Under the sustainment scheme one periscope has been replaced by an L-3 KEO optronic mast, enabling high-definition footage to be collected in both daylight and night conditions.

Hull construction
The unusually shaped hull devolves from the experimental American submarine *Albacore* (1953) and is formed of high-tensile steel. Its anechoic properties have been improved in the sustainment scheme.

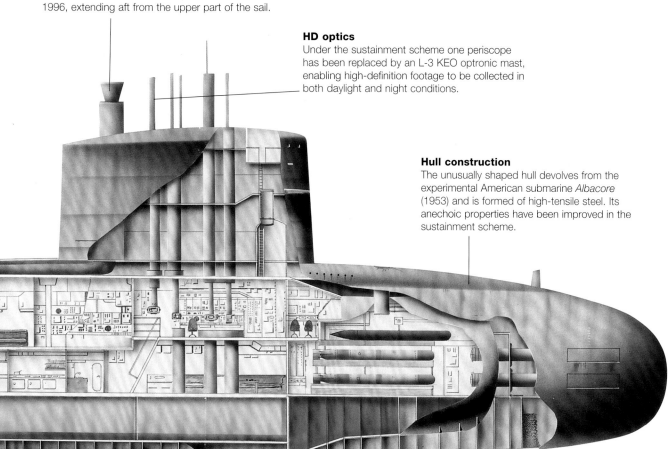

Norwegian exercise on 24 May 2012, 13 submariners and one civilian successfully exited from the submerged *Zeeleeuw* wearing Texcon Armadillo Submarine Emergency Escape Suits with air provided by the HABETaS air systems fitted to the boat.

The Dutch Navy began the Walrus-class sustainment programme in 2013, managed by Imtech Marine with the Nevesbu and Verebus companies to extend the service life of the class by 10 years. The programme will give the boats enhanced intelligence-gathering capabilities and the ability

A Walrus class submarine in the Firth of Clyde, Scotland, in 2011, in the course of a NATO exercise.

to meet modern ergonomic and technological requirements, although it does not include fitting of AIP engines. The refit involves a complete stripping-down for asbestos removal and the installation of new cabling and piping. Among the new equipment is a Mine & Obstacle Avoidance Sonar by ELAC Nautik, a new SHF (Super High Frequency) satellite communication system and a Kollmorgen Model 86 non-hull-penetrating optronic mast system, using television/ thermal cameras and processing features such as electronic zoom, with imagery displayed on multifunctional display screens.

Combat upgrade

A new Combat Management System incorporates multi-mission and multi-task consoles. Under the sustainment programme, the Mk 48 Mod 4 torpedo is replaced by the Mod 7, with improved sonar functions, and usable in both deep and shallow water. *Zeeleeuw* was first to undergo conversion and in refitted form was recommissioned on 3 December 2015. It is currently running evaluation trials prior to the programme being extended to the rest of the class. All the Walrus class are based at the Netherlands' main naval base, Den Helder, in North Holland province.

The Walrus class gained a high reputation following the NATO exercise JTFEX/TMDI99 in 1999, when *Walrus*

Specification

Dimensions:	Length: 67.5m (222ft); Beam: 8.4m (27ft 7in); Draught: 6.6m (21ft 8in)
Displacement:	Surfaced – 2490 tonnes (2450 tons); Submerged – 2800 tonnes (2775 tons)
Propulsion:	Three SEMT Pielstick 12PA4V200SM diesels, 1 Holec main-motor, 5430hp (4000kW); single screw
Speed:	Surfaced – 13 knots (24km/h; 14.9mph); Submerged – 20 knots (37km/h; 23mph)
Range:	10,000nm (18,520km; 11,507 miles) at 9 knots (16.6km/h; 10.3mph)
Armament:	Four 533mm (21in) torpedo tubes, 20 torpedoes or 40 mines
Complement:	49

This close-up shot shows the revised sail design of the Walrus-class submarine.

Lockheed Martin Mk 48

The torpedoes are the upgraded Mod 7 CBASS Mk 48, with a warhead of 290kg (638lb), developed in the USA by Lockheed Martin. This type can be used against both high-performance surface ships and fast deep-diving submarines, is capable of operating with or without wire guidance, and can use either or both active and passive homing. After launch the torpedo carries out target search, acquisition and attack procedures that are effective to a depth of 900m (3000ft), and is programmed with multiple re-attack modes that come on if the target vessel is missed. The Mk 48 has been tested successfully in extreme conditions, including under the Arctic icecap. Range is up to 50km (31 miles) at a speed of 40 knots (92.5km/h; 57.5mph). The boats can also be equipped with the McDonnell Douglas Sub-Harpoon surface-to-surface missile (SSM).

passed the US Navy screening vessels undetected and 'sank' numerous ships, including the nuclear-powered aircraft carrier *Theodore Roosevelt*. It was also reported that the Dutch submarine 'sank' the Los Angeles-class submarine USS *Boise* and other craft including the command ship USS *Mount Whitney*. The submarine then successfully made its escape.

Most of the Walrus deployments have been made under tight security, taking advantage of their stealth characteristics, but they are known to have been active in several ocean regions. Known operations of *Zeeleeuw* include intelligence-gathering in the Caribbean Sea for counter-narcotics operations (2006), and a three-month anti-piracy patrol off the East African coast in September–November 2010 as part of NATO's 'Ocean Shield' task-force.

Following reports that the Dutch government was considering a successor class to the Walrus boats, Saab-Kockums (Sweden) and Damen Schelde (Netherlands) announced in January 2015 that they were collaborating on plans to develop a new AIP-driven submarine to replace the Walrus class after 2015.

▮▮ Le Triomphant (1994)

In 1997 *Le Triomphant* entered service as the first of the French Navy's latest class of SSBN. Three more were commissioned between 2000 and 2010 and since then at least one has been permanently on patrol, armed with 16 M45 ballistic missiles.

First of a class planned to replace the previous *L'Inflexible* class SSBN, *Le Triomphant* was laid down at DCAN, Cherbourg, on 9 June 1989, launched on 26 March 1994 and commissioned on 21 March 1997. The hull is of smooth, streamlined design and formed of a special steel, 100 HLES (high weldable elastic limit – HY 130 in U.S. Standards), with a pressure resistance of 994 MPa (9268 tons/sq ft), developed by Creusot, Loire Industrie and DCAN Cherbourg, to maximize its performance in diving and depth manoeuvring. Operational depth is in

excess of 300m (984ft). It has a nuclear turbo-electric propulsion system based on a Type K15 pressure water reactor supplying 150MW, made by Areva-TA (formerly Technicatome). The auxiliary propulsion system is diesel-electric, with two SEMT-Pielstick 8 PA 4 v 200 SM diesels. A ducted pump-jet propulsion unit is fitted, produced by DCAN Indret and DCAN Cherbourg.

Each operated by two crews ('amber' and 'blue'), the four *Triomphant*-class boats form France's primary nuclear deterrent or second strike force. They were at first fitted

When built, Le Triomphant was the most expensive submarine ever, with a construction cost of 4.8 billion. Total cost of development and construction of the class of four vessels is estimated as close to 100 billion.

Power supply
Le Triomphant was the first submarine to be fitted with a ducted propulsor. The pump-jet system delivers 41,500hp (30,500kW).

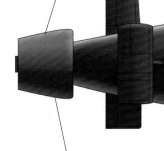

Propeller
The ducted pump-jet propeller reduces disturbance and allows the submarine to achieve a speed of 25 knots (46.2km/h; 28.7mph) underwater.

with 16 vertically launched M45 ballistic missiles supplied by EADS Space Transportation (formerly Aerospatiale), based at Les Mureaux, France. A changeover to the M51 version is due to be complete by 2018. The new missile, three-stage and solid-fuelled like its predecessor, weighs more than 50 tonnes (49 tons) and carries up to 12 independently targetable TN 75 thermonuclear warheads, using a navigation and guidance system developed by Safran Sagem. Its operational range is 8000–10,000km (5000–6200 miles). Following refit in 2016, *Le Triomphant* will be equipped with an upgraded version, the M51.2, which will be mated with a new warhead, the TNO (*Tête Nucléaire Océanique* or Oceanic Nuclear Warhead). With four 533mm (21in) torpedo tubes *Le Triomphant* has the capacity to carry a mixed load of 18 ECAN L5 Mod 3 active/passive homing torpedoes and Exocet missiles. The torpedo, armed with a 150kg (330lb) warhead, has

a range of over 9km (5.5 miles) at a speed of 35 knots (64.8km/h; 40.2mph).

Surveillance system

The electronic support system is supplied by Thales, based in Malakoff, France. DR 3000U is a radar warning receiver (French Navy designation ARUR-13) operating in D to K bands. The search radar operates at I-band, using a masthead antenna array with omnidirectional and monopulse directional antennas and a separate periscope warning antenna. This system provides direction finding with an accuracy greater than 1°. Also fitted to the class is the Thales Underwater Systems (formerly Thomson Marconi Sonar) DMUX 80 bow and flank array sonar suite, providing target ranging and interception capability. The DSUV-61 B low-frequency towed array sonar provides very long-range capability. The countermeasures system

Ballistic missiles
The submarine can fire 16 M51 SLBM missiles from launch tubes behind the conning tower.

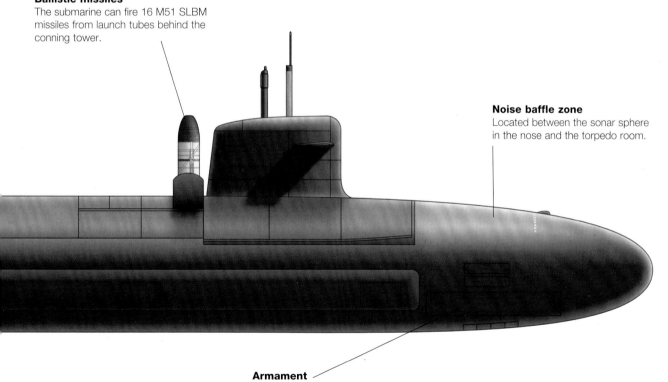

Noise baffle zone
Located between the sonar sphere in the nose and the torpedo room.

Armament
The F21 heavyweight torpedo from DCNS is a dual-purpose anti-ship and anti-submarine weapon. Weighing 1.3 tonnes (1.4 tons), it can be launched in swim-out or push-out modes. It incorporates a new-generation acoustic head from Thales Underwater Systems, in addition to an impact/acoustic fuse warhead. Operational depth is from 10m (33ft) to 500m (1640ft). It has electric propulsion based on a silver oxide-aluminium (AgO-Al) primary battery, with a speed of up to 50 knots (92.5km/h; 57.5mph), a range of over 50km (31 miles) and endurance of one hour.

Le Triomphant

Le Triomphant entering the port of Cherbourg, the location of the Cherbourg Naval Base.

Specification

Dimensions:	Length: 138m (453ft); Beam: 17m (55ft 9in); Draught: 12.5m (41ft)
Displacement:	Surfaced – 12,842 tonnes (12,640 tons); Submerged – 14,565 tonnes (14,335 tons)
Propulsion:	One Type K15 pressurized water reactor supplying 201,150hp (150MW), turbo electric drive; pump-jet propulsor; two SEMT-Pielstick 8 PA 4 v 200 SM diesel auxiliaries.
Speed:	Surfaced – 20 knots (37km/h; 23mph); Submerged – 25 knots (46.2km/h; 28.7mph)
Range:	Unlimited
Armament:	16 M45/TN75 SLBM; four 533mm (21in) torpedo tubes
Complement:	111

is Thomson-CSF ARUR 13/DR 3000U, for interception of incoming missiles, and weapons control is SAD (*Système d'Armes de Dissuasion*) data system (for SLBMs), SAT (*Système d'Armes Tactiques*) and DLA 4A (for anti-ship missiles and torpedoes).

Patrol duties

Operation of France's *Force Océanique Stratégique* (FOST) requires two boats to be on patrol at any time, although on occasions it may be only a single one. Their homeport is at the L'Ile Longue submarine base, located south of Brest harbour. Although major refits are performed at the port of Brest, the base provides support, logistical supply and reconditioning material for the submarines, including the loading and unloading of strategic missiles as well as transfer of fuel components for their nuclear reactors and spare parts for propulsion systems. Each submarine undergoes a routine maintenance period of 40 days at L'Ile Longue after returning from patrol.

In early February 2009 *Le Triomphant* had a glancing collision, underwater in mid-Atlantic, with the British SSGN HMS *Vanguard*. Both submarines were carrying nuclear

Exocet SM39

The Exocet SM39 is deployable in all weather conditions. Target range and bearing data is downloaded from the submarine's SAT tactical data system and the DLA 4A weapon control system into the missile's computer. The missile in its launch capsule is fired from the submarine's torpedo tubes using a gas generator. The launch capsule is propelled away from the submarine and clear of the surface of the sea by a solid propellant motor, then the missile separates from the capsule and the boost motor is ignited. It approaches the target area at speeds over Mach 0.9 in sea-skimming mode using inertial navigation and then active radar homing. Effective range is 50km (31 miles). The Exocet's 165kg (363lb) high-explosive shaped-charge warhead is armed with a delayed impact fuse and a proximity fuse.

Le Triomphant, with crew in protective clothing at work on the open deck.

weapons and both received significant damage (to the sonar dome, the sail and the starboard bow diving plane in the case of *Le Triomphant*), but carried on underwater to their home bases. From March 2013 to March 2015 *Le Triomphant* was in dry dock at Brest, being refitted for the M-51 SLBM, the SYCOBS (*SYstème de COmbat commun Barracuda SNLE*) combat system shared with France's new generation of Barracuda class attack submarines, and including the DCNS F21 new generation heavyweight torpedoes. While at the Ile Longue submarine base for refuelling of the reactor core, a fire broke out in the reactor compartment in November 2015, retarding the boat's return to active service, which is not now expected to be until 2017. The service horizon of the *Triomphant* class extends to 2037, and the French government commissioned preliminary studies for a replacement type in 2012.

Kursk (1994)

Kursk (K-141) was one of the Oscar II class, the largest attack submarines yet built. It was the first Russian nuclear submarine to be completed after the break-up of the Soviet Union in 1990.

Known to the Russians as Project 949 (Granit), the Oscar I class of cruise missile submarine was planned in the early 1970s and its design was produced by the Rubin Design Bureau. The first of two was commissioned in 1981. They were designed to attack NATO carrier battle groups using long-range P-700 (SS-N-19 'Shipwreck') anti-ship missiles, with targeting data provided by the EORSAT satellite system. By 1981 an updated version, Project 949A (Antey) was already in progress. Built between 1985 and 1996, known to NATO as Oscar II, they are quietened and enlarged versions of the Oscar I. As standard with Soviet nuclear submarines, they have double hulls, the outer hydrodynamic one having a weak magnetic signature that prevents detection by Magnetic Anomaly Detection (MAD) systems. A 20.3mm (0.8in) rubber layer between the hulls further helps to reduce detectability, while significant reserve

buoyancy and improved survivability against conventional torpedoes are provided by the 3.5m (11ft 6in) separation between the inner and outer hulls.

Icebreaker

The elongated sail has a reinforced rounded cover for icebreaking and houses multiple retractable masts, including radio-sextant and radar masts in addition to two periscopes, with an open bridge as well as an enclosed bridge station beneath it. The HF and UHF radio-masts, radio direction-finder masts and satellite communication and navigation masts are located on the airshaft that feeds the compressors. Missiles are launched from a submerged position, from tubes fixed at an angle of approximately 40°. The tubes, arranged in two rows of 12, are capped by six hatches on each side

Stern compartment
The survivors of the explosion gathered here, close to the aft escape hatch.

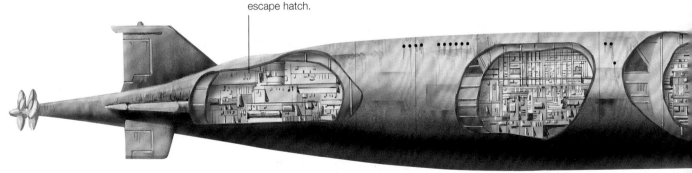

This illustration shows a cutaway
view of the *Kursk* (Oscar II).

of the sail, with each hatch covering a pair of tubes. The launchers are placed between the two hulls. A floating antenna buoy could be sent to the surface to receive radio messages, target designation data and satellite navigation signals at a great depth. The bow horizontal hydroplanes can retract into the hull. The Oscars' pressure hull is divided into 10 major compartments, inside which the main mechanisms have modular design and are insulated by a two-cascade shock-absorbing system. The twin reactors, with an estimated output of 100,000hp (74.5MW) were the most powerful yet

installed in submarines, driving steam turbines and twin propellers.

As attack submarines, these are the largest to be built (only the Typhoon and Ohio missile boats are bigger) and it is notable that construction went on after the collapse of the Soviet Union – a tribute to their general reliability as well as their versatility in uses ranging from shadowing carrier battle groups to attack on coastal and inland targets. From their introduction the principal task of both Oscar types has been to serve as an element of Russia's 'outer layer' defence against American carrier strike groups. The Oscar II

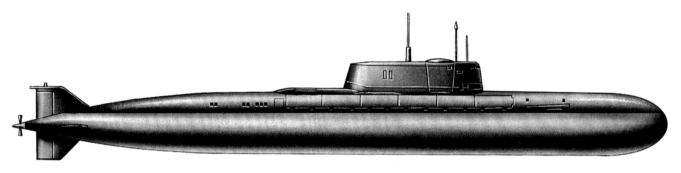

Oscar I profile. Note the closed covers of the missile silos.

Emergency exit
Separable escape module in the sail. This could not be used after the explosion.

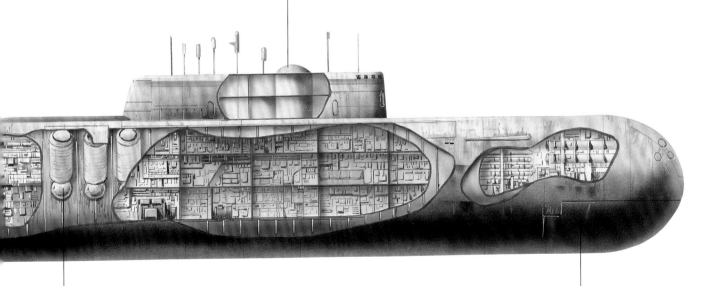

Missile silos
The *Kursk* carries 24 P-700 3M45 missiles.

Torpedo room
This is where the fatal explosion happened on the *Kursk*.

Kursk

Kursk moored at Vidyaevo (Ara Bay) submarine base in May 2000, three months before the disaster.

Specification

Dimensions:	Length: 154m (505ft 2in); Beam: 18.2m (60ft); Draught: 9m (29ft 6in)
Displacement (minimum):	
	Surfaced – 13,600 tonnes (13,400 tons); Submerged – 18,300 tonnes (18,000 tons)
Propulsion:	Two OK-650b reactors, 509,580hp (380MW), steam turbines 100,000hp (7.4MW), two screws
Speed:	Surfaced – 16 knots (29.6km/h; 18.4mph); Submerged – 32 knots (59.2km/h; 36.8mph)
Range:	Unlimited
Armament:	Two 650mm (25.4in) and four 533mm (21in) launch tubes; 24 P-700 3M45 missiles, 24 torpedoes
Complement:	118

submarine was equipped with 24 P-700 3M45 Granit (SS-N-19) cruise missiles with a range of 550km (340 miles). The torpedo tubes fire both torpedoes and shorter range anti-ship missiles, and a combination of some two dozen weapons was carried including the RPK-7 Vodopei (SS-N-16) missile, with a range of 50km (31 miles) powered by a liquid fuel turbojet engine. It can carry either an explosive warhead or a Type 40 torpedo.

K-141 *Kursk* was commissioned on 30 December 1994 and deployed with the Northern Fleet. The Oscar II boats were considered to be highly capable and reliable and the abrupt sinking of *Kursk* during exercises in the Barents Sea on 12 October 2000 was at first attributed to an undersea collision. A violent explosion, equivalent to 4.5 on the Richter scale, was recorded on Norwegian seismographs. Immediate rescue attempts, soon aided by Norway and Britain, were frustrated by surface storms and poor underwater visibility. In total, 23 crewmembers survived the initial event and took refuge in the stern compartment, but attempts to pump oxygen into the hull were unsuccessful and robot vehicles failed to access the emergency hatch in time to rescue them. All 118 persons on board ultimately perished.

In October 2001 the wrecked submarine was raised in a salvage operation carried out by two specialist Dutch companies, Mammoet Worldwide and Smit International, and towed to the naval shipyard in Murmansk. The forward weapons compartment was cut out prior to lifting and other sections were later lifted in May 2002. Wreckage remaining on the seabed was blown up. The nuclear reactors and Granit cruise missiles were all recovered. The cause of the disaster was revealed as the explosion of a Type 65 high test peroxide (HTP) torpedo, triggering another explosion in the weapons compartment, rupturing the hull from bow to sail and causing the vessel to sink. The blast was caused by a leakage of the highly volatile torpedo propellant that

Oscar II-class K-119 *Voronezh* was commissioned in 1989. Following a major refit completed in 2011, it remains in service.

then came in contact with kerosene and metal. Although *Kursk*, in common with other Oscar II boats, had an emergency crew escape capsule located in the sail, the extent of the damage made it impossible to activate.

Extended service life

The Russian Northern Fleet's principal base is at Severomorsk, at the top of the Kola Peninsula near Murmansk, with additional homeports at Kola, Motovskiy, Gremikha and Ura-Guba. In 2014 a former base in the New Siberian Islands was reopened. As of late 2015, at least three Oscar II submarines are understood to be receiving major modernization, including new missiles and new weapon systems. The goal is to extend the boats' service life by 20 years and to bring them up to the technological level of Russia's most modern nuclear-powered undersea vessels. Along with improved acoustic, electronic, navigation and communications systems, Project 949AM submarines are understood to be receiving NPO Mashinostroyeniya 3M55 Oniks (SS-N-26 'Strobile') anti-ship cruise missiles to replace their P-700 3M45 Granit missiles.

SS-N-19 Granit

The SS-N-19 Granit missile has a length of 10.5m (34ft 6in) and weighs 6.9 tonnes (6.8 tons) with a warhead weighing 1000kg (2200lb). Its speed is Mach 1.5. Under the START treaty, nuclear warheads for these missiles have been replaced with high explosive warheads. The missiles, which are launched while the submarine is submerged, are fired from tubes fixed at an angle of approximately 40°. The tubes, arranged in two rows of 12, are each covered by six hatches on each side of the sail, with each hatch covering a pair of tubes. The launchers are placed between the inner pressure hull and the outer hydrodynamic hull.

Accounts of the Oscar IIs' displacement vary and no official figures have been published. Surfaced displacement is between 13,600 tonnes (13,400 tons) and 14,900 tonnes (14,700 tons); submerged displacement is between 18,300 tonnes (18,000 tons) and 24,400 tonnes (24,000 tons).

USS Seawolf (1995)

The culmination of the USA's Cold War attack submarine designs, the Seawolf class was intended to replace the Los Angeles class and to restore US dominance over Russia's new generation of fast stealth submarines. But in changing circumstances, only three were built.

Although it naturally owed much to previous experience, the Seawolf class was the first completely new American submarine design for 30 years. The class leader, USS *Seawolf* (SSN-21) was ordered from the Electric Boat Division of General Dynamics at Groton, Connecticut, in January 1989 and commissioned in July 1997. The second,

Connecticut (SSN-22), was commissioned in December 1998. The Americans had been greatly impressed by the qualities of Russia's Victor and Typhoon classes and the Seawolf project was set up to ensure that the USA continued to have the most effective pursuit and attack submarine type, capable of seeking out and destroying any

Periscopes
Type 6J MOO 3 and Type
18H MOO 1 are fitted.

Boat electronics
The state-of-the-art electronic system features a BSY-2 sonar suite with an active or passive sonar array and a wide-aperture passive flank array. TB-16 and TB-29 surveillance and tactical towed arrays are also fitted. A BPS-16 navigation radar and Raytheon Mk II weapons control system are fitted, and the countermeasures suite includes the Wly-1 advanced torpedo decoy system.

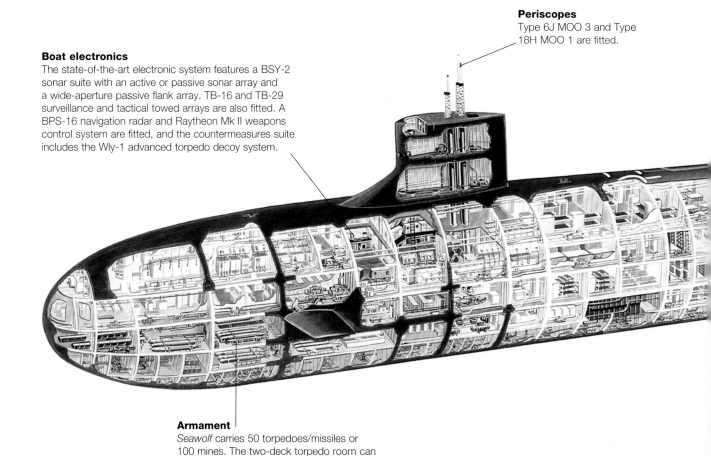

Armament
Seawolf carries 50 torpedoes/missiles or 100 mines. The two-deck torpedo room can engage multiple targets simultaneously through the Raytheon Mk II fire control system.

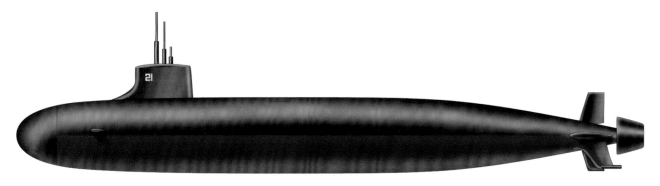

rival ballistic missile boat. Initially 12 were planned, but only three were built before acceptance of changed strategic requirements ended the programme. *Seawolf* is essentially a craft for the open ocean, but with the switch of strategic focus from superpower standoff to regional hotspots around the world, a large fleet of this class would be less effective. In addition, the cost of construction was seen as

USS Seawolf in profile. The anechoic hull covering is not formed of tiles, but is applied as a single overall coating.

Swimmer silo
There is a built-in combat swimmer silo: an internal lock-out chamber that can deploy up to eight combat swimmers and their equipment at one time.

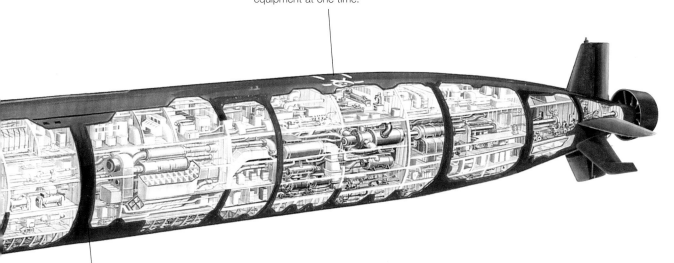

Hull construction
HY-100 steel has a tensile yield strength of 690 MPa (6433 tons/sq ft). Construction of *Seawolf* was dogged by problems of weld cracking and an estimated two years' work on hull construction had to be abandoned until a technical solution was reached.

The Seawolf-class submarines cost around $3 billion each. Only the French Le Triomphant class cost more (though figures for Russian submarines are not published).

USS Seawolf

USS Jimmy Carter (SSN-23) in the Magnetic Silencing Facility at Naval Base Kitsap, Bangor, for a "deperming" treatment, in August 2006.

Specification

Dimensions:	Length: 107m (351ft); Beam: 12m (40ft); Draught: 10.9m (35ft 9in)
Displacement:	Surfaced – 8738 tonnes (8600 tons); Submerged – 9285 tonnes (9138 tons)
Propulsion:	One GE S6W pressurized water reactor, two turbines rated at 52,000hp (38.8MW); one Improved Performance Machinery Program Phase II secondary propulsion motor; propulsor
Speed:	Surfaced – 18 knots (33.3km/h; 20.7mph); Submerged – 35 knots (64.8km/h; 40.2mph)
Range:	Unlimited
Armament:	Eight 660mm (25.9in) launch tubes for Mk 48 torpedoes, Tomahawk or Sub-Harpoon missiles; 50 torpedoes
Complement:	140

unsupportable even for the United States. The cost of the Seawolf class in 1991 was estimated at $33.6 billion (25 per cent of the naval construction budget), making it the most expensive naval building programme ever.

Seawolf is nevertheless a very advanced boat with many features that make it a formidable element in the US ocean armoury, designed for battlespace-preparation roles as well as hunting and surveillance. Its array of sophisticated electronics produces enhanced indications and warning, surveillance and communications capabilities. These platforms are capable of integrating into a battle group's infrastructure or of shifting into a land-battle support role.

New welding materials were used to join the hull subsections and the class are the first attack submarines formed of HY-100 steel rather than the HY-80 used for previous boats. (HY-100 was used in experimental deep-diving submarines during the 1960s.) While the diving depth has been confirmed only as greater than 240m (800ft), it is likely that the craft can operate at double that depth. Powered by a GE PWR S6W reactor and two turbines, it has a pump-jet propulsor and a secondary propulsion submerged motor.

The eight 660mm (25.9in) tubes enable silent 'swimout' launches of Mk 48 torpedoes, but also launch a variety of other missiles including Sub-Harpoon anti-ship missiles and Tomahawk land attack cruise missiles with a range of 1700km (1050 miles), as well as remotely-controlled vehicles. A mix of 50 torpedoes, Sub Harpoons and Tomahawks can be carried. Combat data system, fire control, countermeasures and sonar equipment, all fully up-to-date when *Seawolf* was commissioned in 1997, have been upgraded.

Multi-Mission Platform

The third class member, USS *Jimmy Carter* (SSN23), was laid down at the Electric Boat Yard on 5 December 1998. On 10 December 1999, Electric Boat was awarded an $887 million contract extension to modify the vessel. Commissioned in 2005, it differs from the other two Seawolf class as a result of these modifications. A 30m-(98ft) long hull extension gives *Jimmy Carter* a length only second to the Ohio class in the US Navy submarine fleet. This Multi-Mission Platform extension has been described as a 'moon bay' with an hourglass shaped passage running down the centre. Installed for seabed and Special Forces operations, it has an ocean interface that allows for the operation of a Remotely Operated Vehicle, able to retrieve and deploy weapons, countermeasures and

sensors. Among many other functions, this allows for tapping into seabed fibre-optic cables. SEAL forces can also use the platform for special operations. In 2006 *Jimmy Carter* underwent a 'deperm' in the Magnetic Silencing Facility at Naval Base Kitsap-Bangor: a process that reduces a submarine's electromagnetic signature as it travels through the water. In 2010–12 it went through a major refurbishment. The activities of SSN23 are naturally classified. Between March 2012 and mid-2015 it was reported to have completed five missions vital to national security. The boat earned the Battle Efficiency Award, or Battle 'E', for 2012 and 2013, and won the US Submarine Forces Pacific Retention Excellence Award for 2012 and 2014, while its crew was awarded the Presidential Unit Commendation and the Navy Unit Commendation.

All three remain in service in 2016, with USS *Jimmy Carter* at Naval Base Kitsap, Bangor, and *Seawolf* and *Connecticut* at Bremerton.

In August 2015 *Seawolf* returned from a six-month tour of duty in the Arctic region to undergo a refit at its home base of Bremerton, Washington. New sonar and combat control systems will be installed before it returns to active service in 2018. The life of the class is likely to extend well into the 2030s.

Water propulsion

The pumpjet is a propulsor that was first used on torpedoes and light surface craft, and adapted for submarines – including the UK's Trafalgar-class SSN and the USA's Seawolf SSNs. It is formed by a water intake that is passed through a pump and expelled at high pressure to move the boat forwards. Although a reversing arrangement can be fitted to deflect the flow, pump jet submarines have little reversing power. The pumpjet on Seawolf is both quieter and more efficient than an open propeller, although a propeller might achieve an extra couple of knots. Most submarines need to keep their speed down to as little as 5 knots (9.2km/h; 5.7mph) to avoid detection by passive sonar arrays, while the Seawolf class are credited with being able to cruise at 20 knots (37km/h; 23mph) and still be impossible to locate.

USS *Seawolf* on pre-commissioning sea trials in Narragansett Bay, 3 July 1996.

Type 039 (Song) (1999)

Given the reporting name of Song by NATO, the Type 039 – an ocean-going multi-role SSK – is the first submarine to have been completely designed, built and fitted out in China.

The Type 039 or Song Class attack submarine was built by Wuhan Shipyard (Wuchang Shipyard) for the People's Liberation Army Navy (PLAN) of China. It was the first indigenously built submarine of China. The class is preceded by Type 035 (Ming) and succeeded by Type 041 (Yuan) submarines. The Ming class had been based on the Russian Romeo class, and the Song class shows resemblance to the Russian Kilo class diesel-electric submarine that also features the teardrop shape, a double hull with a T-shaped stern rudder and a single large

Sail
The original Type 039 boat had a stepped sail. On Type 039G the sail is teardrop shaped, narrowing sharply to the rear. Its top deck is open.

Armament
The 039 class are currently equipped with YJ-82 cruise missiles for underwater launching. The YJ-82 is a highly effective surface skimmer with a 120km (75 mile) range, and a warhead of 165kg (363lb). There are six 533mm (21in) bow torpedo tubes for torpedoes and anti-ship missiles, including Yu-3 acoustic-homing anti-submarine torpedoes and Yu-4 passive acoustic-homing anti-ship torpedoes. Yu-4 has a speed of 30 knots (55.5km/h; 34.5mph) and a range of 6km (3.7 miles). The submarine can alternatively carry 24 to 36 tube-launched naval mines.

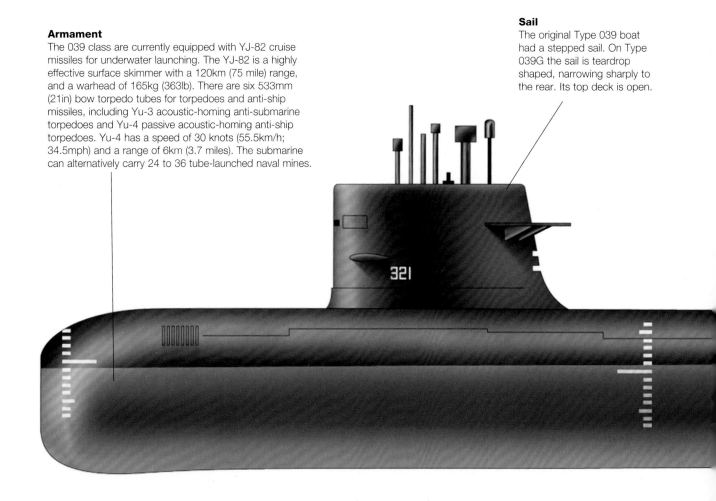

propeller. The keel of the class leader, No. 320, was laid down in 1991. It was launched in May 1994, but was not commissioned until June 1999 due to numerous design and performance problems. Following extensive redesign work after trials of the first vessel, a modified version known as Type 039G was introduced.

The first Type 039G, No. 321, was launched in November 1999 and commissioned in April 2001. This boat is characterized most obviously by a sail without the stepped-down forward section that in No. 320 accommodates the bridge with the forward hydroplanes under it. The new design reduced the acoustic signature and improved the underwater performance of the submarine. Estimated diving depth is 300m (980ft). Construction of a further modified version, Type 039G1,

commenced at Wuchang and Jiangnan Shipyards in 2004, although the alterations are minor. A series of 12 submarines were built at the two shipyards.

Type 039 is the first Chinese submarine built to a teardrop hull design. The body is water-drop shaped and the hull is covered with rubber tiles to absorb active sonar sound waves. The Type 039 is equipped with a diesel-electric propulsion system. Four German MTU 16V 396SE84 diesel engines, mounted on a shock-absorbing base, drive a single large asymmetrical seven-bladed skewed propeller – the first to be fitted on a Chinese submarine – via an electric motor. The submarine is equipped with four alternators. All primary machinery is located on shock-absorbent mountings for reduced vibration and minimized underwater noise radiation.

Song class in profile. It replicates many advanced features found on other diesel-electric drive submarines of the 1990s and has comparable performance.

Sonar
To enhance passive search capabilities, a low frequency sonar of French Thomson-CSF TSM-2255 design is mounted on the flanks. Its maximum range is in excess of 30km (18.6 miles) and it can simultaneously track four targets.

Skew propeller
The propeller is designed to minimize pressure fluctuations on the blade to reduce cavitation (the formation of bubbles and consequent noise).

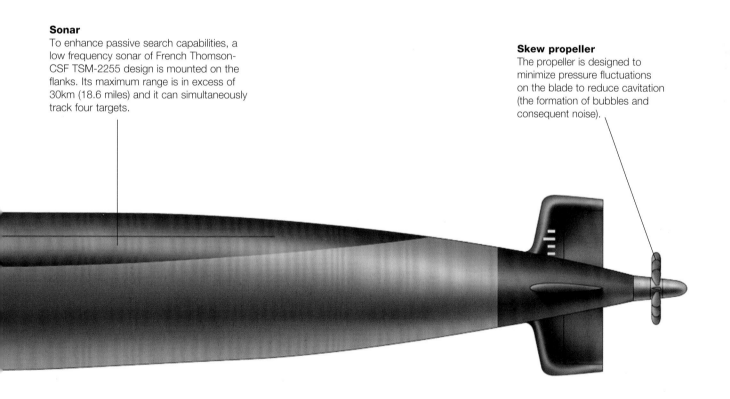

Type 039 (Song)

Crewmen pose on the deck of a Song submarine, at an unidentified location.

Specification

Dimensions:	Length: 74.9m (245ft 8in); Beam: 8.4m (27ft 6in); Draught: 5.3m (17ft 4in)
Displacement:	Surfaced – 1700 tonnes (1673 tons); Submerged – 2286 tonnes (2250 tons)
Propulsion:	Four MTU 16V 396S E84 diesels, 24,360hp (18,148kW); single screw
Speed:	Surfaced – 15 knots (27.7km/h; 17.2mph); Submerged – 22 knots (40.7km/h; 25.3mph)
Range:	Undisclosed
Armament:	Six 533mm (21in) torpedo tubes, 18 torpedoes/missiles or 24–36 mines
Complement:	60

The stealth aspect of the design is further enhanced by the use of anechoic tiling similar to that on the Russian Kilo-class diesel-electric submarines, of which China acquired 12 between 1994 and 2006.

A multi-role combat and command system provides all the data needed for control of the boat and for the firing of torpedoes and missiles. This is likely to be an updated derivative of the combat/command system used in the Ming-class submarines. The integrated sonar system comprises an active/passive medium-frequency spherical bow-mounted equipment and passive low-frequency reach arrays. It is not believed to have a countermeasures suite beyond the Type 921-A radar warning receiver and directional finder.

Six 533mm (21in) bow torpedo tubes are fitted for torpedoes and anti-ship missiles. These tubes can launch Yu-3 acoustic-homing anti-submarine torpedoes and Yu-4 passive acoustic-homing anti-ship torpedoes. Yu-4 has a speed of 30 knots (55.5km/h; 34.5mph) and a range of 6km (3.7 miles). The submarine can also carry 24 to 36 tube-launched naval mines in place of torpedoes.

Type 039 is also armed with the Yingji YJ-82 anti-ship cruise missile launched from the torpedo tubes, reaching a speed of Mach 0.9 and able to strike surface vessels within a range of 80km (50 miles). It carries a 165kg (363lb) warhead.

Territorial mission

Around 13 Song boats are in service, forming the basis of Beijing's modern conventional fleet, along with the 039A or Yuan class currently under development. Their prime use is likely to be in maintaining Chinese claims to islands like the Spratly group in the South China Sea, patrolling territorial waters and monitoring the American observation-ships stationed just off China's territorial limits. The class has more than once proved an embarrassment to the US Navy by its ability to shadow surface vessels without being detected. On 26 October one of the class shadowed the carrier *Kitty Hawk* (CV-63) in the East China Sea, undetected until it surfaced about 5 nautical miles (9km; 5.7 miles) away. In other deployments, a Song-class submarine was engaged with surface ships in anti-piracy patrol off the north-east African coast in September 2014. In October 2014, a member of the class visited Colombo, Sri Lanka, docking at a harbour controlled by a Chinese company. It was escorted by a tender ship, an essential accompaniment for conventional submarines of limited endurance. According to unconfirmed US reports, a Song-class boat may have made a simulated cruise missile attack on the USS *Ronald Reagan* (CVN-76) in the Sea of Japan in late October 2015.

The Song class is no longer in production, superseded by the Type 039A Yuan class, but all 13 remain in active service as of January 2016.

Electronic warfare suite

The submarine is fitted with SRW209 electronic warfare suite comprising electronic support measures, a radar warning receiver and a radio direction finder. The system is fully automatic and manually operated. It operates on S-Ku bands and can be linked with the combat data system. The underwater sensor suite consists of a medium-frequency active/passive bow array, a passive interception and ranging array and two passive flank arrays. The bow-mounted sonar can track up to 12 targets simultaneously, while flank-mounted low-frequency tracks four targets simultaneously to a maximum range of 30km (18.6 miles). The sonar array also performs underwater communication and torpedo approach warning functions. An I-band radar is also fitted for surface search missions.

Song-class submarines advancing in line abreast, in a photo intended to display Chinese naval power.

Dolphin Class (1999)

Israel's Type 800 or Dolphin class submarine is based on the German Type 209, but modified to such an extent that it is really a class in its own right. Further development has produced the larger, AIP-fitted Dolphin II type.

The first of six boats, *Dolphin* was commissioned in 1999 and two more were in service by 2000. These are Dolphin I. A further three, of which two are delivered with a third under construction, are equipped with AIP and known as Dolphin II. With considerable input from the Israeli Navy, the boats were designed by Ingenieurkontor Lübeck Prof Gabler Nachf GmbH (IKL), and all are built by the Howaldtswerke-Deutsche Werft shipyard in Kiel, Germany. The basic design owes much to the German Type 209 submarine, and the second trio have benefited from new automation systems developed for HdW's Type 212, but their increased size and numerous specialized features, some installed in Israel, make the Dolphins effectively a class on their own.

The boats are single-hulled and formed of HY-80 steel, and internal layout is conventional for an up-to-date multi-role submarine, with all torpedo tubes mounted in the bow, in addition to a cylindrical sonar array, and weapons storage immediately aft of a double bulkhead, with crew accommodation on the level above. Command and control rooms are beneath the sail, followed by engine compartments. Two escape towers as well as loading hatches are fitted, and underwater swimmers can be deployed from a wet-and-dry compartment. Modular arrangement of spaces for electronic equipment ensures rapid replacement. The framework supporting the diesel generator and auxiliary equipment such as hydraulic

Fixed planes
Smaller horizontal fixed planes are placed each side of the screw on the Dolphin IIs, to allow for trailing wires or sonar arrays.

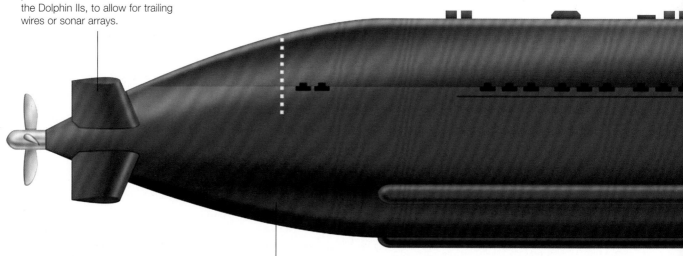

Power supply
The submarine is powered by three 16V 396 SE 84 diesel engines developing 4180hp (3.12MW) sustained power, from MTU (*Motoren und Turbinen Union*) of Munich. There are three 750kW alternators, and a 3822hp (2.85MW) sustained power motor supplied by Siemens.

pumps and compressors is enclosed in a sound absorbent capsule and isolated from the pressure hull. Both sub-classes are powered by three diesel generators driving a single electric motor and propeller. On the Dolphin II boats, a Siemens air-independent propulsion system operates through polymer electrolyte membrane (PEM) fuel cells that combine oxygen and hydrogen to make electricity. Two 120kW modules provide enough power for the submarine to remain underwater without surfacing for potentially weeks at a time. The system works without atmospheric air and is completely exhaust-free, its by-products being only water and heat, although heat emission from the modules, which have an operating temperature of around 80°C, is very low. The system's noise signature lies well under all threshold values. The electrochemical operation of the fuel cells is silent, and the ancillary units are optimized for low noise or incorporated into the sound encapsulation areas.

Based on a German design, constructed in Germany, but with substantial hi-tech instrumentation installed in Israel, the Dolphin-class vessels operate as multi-function submarines, making regular patrols and engaging in special missions.

Periscopes
Search and attack periscopes are supplied by Kollmorgen. The search one is a special development for the Israeli Navy, equipped with infra-red capabilities, ESM (electronic support measures) directional antenna, optic, video and communication antenna.

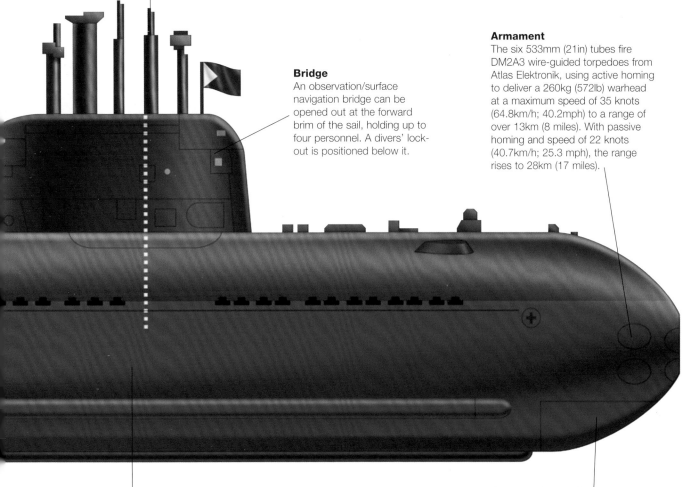

Bridge
An observation/surface navigation bridge can be opened out at the forward brim of the sail, holding up to four personnel. A divers' lock-out is positioned below it.

Armament
The six 533mm (21in) tubes fire DM2A3 wire-guided torpedoes from Atlas Elektronik, using active homing to deliver a 260kg (572lb) warhead at a maximum speed of 35 knots (64.8km/h; 40.2mph) to a range of over 13km (8 miles). With passive homing and speed of 22 knots (40.7km/h; 25.3 mph), the range rises to 28km (17 miles).

Hull
The hull is rated for a diving depth of 350m (1150ft). Underwater endurance is 30 days or more.

Beam and draught
The profile shows Dolphin I. Dolphin II, although 11.6m (38ft) longer, is of the same beam and draught, with a very similar outline.

Dolphin Class

A view of INS *Dolphin* from astern, on its maiden voyage from Kiel to Haifa in May 1998.

Specification

Dimensions:	Length: 68.6m (225ft); Beam: 6.8m (22ft 3in); Draught: 6.2m (20ft 4in)
Displacement:	Surfaced – 2083 tonnes (2050 tons); Submerged – 2438 tonnes (2400 tons)
Propulsion:	Diesel-electric, three V16 396 SE 84 MTU diesel engines, 4180hp (3.12MW), three Siemens (750kW) alternators, one Siemens 3822hp (2.85MW) sustained power motor; HdW/Siemens Air Independent Propulsion system, 402hp (300kW), single screw
Speed:	Surfaced – undisclosed; Submerged – 20 knots (37km/h; 23mph); Snorkelling 11 knots (20.3km/h; 12.6mph)
Range:	surfaced – 8000nm (14,816km; 9206 miles) at 8 knots (14.8km/h; 9.2mph)
Armament:	Four 650mm (25.5in), six 533mm (21in) launch tubes; torpedoes, Harpoon and Triton missiles, mines
Complement:	35

Patrol, surveillance, interception, attack, special operations and minelaying are all regular roles for the submarines in co-operation with IAF, the IDF Intelligence Directorate, Israel's Mossad Agency and IDF special operations units. Two Kollmorgen periscopes are installed, both reaching through the hull to the control station. The sonar system consists of Low Frequency Sonar (LOFAR) with the FAS-3 passive search flank array mounted on the hull on both sides. A bow-mounted cylindrical array complements acoustic detection in medium frequencies and ranges. The Atlas Elektronik Passive Ranging Sonar (PRS-3), consisting of three antennas on each side of the submarine casing, helps to allocate targets in the medium and short ranges. The Intercept Antenna (IA), installed on the casing, detects and analyzes any kind of acoustic transmission to give sufficient alert on threats that might endanger the vessel. Dolphin II boats' sonar suite includes the CSU 90 hull-mounted passive and active search and attack radar supplied by Atlas Elektronik. The submarines' radar warning receiver is the Israeli 4CH(V)2 Timnex electronic support measures system developed by Elbit in Haifa. It receives, identifies, displays and records the radar signal parameters, its system operating over 2GHz to 18GHz frequency bands, while the processor operates at rates up to one million pulses a second.

Each boat carries 16 STN Atlas fibre optic cable guided DM-2A4 torpedoes. The weapons may be swim-out or

A dismountable railing surrounds the sail top for an inspection visit to INS *Dolphin* at its Haifa base by senior officers on 24 November 2013.

Israeli nuclear capability

It is generally assumed, although unconfirmed officially, that Israel possesses nuclear weapons, including tactical warheads that can be fitted to submarine-fired missiles. It seems possible that the 650mm (25.5in) tubes might have been designed to accommodate Israeli-built long-range cruise missiles (SLCMs). The Dolphins reputedly carry a version of the Popeye Turbo cruise missile. In June 2012, the German magazine *Spiegel* claimed that Dolphin-class submarines are equipped with hydraulic ejection systems that enable the underwater launch of cruise missiles with nuclear warheads. Popeye was first developed in 1985, and submarine-launched for the first time in 2002 in the Indian Ocean. As an SLCM it is believed to have a range of up to 1500km (930 miles) and to carry a 200kg (440lb) payload, enough to accommodate a nuclear warhead.

ejected by hydraulic piston. Quick reloading is possible with the Embarkation and Storage System, which is installed behind the tubes. Mines can be carried instead of torpedoes. Anti-ship Harpoon and anti-helicopter Triton missiles are also believed to be carried. The weapon control system is the ISUS 90-1 TCS by STN Atlas Elektronik for automatic sensor management, fire control and navigation.

First of the Dolphin II boats, INS *Tanin* reached the port of Haifa in September 2014, after a long four-week voyage from Germany, and INS *Rahav* followed a year later. Both were fitted with only a part of the systems they were designed to contain. Communication, warfare and mainly classified Israeli-made weapon systems were installed after delivery. Commissioning of *Rahav* enabled the Israeli Navy to maintain one submarine on patrol at sea at any given time. The class is normally stationed at Haifa on the Mediterranean coast, but is deployed in accordance with perceived security requirements and has been known to operate in the Red Sea from Eilat. Missions are never disclosed but unconfirmed reports were made in July 2013 that an Israeli submarine had fired missiles at the Syrian port of Latakia to destroy a consignment of 50 Yakhont P-800 anti-ship missiles from Russia.

Type 212A (2002)

In commission with the German and Italian navies, the Type 212 is a multi-role submarine with highly sophisticated electronics. It was the first submarine to use AIP propulsion in regular service, making it capable of long-distance submerged passage to an area of operation.

Ingenieurkontor Lübeck (IKL) has a long connection with German submarine design and after World War II was developed by the former *Kriegsmarine* engineer Ulrich Gabler into a leading design bureau, first for export, then home-commissioned submarine designs. Now a subsidiary of ThyssenKrupp Marine Systems, it remains among the world leaders in submarine technology. Type 212A is an evolved double-hulled design, stemming from the Type 209 of the 1960s. The original brief for Type 212 came in the early 1990s from the Bundesmarine (German Navy) specifying a high-performance diesel-electric submarine that would also have AIP drive. Later, Italian participation in the project resulted in a change of specification and its designation as 212A. While the German requirement was for a submarine to operate in the shallow and cold

Baltic Sea, the Italian Navy wanted one for the deeper and warmer Mediterranean. Fusing of these requirements produced a high-capacity boat, equally effective in deep submerged positions far offshore or in coastal waters as shallow as 17m (55ft).

Extreme attention has been paid to efficiency and energy management on board, and the boats are managed by a relatively small crew of 22 and five officers. The pressure

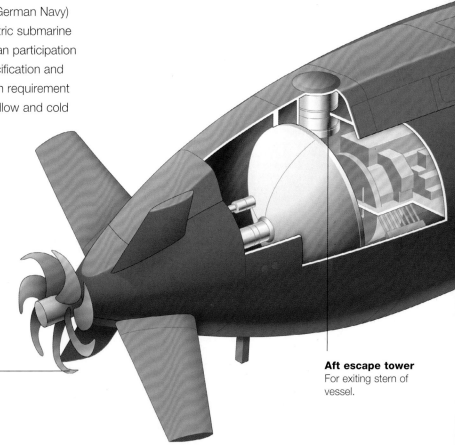

The Type 212A, with its non-magnetic hull and AIP propulsion, is claimed to be the most silent of present-day submarines.

Propeller
The seven-blade propeller is designed for silent operation.

Aft escape tower
For exiting stern of vessel.

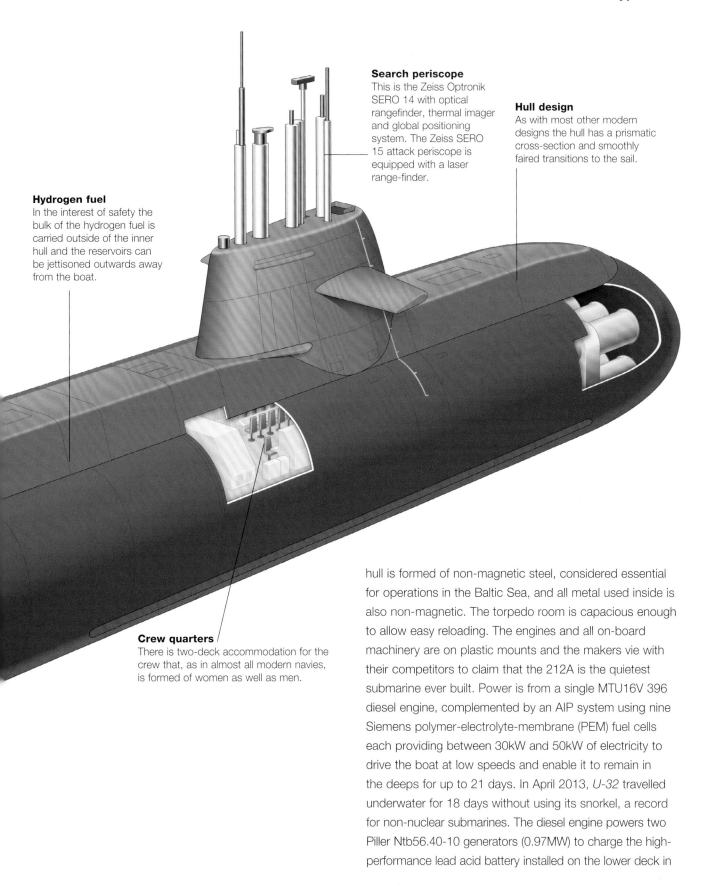

Search periscope
This is the Zeiss Optronik
SERO 14 with optical
rangefinder, thermal imager
and global positioning
system. The Zeiss SERO
15 attack periscope is
equipped with a laser
range-finder.

Hull design
As with most other modern
designs the hull has a prismatic
cross-section and smoothly
faired transitions to the sail.

Hydrogen fuel
In the interest of safety the
bulk of the hydrogen fuel is
carried outside of the inner
hull and the reservoirs can
be jettisoned outwards away
from the boat.

Crew quarters
There is two-deck accommodation for the
crew that, as in almost all modern navies,
is formed of women as well as men.

hull is formed of non-magnetic steel, considered essential for operations in the Baltic Sea, and all metal used inside is also non-magnetic. The torpedo room is capacious enough to allow easy reloading. The engines and all on-board machinery are on plastic mounts and the makers vie with their competitors to claim that the 212A is the quietest submarine ever built. Power is from a single MTU16V 396 diesel engine, complemented by an AIP system using nine Siemens polymer-electrolyte-membrane (PEM) fuel cells each providing between 30kW and 50kW of electricity to drive the boat at low speeds and enable it to remain in the deeps for up to 21 days. In April 2013, *U-32* travelled underwater for 18 days without using its snorkel, a record for non-nuclear submarines. The diesel engine powers two Piller Ntb56.40-10 generators (0.97MW) to charge the high-performance lead acid battery installed on the lower deck in

Type 212A

U-31, launched on 20 March 2002, was the first Type 212A to be commissioned into the Federal German Navy, on 19 October 2005.

the forward section. For bursts of high speed a connection can be made from the battery to the propeller motor, which is directly coupled to the seven-bladed screwback propeller.

Germany's Type 212A boats were constructed by ThyssenKrupp Marine Systems Yards at Kiel (HdW) and Emden (TNSW), with HdW responsible for the bow sections and TNSW for the stern sections. HdW assembled the first

and third vessels, TNSW the second and fourth. *U-31*, the first of the class, was launched in March 2002 and commissioned in October 2005. By May 2007 *U-32*, *U-33* and *U-34* were also commissioned. In September 2006, the German Navy ordered two further 212A submarines. They are 1.2m (4ft) longer to provide space for a new reconnaissance mast. *U-35* was delivered in November 2011 and *U-36* was launched in May 2013. Four U-212A submarines have been built by Fincantieri of Trieste for the Italian Navy. The first, S526 *Salvatore Todaro*, was launched in November 2003 and commissioned in June 2005. The second, *Scire*, was commissioned in February 2007. In 2008, the Italian government ordered two more submarines of the class – *Pietro Venuti*, launched in October 2014, and *Romeo Romei*, launched in July 2015. Both are expected to be commissioned in 2016.

Cutting-edge sonar

The type 212A carries leading-edge technology. The first batch are equipped with an integrated DBQS sonar system that has a cylindrical array for passive medium-frequency detection, a sail-mounted TAS-3 low-frequency towed sonar array, FAS-3 flank array sonar for low/medium-frequency detection, passive ranging sonar and a hostile sonar intercept system. The active high-frequency mine detection sonar is the Atlas Elektronik MOA 3070. A highly integrated command and weapons control system is supplied by Kongsberg Defence & Aerospace of Norway under the trade name MSI-90U. Interfacing with sensors, weapons and navigation systems, the system is based on a high-performance databus and a distributed computer system. There are six torpedo tubes in two groups of three, and a water ram expulsion system is used for torpedo launches. The submarine can fire the fibre-optic guided DM2A4 'Seehecht' heavyweight torpedo from Atlas Elektronik, the WASS A184 Mod.3 and WASS Black Shark torpedoes; also the fibre-optic-guided IDAS submarine-launched anti-helicopter missile, developed by Diehl BGT Defence, HdW and Kongsberg Defence & Aerospace and first tested in 2008 on *U-33*.

Specification

Dimensions:	Length: 56m (183ft 9in); Beam: 7m (23ft); Draught: 6m (19ft 8in)
Displacement:	Surfaced – 1450 tonnes (1430 tons); Submerged – 1830 tonnes (1800 tons)
Propulsion:	One MTU 16v 396 turbocharged diesel generator set developing 2881hp (2150kW), one Siemens Permasyn (synchronous motor with permanent magnet excitation) Type FR6439 motor, 4023hp (3MW); HdW/Siemens Air Independent Propulsion system, 402hp (300kW)
Speed:	Surfaced – 12 knots (22.2km/h; 13.8mph); Submerged – 20 knots (37km/h; 23mph)
Range:	8000nm (14,816km; 9206 miles) at 8 knots (14.8km/h; 9.2mph)
Armament:	Six 533mm (21in) tubes for 24 Atlas Elektronik DM2A4 torpedoes Siluri Whitehead A184 Mod3
Complement:	27–30

Due to changing mission requirements and on-going advances in technology, a number of modifications and enhancements were made to the second series of Class 212A. The Atlas Elektronik DBQS 40 electro-acoustic suite has been updated to the fully digitized CSU 90-138 version; and the Kongsberg MSI-90U Mk 2 submarine combat management system (CMS), which offers the ability

The Type 214, shown here, is the export version of the Type 212A, slightly larger, but with a conventional steel hull and some differences in technology. Greece, Korea and Portugal are purchasers.

FL1800U electronic warfare system

EADS Systems & Defence Electronics and Thales Defence were awarded a contract to develop the FL1800U electronic warfare system for U212A submarines. The 1800U is a submarine version of the FL1800 S-II also in service on the Brandenburg and Bremen-class frigates. A consortium led by ATLAS Elektronik and ELAC were responsible for the development of the TAU 2000 torpedo countermeasures system. It has four launch containers, each with up to 10 discharge tubes equipped with effectors. The effectors are small underwater vehicles, similar in appearance to a torpedo, but in fact jammers and decoys with hydrophones and acoustic emitters. Multiple effectors are deployed in order to counter torpedoes in re-attack mode.

to control the boats' periscopes from the CMS consoles. The navigation system has also been improved, with the installation of ECDIS digital cartography. The communications suite has been augmented by an SHF-band SATCOM-dedicated mast and Link 16 Joint Range Extension Applications Protocol-C (JREAP-C) capabilities. The Indra MRBR 800 has been installed as the electronic support measures (ESM) system. U-35 and U-36 are fitted with the Callisto B submarine communication system supplied by Gabler Maschinenbau, suitable for use in Network Centric Warfare scenarios; installation of the integrated German Sonar and Command Weapon and Control System; substitution of the flank array with a superficial lateral antenna; replacement of one periscope by an OMS 100 optronic surveillance mast; integration of a diver lock-out system; and fitting of the boats for action in tropical waters.

The German Navy currently operates five Type 212A submarines, commissioned between 2004 and 2015 and based at Eckernförde on the Baltic coast. The squadron will increase to six boats when U-36, still undergoing sea trials at the end of 2015, is commissioned into the fleet. From the end of 2016 the Italian Navy will deploy at least three.

🇺🇸 USS Virginia (2003)

The Virginia class is intended to assume the US Navy's attack- and multi-mission submarine role in the post-Cold War context. Its use of modular construction and commercial off-the-shelf technology is intended both to hold down costs and to provide flexibility in updating its electronic systems.

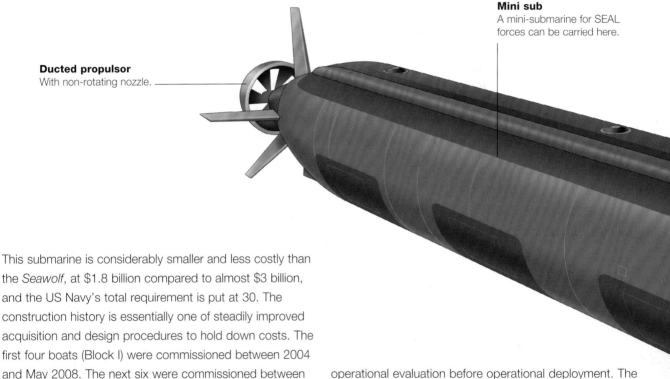

Mini sub
A mini-submarine for SEAL forces can be carried here.

Ducted propulsor
With non-rotating nozzle.

This submarine is considerably smaller and less costly than the *Seawolf*, at $1.8 billion compared to almost $3 billion, and the US Navy's total requirement is put at 30. The construction history is essentially one of steadily improved acquisition and design procedures to hold down costs. The first four boats (Block I) were commissioned between 2004 and May 2008. The next six were commissioned between 2008 and 2013. Commissioning of the seven Block III boats began in 2014. General Dynamics Electric Boat is expected to complete the deliveries by 2023. Virginia-class boats are built jointly by General Dynamics' Electric Boat Division of Groton, Connecticut, and Quonset Point, Rhode Island, and Newport News Shipbuilding, Virginia. Each builds specific sections of each boat, and takes turns in building the reactor compartments and completing final assembly.

SEAL support

USS *Virginia* (SSN-774) was laid down at Groton in September 1999, launched in August 2003 and commissioned in October 2004. It underwent a three-year operational evaluation before operational deployment. The hull contains a series of structurally integrated enclosures, which accommodate standard width equipment, 48.26cm and 61cm (19in and 24in) for ease of installation, repair and upgrade of the submarine's systems. Large isolated modular deck structures are fitted, for example the command centre is installed as a single unit resting on cushioned mounting points. It is the first US submarine to have a built-in Navy SEAL staging area, allowing a nine-man team to enter and leave the boat. An integral lock-out/lock-in chamber, incorporated into the hull, can hold a mini-submarine, such as Northrop Grumman's Oceanic and Naval Systems advanced SEAL delivery system (ASDS), to transfer or land Special Forces.

Multi-function mast
The multi-function mast incorporates submarine high data rate (sub HDR) multiband satellite communications systems allowing simultaneous communication at super high frequency (SHF) and extremely high frequency (EHF).

Design of the class was accomplished by the engineering and design and build teams at Electric Boat, working in partnership with the Naval Sea Systems Command, NAVSEA. For the first time, computer-assisted design (CAD) and visualization techniques were extensively used in US submarine design.

Photonic masts
The submarines have two Kollmorgen AN/BVS-1 photonic masts, rather than optical periscopes. Sensors mounted on the non-hull-penetrating photonic mast include LLTV (low-light TV), thermal imager and laser rangefinder.

Airlock chamber
A built-in nine-man airlock chamber allows access and egress.

Electromagnetic reduction
From USS California (SSN-781) an advanced electromagnetic signature reduction system has been incorporated, and retrofitted in earlier boats.

Bow and chin sonar arrays
For detecting other vessels.

USS *Virginia* at sea. The deck markings indicate the location of rescue hatches.

Specification

Dimensions:	Length: 115m (377ft 3in); Beam: 10m (33ft); Draught: 9.7m (32ft)
Displacement:	Surfaced – undisclosed; Submerged – 7900 tonnes (7800 tons)
Propulsion:	One S9G pressurized water reactor, 40,000hp (29.4MW); two steam turbines; United Defense pump jet propulsor
Speed:	Surfaced – undisclosed; Submerged – 25 knots (46.2km/h; 28.7mph)
Range:	Unlimited
Armament:	12 vertical BGM-109 Tomahawk cruise missile tubes; four 53mm (21in) torpedo tubes; 38 weapons
Complement:	135

The class is powered by ninth-generation (S9G) GE pressurized water reactors, designed not to require refuelling for the hull's lifetime, providing steam to two turbines. The noise level of the Virginias is the same as that of the Seawolf class, and an acoustic signature lower than Russia's Improved Akula Class and fourth-generation attack submarines is claimed. *Virginia* incorporates newly designed anechoic coatings, isolated deck structures and a new design of United Defense pump jet propulsor. However in August 2014 an American submarine, said by the Russians to be a Virginia-class, was detected within Russian territorial waters in the Barents Sea.

Rather than deep-sea encounters, coastal and hotspot operations were considered most probable for the class, and these requirements are reflected in the on-board equipment. The very extensive sonar suite comprises bow-mounted active and passive array, lightweight wide aperture passive flank arrays, high-frequency active arrays on keel and fin, TB 16 towed array and the Lockheed Martin TB-29A thin-line towed array, with the AN/BQQ-10(V4) sonar processing system. The flank arrays use fibre-optics, instead of traditional ceramic hydrophone sensors. A Sperry Marine AN/BPS-16(V)4 navigation radar, operating at I-band, is fitted. *Virginia*'s command and control systems module (CCSM) integrates all of the vessel's systems – sensors, countermeasure technology, navigation and weapon control. It is based on open system architecture (OSA) with Q-70 colour common display consoles. The control suite is equipped with touch screens. Steering and diving control is via a four-button, two-axis joystick.

Weapons system

Weapons control is provided by Raytheon with a derivative of the CCS Mk 2 combat system, the AN/BYG-1 combat control system. The submarine has 12 vertical missile launch tubes with capacity to launch 16 Tomahawk cruise missiles (SLCM) in a single salvo. Four 533mm (21in) torpedo tubes can launch Mk48 ADCAP Mod 6 heavyweight torpedoes, of which 26 are carried; as well as sub-Harpoon anti-ship missiles. Mk60 CAPTOR mines may also be discharged. Virginia is fitted with the AN/WLY-1 acoustic countermeasures system developed by Northrop Grumman, which provides range and bearing data, along with the mast-mounted AN/BLQ-10 electronic support measures (ESM) system from Lockheed Martin Integrated Systems, providing full spectrum radar processing, automatic threat warning and situation assessment. The Boeing long-term mine reconnaissance system (LMRS) deploys two 6m (19ft 4in) autonomous unmanned underwater vehicles, and an 18m (58ft 4in) robotic recovery arm, with support electronics.

From 2019 new boats will form Block IV, with an additional mid-body section, the Virginia Payload Module (VPM), containing four large-diameter, vertical launch tubes to store and fire additional Tomahawk cruise missiles or other payloads, including large-diameter unmanned underwater vehicles (LDUUVs). Future Virginias may also have integrated electric power systems, in which the reactor powers electric generators rather than turbines, and electricity can then be distributed across all systems as required, with an electric motor driving the propulsor.

Cost-effective redesign

As part of the Virginia-class Block III contract, the US Navy redesigned approximately 20 per cent of the submarine to reduce future acquisition costs and improve operational effectiveness. Most of the changes were made in the bow where the air-backed sonar sphere has been replaced with a water-backed Large Aperture Bow (LAB) array, reducing acquisition and life-cycle costs and providing enhanced passive detection capabilities. The redesigned bow also replaces the 12 Vertical Launch System (VLS) tubes with two large-diameter 213.3cm (84in) Virginia Payload Tubes (VPTs), each capable of launching six Tomahawk cruise missiles. The VPTs simplify construction, reduce acquisition costs and offer greater payload flexibility. These alterations were successfully tested during sea trials in North Dakota in August 2014.

USS *Virginia* arriving at Portsmouth Naval Shipyard on 7 September 2010 for a major overhaul. It returned to active service on 5 May 2012.

Scorpène (2005)

Originally a French–Spanish project, now French, this class of diesel-electric attack submarine has been sold to several navies and is a strong contender in the competition to secure further orders.

The Scorpène ('Scorpion-fish') class of diesel-electric attack submarine, originally a French–Spanish project between Navantia (Spain) and the French DCNS (formerly DCN) company, has been wholly under DCNS management since 2010. It is an export design and a strong contender in the international market for non-nuclear submarines. The basic form is the CM-2000, with conventional diesel-electric engines, but also on offer are

Armament
Black Shark torpedoes from Finmeccanica subsidiary Whitehead Alenia Sistemi Subacquei (WASS) are carried by the Chilean and Malaysian Scorpènes. This is a dual-purpose, wire-guided torpedo fitted with Astra active/passive acoustic head and a multi-target guidance and control unit incorporating a counter-countermeasures system. Its electrical propulsion system is based on a silver oxide and aluminium battery.

Profile
The profile shows the AM-2000 form of Scorpène. Incorporation of AIP propulsion lengthens the hull by 8.3m (27ft 2in) compared with the CM-2000.

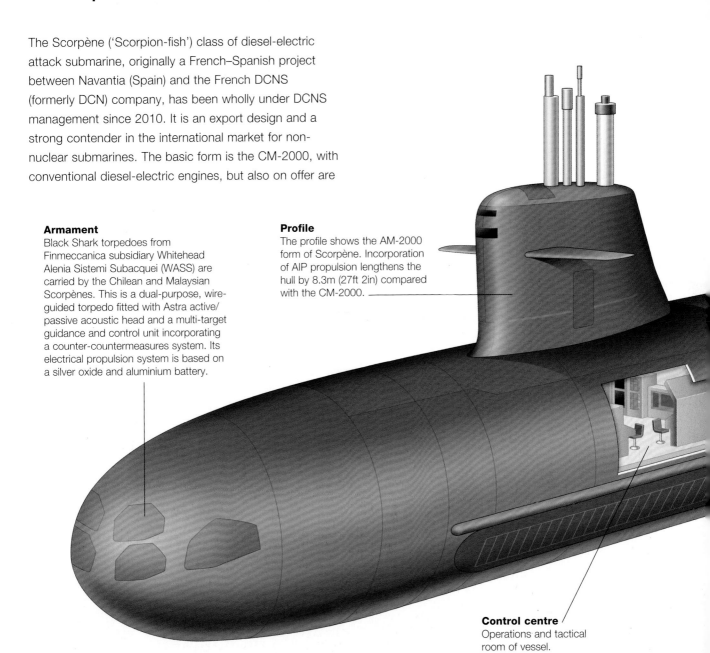

Control centre
Operations and tactical room of vessel.

the AM-2000, with the French MESMA system of AIP (air-independent propulsion); the CA-2000, a smaller version for coastal work; and the S-BR, a larger version supplied to the Brazilian Navy, but without AIP.

The Spanish government ordered four in 2003, then subsequently cancelled the order in favour of the similar S-80 Spanish-designed submarine, also built by Navantia (a design error has delayed this project until 2018). As of December 2015, two Scorpènes had been built for the Chilean Navy, commissioned in 2005 and 2006, and two for the Malaysian Navy, commissioned in 2007 and 2008. Two were under construction in Brazil, laid down in 2010 and 2013, with two more planned. India has six planned in collaboration between DCNS and the state-run Mazagon Docks (MDL), with one, *Kalvari*, launched on 6 April 2015 and two others under construction. In December 2015 the Indian government announced it would bring its Scorpène fleet up to nine. Other countries said to be interested in acquiring Scorpène are Saudi Arabia, Indonesia and Poland.

The submarine is designed with the aim of achieving an average 240 days a year at sea. Maximum diving depth is 350m (1150ft), exceeding that of some of Scorpène's rivals. There is no limit to the duration of dives

Power supply
MTU 16V 396 SE84 diesels and GM synchronous motors with permanent magnets power the Chilean Scorpènes. SEMT Pielstick 12 PA4 V 200 SMDS diesels can also be installed.

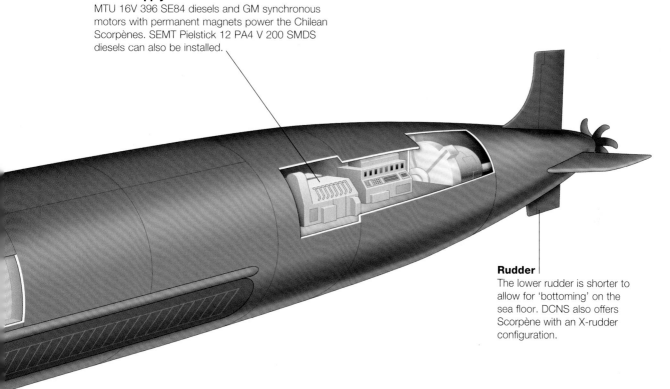

Rudder
The lower rudder is shorter to allow for 'bottoming' on the sea floor. DCNS also offers Scorpène with an X-rudder configuration.

Scorpène-type submarines are in service with the Chilean and Malaysian navies, fitting out with the Indian Navy, and under construction for the Brazilian Navy.

Scorpène

at a maximum depth. A connection point for a diving bell or deep submergence rescue vehicle (DSRV) allows collective rescue operations. Hull plates of HLES 80 high-yield stress-specific steel keeps down the weight of the pressure hull, allowing a larger load of fuel and weapons.

Specification

Dimensions:	Length: 70m (230ft); Beam 6.2m (20ft 4in); Draught: 5.8m (19ft)
Displacement:	Surfaced – 1870 tonnes (1840 tons); Submerged – 2032 tonnes (2000 tons)
Propulsion:	Two diesel engines, 1675hp (1250kW), electric motor, 3886hp (2900kW); AIP propulsion unit; single screw
Speed:	Surfaced – 12 knots (22.2km/h; 13.8mph); Submerged – 20 knots (37km/h; 23mph)
Range:	6500nm (12,038km; 7480 miles) at 8 knots (14.8km/h; 9.2mph)
Armament:	Six 533mm (21in) launch tubes for 18 torpedoes or SM39 Exocet anti-ship missiles or 30 mines
Complement:	31

With the Andes in the background, one of the two Scorpène submarines, *O'Higgins* and *Carrera*, which have been in service with the Chilean Navy since 2006.

The reduced complement – 31, with teams of nine for each watch – holds down training costs and improves combat efficiency by increasing available space for technical equipment and enabling a larger weapons load.

Low noise

The forms of hull, sail and appendages, including the 'albacore' bow shape and optimized propeller, have been designed to produce minimum hydrodynamic noise. Internal decks have suspended mounts, and all mechanical and electrical items of equipment are mounted on elastic supports, which are in turn mounted on uncoupled blocks and suspended platforms, both minimizing noise and vibration and also providing better shock protection to the machinery.

When dived, the Scorpène's advanced hydrodynamics make for extremely low radiated noise and give it the capability to carry out anti-submarine and anti-surface ship warfare operations in closed or open sea conditions, as well as to work with Special Forces in coastal waters.

The maximum operational lifespan of the type is 35 years. As an attack submarine it can carry 18 torpedoes and missiles or 30 mines. There are six bow-located 533mm (21in) torpedo tubes providing salvo launch capability. Positive discharge launching is by an air turbine pump. At least two of the tubes are fitted with a pneumatic ram positive discharge system for the launch of SM 39 anti-ship missiles and torpedoes. Depending on variants, the other tubes are of the swim-out variety. The SUBTICS combat management system, with up to six multifunction common consoles and a centrally situated tactical table, is collocated with the platform-control facilities. Composed of a command and tactical data handling system, a weapon control system and an integrated suite of acoustic sensors, it has an interface to a set of air surface detection sensors and to the integrated navigation system. The system can also download data from external sources.

The integrated navigation system combines data from global positioning systems, the log, depth measurement and the ship's trim/list monitoring system. The Scorpène monitors its environment, including seawater density and temperature and its own noise signature. The sonar suite includes a long-range passive cylindrical array, an intercept sonar, active sonar, distributed array, flank array, a high-resolution sonar for mine and obstacle avoidance and a towed array. The vessel features automatic control mode of rudders and propulsion, continuous monitoring of propulsion systems and platform installations and continuous centralized surveillance of all potential hazards (leaks, fires, presence of gases, etc.) and the status of installations that affect its safety while submerged.

Construction deals for Scorpène in Brazil, India and Malaysia have been troubled by accusations of corruption and bribery in the tendering process. The Brazilian contract alone is worth some €6.7 billion. These cases are still under investigation in these countries and at the Tribunal de Grande Instance courthouse in Paris.

Extended submergence

The MESMA anaerobic system, in which heat in the primary circuit is produced by burning ethanol with oxygen, can be installed either at the start of the submarine's construction or in a later modernization to convert the CM-2000 to an AM-2000 build standard. With the MESMA system the AM-2000 submarine can stay submerged on underwater patrol three times longer than the CM-2000. As an alternative to MESMA, Stirling-type engines can also be fitted. The length of the converted boat is increased to 70m (229ft 6in), and its submerged displacement to 1870 tonnes (1840 tons), against the 61.7m (202ft 4in) and the 1565 tonnes (1540 tons) of the CM2000.

India's first Scorpène type, INS *Kalvari*, was floated at Mazagon Dock Shipbuilders, Mumbai, on 28 October 2015.

Astute Class (2007)

Britain's latest fast-attack SSN class is named after HMS *Astute*, and is intended to be formed of seven boats over a construction period extending towards 2020 and with a service life continuing towards the mid-century.

The largest, most advanced and most powerful attack submarines ever operated by the British Royal Navy, this class replaces the seven Trafalgar-class submarines introduced in 1977–86. Construction delays and cost overruns are familiar features of new submarine programmes in all countries. With the Astute class, design difficulties including the failure of a 3D CAD system, and unexpected technical problems and deficiencies in programme management, required considerable design assistance from General Dynamics Electric Boat and the US Navy. By November 2009 the programme was 57 months behind schedule and more than 50 per cent (£1.35 billion) over its original budget. HMS *Astute* was laid down on 31 January 2001 at BAE Systems, Barrow-in-Furness,

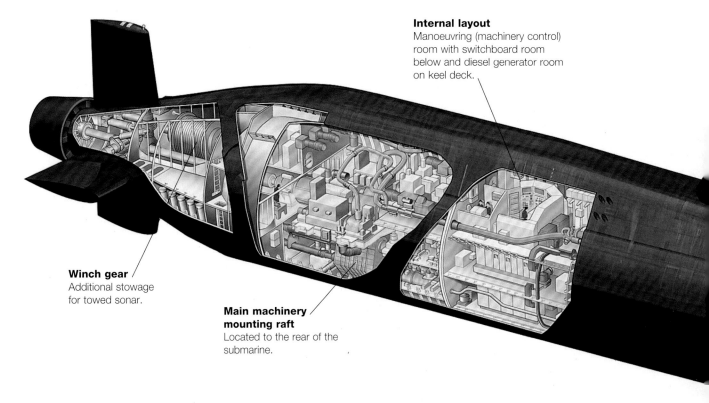

Internal layout
Manoeuvring (machinery control) room with switchboard room below and diesel generator room on keel deck.

Winch gear
Additional stowage for towed sonar.

Main machinery mounting raft
Located to the rear of the submarine.

As a fast-attack SSN, HMS *Astute* has both land and sea combat capacity in its missile stocks, backed up by a high level of combat management and countermeasures systems.

and launched on 8 June 2007. It was commissioned on 27 August 2010, but was not formally brought into active service until February 2014.

Few details of *Astute*'s design and structure have been published. The steel hull is said to be of 31.78cm (12in) thickness in places, and is covered with 39,000 acoustic tiles. The nuclear reactor is the Rolls-Royce PWR2, first developed in 1985 for the Vanguard SSBNs, linked to the GEC-Alstom steam turbine system designed originally for the Trafalgar class SSN. On *Trafalgar* the turbines gave a top speed of 32.5 knots (60.1km/h; 37.4mph) but *Astute*'s top speed was said to be 29 knots (53.7km/h; 33.3mph). A single pump-jet propulsor drives the craft, more quietly than a propeller would but with some loss of speed. There

are two diesel alternators, one emergency drive motor and one auxiliary retractable propeller.

Land and sea attack capability

Six 533mm (21in) torpedo tubes are fitted and 38 weapons can be stored. Tomahawk Block IV land attack missiles and Spearfish heavyweight torpedoes give it land and sea attack capacity. Tomahawk has a range of up to 609km (1000 miles) and a maximum velocity of 880km/h (550mph). Block IV includes a two-way satellite link that allows reprogramming of the missile in flight and transmission of battle damage indication (BDI) imagery. The Spearfish torpedo from BAE Systems is wire-guided with an active/passive homing head. Its range is 65km (40 miles) at a

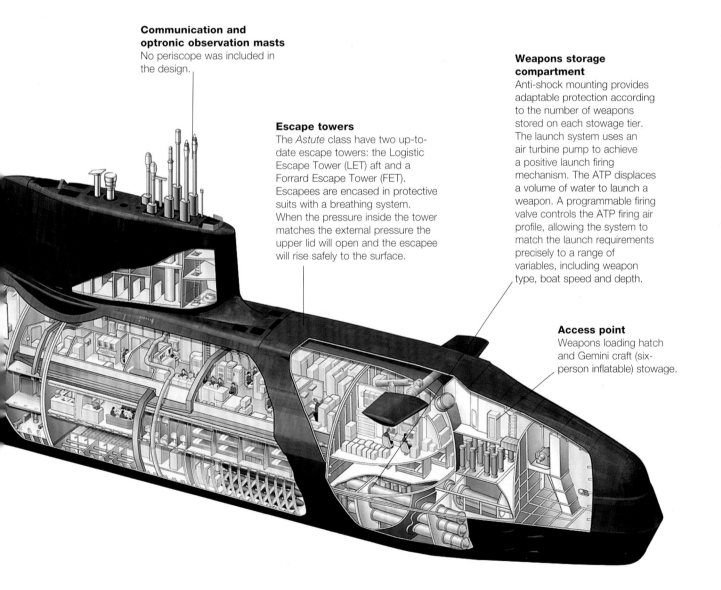

Communication and optronic observation masts
No periscope was included in the design.

Escape towers
The *Astute* class have two up-to-date escape towers: the Logistic Escape Tower (LET) aft and a Forrard Escape Tower (FET). Escapees are encased in protective suits with a breathing system. When the pressure inside the tower matches the external pressure the upper lid will open and the escapee will rise safely to the surface.

Weapons storage compartment
Anti-shock mounting provides adaptable protection according to the number of weapons stored on each stowage tier. The launch system uses an air turbine pump to achieve a positive launch firing mechanism. The ATP displaces a volume of water to launch a weapon. A programmable firing valve controls the ATP firing air profile, allowing the system to match the launch requirements precisely to a range of variables, including weapon type, boat speed and depth.

Access point
Weapons loading hatch and Gemini craft (six-person inflatable) stowage.

Astute Class

About to take to the water – *Astute* at the BAE Systems
construction yard, Barrow-in-Furness, June 2007.

Specification

Dimensions:	Length: 97m (318ft); Beam: 11.3m (37ft); Draught: 10m (33ft)
Displacement:	Surfaced – 7000 tonnes (6889 tons); Submerged – 7400 tonnes (7283 tons)
Propulsion:	One RR PWR2 Core H reactor, two turbines, single shaft, propulsor
Speed:	Surfaced – undisclosed; Submerged – 29 knots (53.7km/h; 33.3mph)
Range:	Unlimited
Armament:	Six 533mm (21in) launch tubes for Spearfish torpedoes/Tomahawk Block IV TLAM; 38 weapons
Complement:	135

speed of 60 knots (111.1km/h; 69mph). Spearfish is fitted with a directed-energy warhead.

Comprehensive countermeasures include decoys and electronic support measures (ESM). The ESM system is the Thales Sensors Outfit UAP(4), with two multifunction antenna arrays mounted on the two optronics masts. The CM010 mast includes thermal imaging, low light TV and colour CCD TV sensors. The Royal Navy's Eddystone Communications band Electronic Support Measures (CESM) system provides advanced communications, signal intercept, recognition, direction finding and monitoring capability. *Astute* is fitted with I-band navigation radars.

The sonar is the Thales Underwater Systems 2076, a software-intensive system with integrated passive/active search and attack suite comprising bow, intercept, flank and towed arrays; also the latest version of the Thales S2076 integrated suite. An Atlas Hydrographic DESO 25 high-precision echo sounder gives precise depth measurements down to 10,000m (32,800ft). Raytheon Systems provide the Successor IFF (identification friend or foe) naval transponder system for the class.

In late 2011 *Astute* was sent to the US Navy Atlantic Undersea Test and Evaluation Center in the Bahamas where it spent five months on tests and exercises, including underwater detection trials conducted with USS *New Mexico*. These were said to confirm *Astute*'s advanced sonar systems to be as good as or better than any other in use.

Astute's first deployment on active service was from February to September 2014. Its cruise took it to the Mediterranean Sea where it joined units of the US Mediterranean Fleet in exercises using the Tomahawk Land Attack Missile (TLAM) for potential anti-terrorist operations, then proceeded to the Gulf of Oman to conduct ASW exercises. There were more of these on the return leg through the Mediterranean. *Astute* was carrying a DDS deck-mounted, semi-recessed pod containing a miniature submarine and other specialized equipment for use by Special Boat Service (SBS) teams. This cruise was said to confirm the boat as a fully operational front-line unit capable of conducting operations at a superior level. New equipment such as the optronics mast has proved particularly effective at night, enabling *Astute* to perform complex manoeuvres even in pitch darkness.

All five Astute submarines are expected to be operational by 2022, when the last four serving Trafalgar-class boats are to be decommissioned. Boats of the class from No. 4, *Audacious*, onwards will have a 'common combat system' in which the command, navigation and sonar system use a shared computer environment. Already retrofitted to *Artful*, these will also be installed on *Astute* and *Ambush*. In November 2015 the contract for a fifth Astute class boat, HMS *Anson*, was awarded to BAE Systems, at a price of £1.3 billion.

Quality control problems

Aspects of the design, including the use of a reactor made in the 1980s for a much larger SSBN, have been criticized, as have some serious failures in quality control during construction. Details of *Astute*'s technical problems are, of course, classified, but it is known that a mismatch between the powerful reactor and under-size steam turbines means she cannot reach her full design speed. Ministry of Defence statements refer to teething troubles inevitable in the first boat of a new class, although

an MoD document of 16 November 2012 noted numerous Quality Assessment issues to do with actual and potential corrosion. In March 2014 it was admitted that there is a problem that may reduce the life expectancy of the Vanguard- and Astute-class PWR2 reactors, possibly requiring costly mid-life nuclear refuelling, something the new design was supposed to avoid.

Astute close to its home base at Faslane, Scotland.

Type 094 (Jin Class) (2007)

China's second-generation nuclear-powered SSBN has significantly extended the country's range of potential strategic engagement.

The first Chinese designed and built nuclear-powered attack submarine (Han class) began sea trials in August 1971. It was a major steppingstone towards development of a Chinese nuclear-powered, submarine-launched ballistic missile (SSBN) force. Such a force would enhance Beijing's assurance of an effective retaliatory capability, as well as strengthening its deterrent posture.

In 1981 the Type 092 (Xia class) SSBN, derived from the Han class with the hull lengthened to accommodate missile tubes, became operational. The Type 093 (Shang-

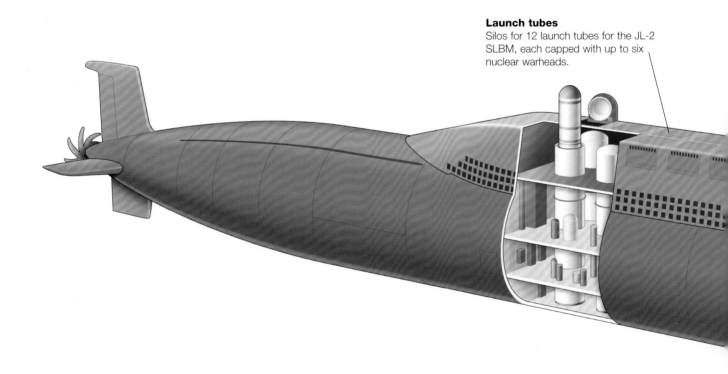

Launch tubes
Silos for 12 launch tubes for the JL-2 SLBM, each capped with up to six nuclear warheads.

No details about the Jin's internal arrangements have been officially released, but analysis of external images enables experts to make conjectures about the internal layout and key features, with a high degree of probability.

class) nuclear-powered attack submarine (SSN) followed, although none are yet commissioned. The Type 092 was initially armed with 12 JL-1 (CSS-N-3) SLBMs. A major update of the class started in 1995 to fit the new JL-2 SLBM system, with the upgrade completed in 1998. The JL-2 (CSS-NX-4) SLBM is reported to carry three or four MIRV (90kT each) or a single 250kt warhead with a range of 8000km (5000 miles). Operations have been limited and the Xia has never sailed beyond Chinese regional waters.

Jin class

The Type 094 (NATO reporting name Jin class) SSBN is a more effective craft. Three are in service and eight may be commissioned by 2020. The Jin class, carrying the JL-2 submarine launched ballistic missile (SLBM) with a range capable of reaching the US, give China its first credible sea-based nuclear deterrent. Nuclear deterrence patrols are thought to have begun in October 2015. Secrecy surrounds the Chinese nuclear submarine

Hull construction
The Jin hull is modelled on that of the Xia class, but the design is smoother, more integrated and sophisticated.

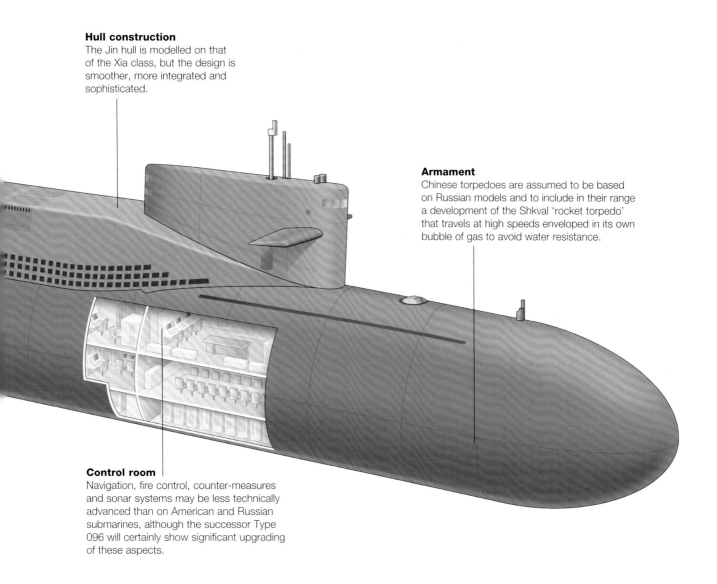

Armament
Chinese torpedoes are assumed to be based on Russian models and to include in their range a development of the Shkval 'rocket torpedo' that travels at high speeds enveloped in its own bubble of gas to avoid water resistance.

Control room
Navigation, fire control, counter-measures and sonar systems may be less technically advanced than on American and Russian submarines, although the successor Type 096 will certainly show significant upgrading of these aspects.

Type 094 (Jin Class)

A Type 094 at sea. It shows typical basic features of a ballistic missile submarine, with a raised fairing over the missile launchers. The sail is partly merged into the fairing to improve hydrodynamics.

programme and most information comes from Western or Russian sources. Development of the Jin class possibly began in the early 1980s as an improved successor to the Xia class. Some Western observers have suggested that design work was assisted by the Russian Rubin Design Bureau in St Petersburg, but this is unconfirmed.

Construction of the lead vessel began in 1999, it was launched in 2004 and the first boat was commissioned in 2010. Currently at least three hulls of the class have been identified. The second vessel of the class was launched in 2007. The Jin class reportedly will carry 12 JL-2 (NATO designation CSS-N-5 Sabbot) SLBMs. Other armament includes six 533mm (21in) torpedo tubes. American intelligence suggests that the PLAN (People's Liberation Army Navy) is also developing a typical range of countermeasures including decoys, chaff, electronic jamming and thermal shielding.

Like other governments that have made vast investments in nuclear submarines, the Chinese government is eager to play up the Jin's abilities, while giving away few details of its features and performance. Armed with the JL-2, the submarine is "a trump card which makes our motherland proud and our adversaries terrified", Admiral Wu Shengli, commander of the Chinese Navy, is quoted as having said.

Apart from how many Jin SSBNs China will build, a key question is whether the Chinese government will use

Specification

Dimensions (estimated):
Length: 135m (442ft 11in); Beam: 12.5m (41ft); Draught: 8m (26ft 3in)

Displacement (estimated):
Surfaced – 8128 tonnes (8000 tons); Submerged – 11,176 tonnes (11,000 tons)

Propulsion:	Nuclear reactor, single screw
Speed:	Surfaced – undisclosed; Submerged – 20 knots+ (37km/h+; 23mph+) (estimated)
Range:	Unlimited
Armament:	12 JL-2 SLBMs; six 533mm (21in) torpedo tubes
Complement:	Undisclosed

Two Type 094 Jin-class submarines moored at the Hainan Island naval complex. The nearer has its missile tubes open. These submarines carry twelve JL-2 SLBMs with a range of 7200 km (4500 miles).

them in the same way as Western nuclear-armed states have been operating their SSBNs for decades – deployed

Concealed submarine base

Since 2000 China has built a massive infrastructure of facilities to service its SSBN fleet. This includes extending and modernizing naval bases, with submarine hull demagnetization equipment, underground facilities and high-bay buildings for missile storage and handling. Tunnels and covered railway lines conceal activities from spy satellites. The Jin SSBNs have been observed at four sites: the Bohai shipyard at Huludao on the Bohai Sea where they are built; the Xiaopingdao naval base near Dalian where they are fitted out for missile launch tests; the North Sea Fleet base at Jianggezhuang near Qingdao where one Jin SSBN is stationed along with the Xia-class SSBN from the 1980s; and at the South Sea Fleet base at Longpo on Hainan Island where at least one Jin SSBN has been based since 2008.

continuously at sea with nuclear-armed ballistic missiles – or continue China's long-standing practice of not deploying nuclear weapons outside Chinese territory, instead keeping them in central storage for deployment in a crisis.

New role

It is also anticipated that the Jins will be used to demonstrate Chinese power in the West Philippine Sea, where there are numerous sites of territorial dispute involving China, the Philippines, Japan and Taiwan. This sea has large extents of very deep water, with a maximum depth of about 4000m (13,000ft) giving ample movement room for nuclear submarines. Each Jin-class boat is able to conduct patrols lasting approximately 60 days, and with five submarines to deploy, near-continuous at-sea deterrence can be maintained, although refit time may present problems.

Meanwhile it has been reported that the design of a successor SSBN class, Type 096 (Tang class), is already in progress for entry into service in the 2020s. It may be that production of further Jin-class boats will be curtailed in anticipation of delivery of this more advanced type that will be able to launch missiles from under the Arctic icecap and will be much quieter in operation. It is clear that China is fully embarked on being a global strategic power through use of a modern nuclear submarine fleet as part of their nuclear strike capability.

# **Soryu** (2009)

The first boat, named after the Japanese Imperial Navy aircraft carrier *Soryu*, was commissioned in 2009. Translated from Japanese it means 'Blue Dragon'. A class of 10 is planned, all of them named after dragons in Japanese mythology.

Japan's post-war submarines have followed a steady design progression, each class slightly larger and more comprehensively equipped than the preceding one, and with a steadily increasing use of Japanese-made components and systems. The Soryu class have the largest displacement of any Japanese submarines since World War II. Its introduction has coincided with a change in Japanese naval planning. Earlier types were seen primarily as coastal defence craft, but rising tensions and territorial disputes in the Western Pacific region have prompted Japanese

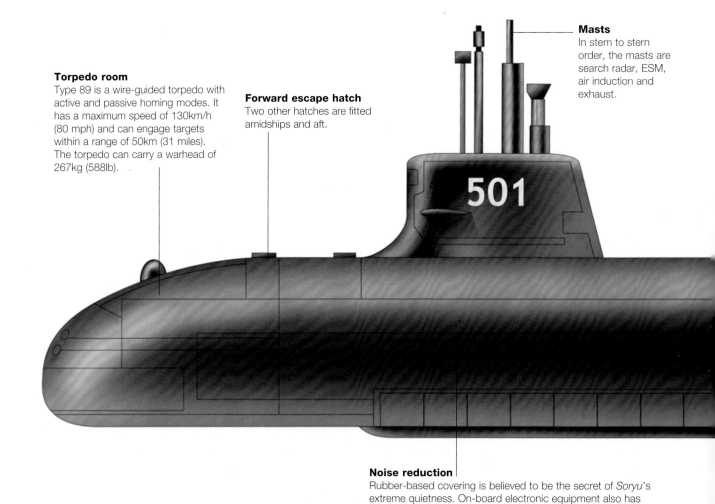

Torpedo room
Type 89 is a wire-guided torpedo with active and passive homing modes. It has a maximum speed of 130km/h (80 mph) and can engage targets within a range of 50km (31 miles). The torpedo can carry a warhead of 267kg (588lb).

Forward escape hatch
Two other hatches are fitted amidships and aft.

Masts
In stem to stern order, the masts are search radar, ESM, air induction and exhaust.

Noise reduction
Rubber-based covering is believed to be the secret of *Soryu*'s extreme quietness. On-board electronic equipment also has this covering to mute any noise. Even the light bulbs have had their sound signatures extracted.

strategists to take a wider view, for which the Soryu class's range and capacities are well fitted. The Japanese Maritime Self-Defence Force (JMSDF) is looking towards an enlarged fleet of 22 SSKs, and by 2015 a total of eight of this class had been built or were on order.

The vessel can be distinguished from the preceding Oyashio class by the X-shape rudder configuration, first used on the Swedish Gotland class. The functions of this are computer-enhanced, giving the vessel exceptional manoeuvrability and close-to-seabed operation. The combination of hydrodynamic design, anechoic coating of the hull, isolation of potentially noisy mechanical components and a silent AIP engine results in a very high level of stealth capacity. Operational depth has been unofficially estimated as 500m (1640ft).

The class leader, Soryu, was laid down at the Kawasaki Shipyard, Kobe, on 31 March 2005, launched on 5 December 2007 and commissioned on 30 March 2009. Five more were in service by March 2015, all delivered on time and without exceeding budgeted costs, a rare achievement in present-day submarine construction. Soryu is powered by a diesel-electric propulsion system. Two Kawasaki 12V 25/25 SB-type diesel engines and four Kawasaki Kockums V4-275R Stirling engines provide total power outputs of 3900hp (2900kW) surfaced and 8000hp (6000kW) submerged. The Stirling external combustion engines are air-independent propulsion units, silent and almost vibration-free. They generate heat in a separate combustion chamber and transfer to the engine working gas, operating in a completely closed system.

The Soryu class are extremely advanced submarines. For the first time, Japanese submarines are available for purchase, by countries in alliance with Japan, at a cost of around $540 million each.

Hull construction
Like the Oyashio class, the Soryu class has a 'hybrid' hull structure that is partially double and partially single. The hull is divided into six compartments.

Exhaust discharge
Stirling-AIP burns pure oxygen and diesel fuel in a pressurized combustion chamber whose pressure is higher than the external water pressure, allowing exhaust products to be discharged overboard without using a compressor to dissolve in the sea. This procedure reduces infrared signature and noise emission levels.

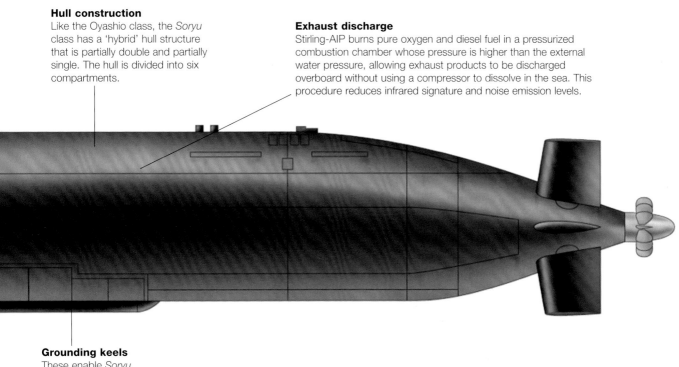

Grounding keels
These enable Soryu to sit silently on the seabed.

A Soryu-class boat making full surface speed. Under the surface it would be almost undetectable.

Specification

Dimensions:	84m (275ft 7in); Beam: 9.1m (30ft); Draught: 8.5m (27ft 11in)
Displacement:	surfaced – 2900 tonnes (2854 tons); submerged – 4200 tonnes (4134 tons)
Propulsion:	Two Kawasaki 12V 25/25 SB-type diesels; 4 Kawasaki-Kockums V4-275R Stirling engines; single screw
Speed:	Surfaced – 13 knots (24km/h; 14.9mph); Submerged – 20 knots (37km/h; 23mph)
Range:	6100nm (11,297km; 7019 miles) at 6.5 knots (12km/h; 7.4mph)
Armament:	Six 533mm (21in) launch tubes for torpedoes, Sub-Harpoon missiles, mines
Complement:	65

Expansion of the gas forces the pistons to move, thus producing mechanical energy. *Soryu*'s increase in size over the Oyashio-class boats is chiefly in order to house this propulsion system, which allows the submarine to stay submerged for longer periods of time – up to 14 days – without surfacing to charge the batteries.

The Stirling system is produced under licence by Kawasaki Heavy Industries, and it was decided in 2014 to replace it in the final four of the Soryu class with Japanese-developed lithium-ion batteries, which are more powerful and require far lower maintenance than lead-acid batteries. JMSDF engineers were said to view AIP technology, which reduces the speed of submerged submarines to just a few knots, as too slow for emerging strategic uses and excessively maintenance-intensive. Anticipated improvements in batteries are considered to make this technology a better long-term option.

The class is armed with six HU-606 533mm (21in) torpedo tubes for the Type 89 torpedoes and UGM-84 Sub-Harpoon anti-ship missiles. Type 89 is a wire-guided torpedo with active and passive homing modes. It has a maximum speed of 130km/h (80mph), can engage targets within a range of 50km (31 miles) and carry a high-explosive warhead of 267kg (588lb). The Harpoon has a range of over 124km (77 miles) and speed of 864km/h (536mph). Weapon stowage capacity is believed to be the equivalent of 20 heavyweight torpedoes/Harpoon missiles or 10 torpedoes/Harpoon missiles plus 20 (smaller) mines.

Sonar suite

The submarine is equipped with a ZPS-6F navigation or surface search radar. The sonar suite integrates four low frequency flank arrays, a bow-array and a towed array sonar. Countermeasures feature ZLR-3-6 electronic support measures (ESM) systems. There are two 76mm (3in) underwater countermeasure launcher tubes installed for launching acoustic device countermeasures (ADCs) to act against both sonar pulses and actual weapons.

With the Soryu class the Japanese government has moved into the arena of international arms sales to countries considered friendly. As of December 2015 the Australian government was considering whether to buy Japanese, German or French submarines to replace its six Collins-class submarines. Strategic military and diplomatic considerations and intense public-relations campaigns have made it far more than a conventional decision based on cost and performance.

As part of any deal, Japan had agreed to share information about classified technologies on the Soryu class with Australia – the first time it has agreed to share classified information with any country other than the United States. The modified version of the Soryu class is regarded as more technically sophisticated than its competitors – Germany's Type 214 submarine from ThyssenKrupp Marine Systems (TKMS) and France's Scorpène-class from DCNS. However, it is also more expensive at $540 million, compared to the Type 214 at $330 million and the Scorpène at $450 million. But at 4267 tonnes (4200 tons) submerged, the Soryu class is considerably larger than its rivals, can carry a heavier weapons load with a greater range and has comparable stealth characteristics. India and Taiwan are also believed to have expressed interest in acquiring Soryu-class vessels.

US–Japanese exercises

Japan's Maritime Self-Defence Force submarines are grouped in two flotillas, based at Kure and Yokosuka. Their operations are closely linked with those of the US Navy, with which they conduct regular exercises. Japanese submariners are experts in navigating across topographically complicated sea floors with steep hills, plunging gorges and conflicting ocean currents, in total darkness. Using a mix of information from US reconnaissance satellites and other intelligence sources, MSDF submarines track the movements of submarines and surface ships. Critical patrol areas for the Soryu class are the passageways between the East China Sea and the Pacific Ocean – the Tsushima Strait, the Miyako Strait between Okinawa Island and Miyako Island, and the Osumi Strait off the southern tip of Kyushu.

With garlanded sail, Soryu-class *Hakuryu* (commissioned 14 March 2011) arrives at Joint Base Pearl Harbor-Hickam on a goodwill visit on 6 February 2013.

Project 885 Yasen Class
(2014)

Russia's fourth generation of fast-attack nuclear submarine is a formidable multi-purpose vessel with enhanced stealth characteristics and the ability to launch 24 MIRV cruise missiles.

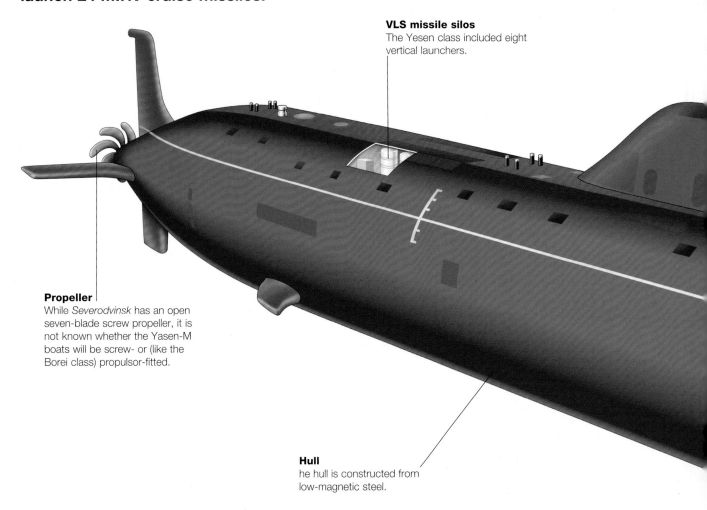

VLS missile silos
The Yesen class included eight vertical launchers.

Propeller
While *Severodvinsk* has an open seven-blade screw propeller, it is not known whether the Yasen-M boats will be screw- or (like the Borei class) propulsor-fitted.

Hull
he hull is constructed from low-magnetic steel.

The Yasen in profile clearly shows its Russian lineage, but it is a formidable and very up-to-date twenty-first century submarine in its Yasen-M form.

Project 885 Yasen ('Ash Tree'), designated Granay by NATO, draws on experience with the high-speed Akula class. The Malakhit Design Bureau was responsible for the planning. The first boat was laid down in 1992 at the Sevmash Yard in Severodvinsk, but financial difficulties and disagreements over naval priorities meant that work slowed down and was suspended in 1996, not resuming until 2003. The lead boat, named *Severodvinsk*

in 1993, was launched in 2010 and commissioned into the Northern Fleet as K-560 on 17 June 2014. By then doubts over the future of Project 885 had been resolved and by 2016 a further four Yasens were under construction, with a fifth on order. Ultimately the class may consist of 12 boats. With many alterations and additions to the design made since the original plans of the early 1990s, they are known as Yasen-M.

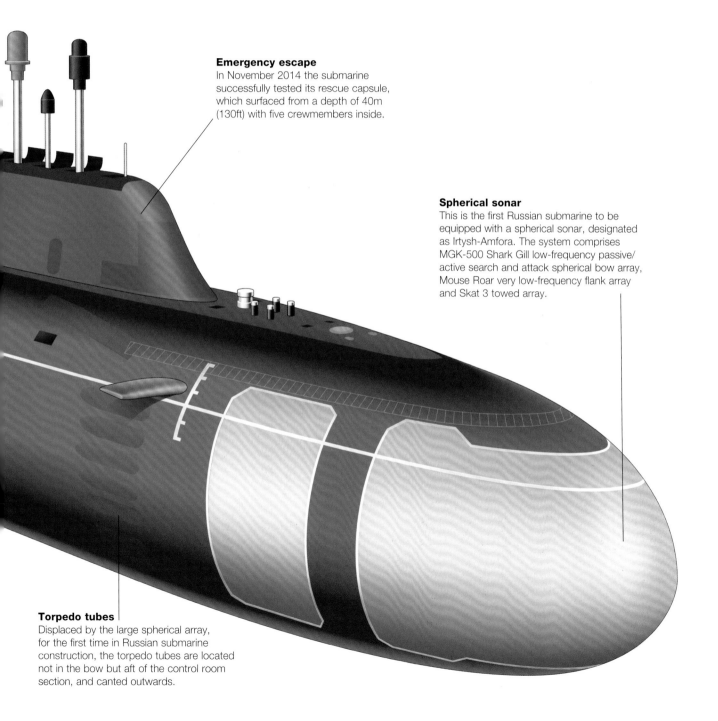

Emergency escape
In November 2014 the submarine successfully tested its rescue capsule, which surfaced from a depth of 40m (130ft) with five crewmembers inside.

Spherical sonar
This is the first Russian submarine to be equipped with a spherical sonar, designated as Irtysh-Amfora. The system comprises MGK-500 Shark Gill low-frequency passive/active search and attack spherical bow array, Mouse Roar very low-frequency flank array and Skat 3 towed array.

Torpedo tubes
Displaced by the large spherical array, for the first time in Russian submarine construction, the torpedo tubes are located not in the bow but aft of the control room section, and canted outwards.

Severodvinsk sets out on patrol from its home base. It is assigned to the 11th Submarine Division, at Bloshaya Lopatka on the Zapadnaya Litsa fjord, located on the Barents Sea coast of the Kola Peninsula.

Specification

Dimensions:	Length: 119m (390ft 5in); Beam: 13.5m (44ft 3in); Draught: 8.4m (27ft 6in)
Displacement:	Surfaced – 8737 tonnes (8600 tons); Submerged – 14,021 tonnes (13,800 tons)
Propulsion:	One KPM pressurized water reactor 43,000hp (200MW); single screw
Speed:	Surfaced – 20 knots (37km/h); Submerged – 35 knots (64.8km/h; 40.2mph); silent – 28 knots (51.8km/h; 32.2mph)
Range:	Unlimited
Armament:	Eight silos for SL weapons; eight 650mm (25.3in) and two 533mm (21in) torpedo tubes
Complement:	90

Handing over of the first Yasen-M, K-561 *Kazan*, has been delayed from 2017 to 2018. In 2011, the Defence Minister criticized the ever-increasing cost of both the Yasen- and Borei-class submarines, describing the huge increase in cost between the first and the second Yasen-class boats as 'incomprehensible'. External observers have estimated the cost per boat as ranging from the equivalent of $1 billion to $3 billion. While Russia would no doubt like to reclaim some of the vast investment associated with the project, reports of a potential sale of a Yasen to India or Indonesia seem improbable.

Only the most basic technical details about the class have been officially released. Its hull is constructed from low-magnetic steel alloy, and it is powered by a new KPM type pressurized water reactor, developed by the OKBM Afrikantov company in Nizhny Novgorod. Rated at 200MW, the reactor drives steam turbines and a single propeller.

Its core life is 25–30 years and it will not need refuelling during the boat's lifetime. The propulsion system provides a maximum submerged speed of 35 knots (64.8km/h; 40.2mph) and a surface speed of 20 knots (37km/h; 23mph). Operating depth has been estimated

The Yasen-class submarine *Severodvinsk* photographed against an Arctic sky.

at 450m (1475ft); maximum safe depth 550m (1800ft); and never-exceed depth at 660m (2165ft). American reports describe the class as the quietest yet built by Russia, although with a higher noise profile than the US Navy's Virginia and Seawolf classes. While this may be the case, the noise-profile of the Yasen-M boats is not yet established. It is notable that in late 2012, an Akula allegedly remained undetected for several weeks while conducting operations in the Gulf of Mexico.

Weapons load

It is reported that a total of 30 torpedoes and anti-ship missiles are carried in a variety according to the type of target. The central part of the hull, aft of the sail, holds eight vertical triple-launch silos for 3M-14E Biryuza or P-800 Oniks anti-ship missiles. Six 650mm (25.3in) and two 533mm (21in) torpedo tubes can discharge VA-111 Shkval rocket torpedoes, SAET-60M, Type 65-76, Type 65K torpedoes and RPK-7 Veter anti-submarine rockets.

VA-111 Shkval rocket-torpedo

The Yasen class carries highly sophisticated weaponry, which is still being updated. The VA-111 Shkval rocket-torpedo is 8.2m (26ft 11in) long, with a diameter of 533mm (21in). It weighs 2700kg (5950lb) and can carry a 210kg (462lb) warhead. It has a speed of 200 knots (370km/h; 230mph) and in its latest form has a range of 11–15km (7–9 miles). The P-800 Oniks anti-ship missile travels at supersonic speed up to Mach 2.5 over a maximum range of 300km (186 miles) and is fitted with an active/passive radar seeker and a 200kg (440lb) warhead. Novator RK-55 Granat nuclear-capable subsonic land attack cruise missiles with a 2880km (1800 mile) range can be carried. The torpedo tubes can also launch the 3M14 Kalibr and 3M54 Biryuza land attack and anti-ship missiles, with a range of around 486km (300 miles). The class is also believed to have effective defences against submarine and air attack.

Electronic countermeasures equipment includes a Rim Hat radar intercept receiver, a Snoop Pair surface search radar and a Myedvyeditsa-971 Radar.

The Yasen class can be deployed in anti-submarine warfare, anti-surface warfare, surveillance operations and special missions. Details of the actual activities of *Severodvinsk* are not known, but since 2014 patrols of world oceans by Russian submarines have been greatly stepped up. From January 2014 to March 2015 the intensity of such patrols was officially reported as having increased by almost 50 per cent as compared to 2013. Some Western analysts have suggested that even if part of the Yasen-M brief is to get a relatively cheaper submarine, the whole concept of the Yasen-class is at odds with the geopolitical realities of the 21st century, since they were originally designed as attack submarines to confront the advanced naval capabilities of the United States during the Cold War.

In the Russian view, however, to obtain strike and stealth parity with the Seawolf and Virginia classes (and their successors) is a priority worth the cost. The Russian government is also looking beyond the Yasens to a fifth generation of nuclear submarines, and has commissioned preliminary work from the Malakhit Bureau on a submarine that can be adapted to carry missile systems either as an interceptor of other undersea craft or as a 'carrier killer' to destroy large surface ships.

⬜🇮🇳 INS Arihant (2015)

With the home-built SSBN *Arihant*, India has become the sixth country to construct and operate nuclear submarines, and an ongoing programme for further vessels, both missile carriers and attack boats, has been announced by the Indian government.

The Indian Navy's Advanced Technology Vessel (ATV) Project for the design and construction of a nuclear submarine was first made public in 1998. Originally planned to be a fast attack vessel, the project was altered to a missile-carrying submarine (SSBN) following a review of strategic requirements. The project was jointly developed by the Indian Navy, Bhabha Atomic Research Centre (BARC) and Defence Research and Development Organisation (DRDO), with substantial design input from the Malakhit design bureau of St

Propeller
Arihant is driven via a seven-bladed fixed-pitch propeller with cruciform vortex dissipators. An emergency back-up drive is provided by two diesel engines of 496hp (370kW) giving a speed of 4 knots (7.4km/h; 4.6mph).

AB-2 steel
AB-2 is a high-yield strength, low-carbon, low-alloy steel with nickel, molybdenum and chromium. It has excellent weldability and good ductility even in welded sections. Its yield strength of 690 MPa (6433 tons/sq ft) is equivalent to the USA's HY-100 rating.

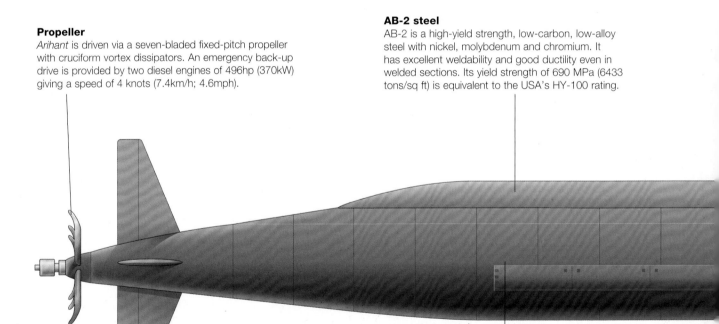

Reactor compartment
The 42m (137ft 9in) long and 8m (26ft 3in) in diameter, the compartment holds the cooling-water tank, the reactor itself and the cooling system. There is a main control room and an auxiliary control room. The complete power and propulsion plant and associated systems occupy the rear half of the hull.

Petersburg. The pressure hull was fabricated from high-yield AB grade steel obtained from Russia. The power unit is an 80MW pressurized water reactor, whose operational life is 20–25 years, although refuelling of the core will be required. *Arihant*'s onboard reactor achieved criticality on 10 August 2013. The Proto-type Testing Centre (PTC) at the Indira Gandhi Centre was used to test the submarine's turbines and propellers. A similar facility was operational at Vishakapatnam to test the main turbines and gearing. The vessel's cost, so far, is in the region of $3 billion, although it is officially anticipated that subsequent boats of the class will be less expensive. INS *Arihant* (which means 'Destroyer of Enemies' in Sanskrit) was first floated on 26 July 2009 at the Navy Shipbuilding Centre, Vishakhapatnam, and began sea trials in 2015.

India's Advanced Technology Vessel (ATV) is intended to be the precursor of further SSBNs, whose design and equipment will be adapted from experience gained with *Arihant*.

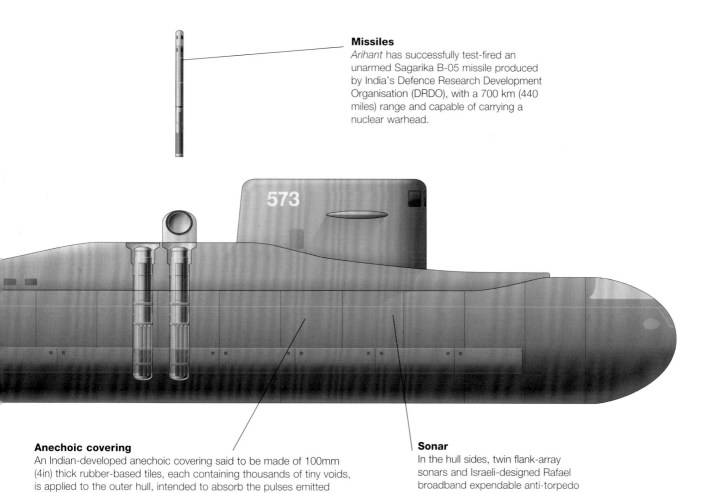

Missiles

Arihant has successfully test-fired an unarmed Sagarika B-05 missile produced by India's Defence Research Development Organisation (DRDO), with a 700 km (440 miles) range and capable of carrying a nuclear warhead.

Anechoic covering

An Indian-developed anechoic covering said to be made of 100mm (4in) thick rubber-based tiles, each containing thousands of tiny voids, is applied to the outer hull, intended to absorb the pulses emitted by active sonar, and reduce and distort the return signal, while also attenuating the sounds emitted by the vessel itself.

Sonar

In the hull sides, twin flank-array sonars and Israeli-designed Rafael broadband expendable anti-torpedo countermeasures are fitted.

INS Arihant

Specification

Dimensions:	Length: 110m (361ft); Beam: 11m (36ft); Draught: 9m (29ft 6in)
Displacement:	Surfaced – 6000 tons (5900 tons); Submerged – undisclosed
Propulsion:	One pressurized water reactor, 111,000hp (83MW), single screw
Speed:	Surfaced – 15 knots (27.7km/h; 17.2mph); Submerged – 24 knots (44.4km/h; 27.6mph)
Range:	Unlimited
Armament:	Six 533mm (21in) launch tubes; 30 torpedoes; 12 K-15 SLBM
Complement:	96

Arihant in the course of sea trials. It is interesting to compare its shape with the contemporary Chinese Jin class.

As a multi-role platform *Arihant* is designed for long-distance interdiction and surveillance, both of submerged targets as well as principal surface combatants. It can also facilitate Special Forces operations by covertly landing such forces ashore. With underwater ballistic missile launch capability, the boat carries 12 K-15 Sagarika submarine-launched ballistic missiles (SLBMs). With a 1000kg (2200lb) warhead it has a 700–750km (434–465 mile) range – a significant limitation, since the submarine has to move close to enemy shores to launch its missiles, although with a 180kg (396lb) warhead the range extends to 1900km (1200 miles). The K-15 will be replaced in the future by the 3500km (2170 mile) range K-X missile. A four-tube vertical launch system is installed aft of the sail, with each tube able to accommodate three canisters for the shorter-range BO-5 SLBM, which has a 700km (434 mile) range. *Arihant* will also carry a range of anti-ship and land-attack cruise missiles and torpedoes, with six 533mm (21in) tubes set in the bows. *Arihant* is fitted with a combination of two sonar systems – Ushus and Panchendriya. Ushus is state-of-the-art sonar designed for the Russian Kilo class diesel-electric submarines. Panchendriya is a unified submarine sonar and tactical control system, which includes all types of sonar (passive, surveillance, ranging, intercept and active). It also features an underwater communications system.

Sea trials began in December 2014 and were reported in November 2015 as going well. While recording satisfaction, a senior naval spokesman added that he is "not in a position to give timelines with regard to the completion of INS *Arihant* trials or what happens thereafter." The double hull has been tested to a depth of 300m (980ft). Other tests include firing of the Nirbhay long-range subsonic cruise missile with a range of 1000km (620 miles). Tests are also believed to involve the K-15 Sagarika SLBMs; and could also include the K-4, an intermediate-range nuclear-capable SLBM under development by DRD with a range of up to 3500km (2170 miles). Commissioning of *Arihant* has been put back to 2016. The crew underwent training at

Learning from the Russians

Although India emphasizes the extent to which indigenous industry and technology have been involved in the ATV programme, the importance of Russian expertise in nuclear submarine design and building has been vital. In 2012 the Indian Navy acquired a Project 971 Shchuka-B (designated Akula by NATO) nuclear attack submarine from the Russian Navy, with an option to buy the vessel after the lease expires. Up to 300 Indian Navy personnel were trained in Russia for the operation of this submarine, which was renamed Chakra II. Arihant, although Indian-designed, owes a good deal to the Shchuka-B class. Unconfirmed reports suggest that India will lease another submarine of this class from Russia.

an indigenously-developed simulator in the School for Advanced Underwater Warfare (SAUW) at the naval base in Vizag, and also on the INS *Chakra*, an Akula II class nuclear-powered attack submarine being taken on a 10-year lease from Russia.

Expanding the class

As early as 2008 it was being suggested that the vessel was essentially a prototype – 'a technology demonstrator' rather than a fully operational SSBN, necessary to push India's scientific and industrial infrastructure to a level that meets the challenge of advanced technology – and that subsequent nuclear submarines of the Indian Navy will incorporate many improvements, not least to the boat's substantial noise levels. A more powerful reactor and turbine machinery will also be needed to achieve fast attack speeds on SSGN versions. The Vishakhapatnam Yard has INS *Aridhaman*, the second vessel of the Arihant class, under construction, which will have eight rather than four launch tubes. In late 2015 the Indian government announced its intention to build two further Arihant-class submarines. Up to six SSBNs of the class have been proposed, with three expected to be active by 2023. The government has also approved the production of six new SSN, or nuclear attack submarines, faster and leaner than the SSBNs. These will require a more powerful reactor.

Several factors have influenced India's decision to undertake the immensely expensive step of forming a SSBN force, completing the 'nuclear triad' of fighter-bombers carrying nuclear bombs, ICBMs and SLBMs. Most important are the regional tensions with Pakistan and India's concern about China's extension of its submarine fleet and its strategic role. In response to the Indian–Russian co-operation that has resulted in the Arihant class, Pakistan has for some years been negotiating with China over nuclear missile and submarine technology, and in October 2015 an agreement was announced for the purchase of eight modified Type 41 Yuan-class diesel-electric attack submarines from China (export model is the S20) capable of firing guided missiles with nuclear warheads. While this may result in a standoff position of mutual deterrence between India and Pakistan, it is an indication of the ways in which submarine technology both shapes and is driven by new global strategies.

Name Index

General Index

Index

Index